PRAISE FOR THE AUTHOR

A superbly crafted nonfiction drama that transcends true-crime genre expectations...

  KIRKUS REVIEWS (STARRED REVIEW
  FOR *THE EDGE OF MALICE*)

A work of compelling immediacy... Miraldi crafts an engaging courtroom drama that offers both a gripping legal narrative and a vivid glimpse into a bygone era. Avoiding the melodramatic tone of lesser true crime, he relies on careful pacing and deep research to hold the reader's interest. A standout for fans of cerebral, up-market crime writing.

  BLUEINK REVIEWS *(FOR THE EDGE OF*
  INNOCENCE)

A convincing and tense drama with strong characterisation... Miraldi makes complex legal material accessible and engaging. It becomes something of a page-turner and builds to a gripping climax. There is a force of intellect behind it that is appealing —offering insight into the jury system and mid-century American life. A very impressive book.

  RUBERY BOOK AWARD JUDGES, 2018
  BOOK OF THE YEAR (FOR *THE EDGE OF*
  INNOCENCE)

THE EDGE OF GUILT

DAVID MIRALDI

The Edge of Guilt

Copyright © 2025 by David Miraldi

All rights reserved.

No part of this publication may be reproduced, stored in a retrieval system, or transmitted in any form or by any means—electronic, mechanical, photocopying, recording, or otherwise—without the prior written permission of the publisher, except in the case of brief quotations used in critical articles or reviews.

This is a work of fiction. Although *The Edge of Guilt* is inspired by real court cases, the story and characters are entirely fictional. Any resemblance to actual persons, living or dead, is purely coincidental.

Library of Congress Control Number: 2025907415

ISBNs
Paperback: 979-8-9887660-6-3
Hardcover: 979-8-9887660-7-0
eBook: 979-8-9887660-5-6
Audio: 979-8-9887660-8-7

Cover design by Nick Venables [https://www.nickvenablesbookdesign.com/]

Title Production by The Book Whisperer [https://BookWhisperer.ink]

CONTENTS

Author's Note   vii

PART ONE

1. April 20, 2017   3
   Paul Schofield and Wendy Schofield
2. April 20, 2017   13
   Cindy Zurcher
3. April 20, 2017   19
   Paul Schofield
4. April 20, 2017   31
   Cindy Zurcher
5. April 26, 2017   39
   Paul Schofield
6. April 30, 2017   45
   Susie Phillips
7. April 30, 2017   49
   Paul Schofield
8. May 24, 2017   59
   Paul Schofield

PART TWO

9. July 19, 2017   73
   Robert Ingram
10. August 9, 2017   85
    Tom Wilchuck
11. November 15, 2017   95
    Wendy Schofield
12. March 1, 2018   101
    Tom Wilchuck
13. April 23, 2018   107
    Cindy Zurcher
14. August 14, 2018   115
    Paul Schofield
15. September 5, 2018   123
    Paul Schofield

16. October 17, 2018   129
    Paul Schofield
17. February 19, 2019   135
    Paul Schofield
18. February 19, 2019   147
    Cindy Zurcher
19. February 19, 2019   155
    Wendy Schofield

PART THREE

20. September 16, 2019   171
    Wendy Schofield
21. September 23, 2019   177
    Tom Wilchuck
22. September 24, 2019   191
    Susie Phillips
23. September 24, 2019   201
    Robert Ingram
24. September 24, 2019   215
    Cindy Zurcher
25. September 25, 2019   225
    Paul Schofield
26. September 25, 2019   235
    Wendy Schofield
27. September 26, 2019   251
    Paul Schofield
28. September 26, 2019   263
    Robert Ingram and Paul Schofield
29. September 27, 2019   271
    Wendy Schofield, Robert Ingram, and Paul Schofield
30. September 27, 2019   291
    Paul Schofield

Epilogue   297

Also by David Miraldi   299
About the Author   301

AUTHOR'S NOTE

Although *The Edge of Guilt* is a work of fiction, the story is inspired by a composite of real court cases involving negligence, medical malpractice, and psychiatric care. Names, characters, and specific circumstances have been altered to protect privacy, but the emotional and ethical realities are authentically portrayed.

These fictionalized events reflect the difficult truths faced by many families, practitioners, and legal professionals navigating the intersections of mental health, accountability, and justice.

GUILT

The fact or state of having done something wrong or committed a crime

A painful feeling of self-reproach from a belief that one has done something wrong or immoral, such as causing harm to another person

Conduct that involves guilt, crime, or sin

Source:Collinsdictionary.com

PART ONE
THE CASE

CHAPTER 1
APRIL 20, 2017
PAUL SCHOFIELD AND WENDY SCHOFIELD

It is an innocent question from his eleven-year-old daughter, yet it rankles Paul Schofield. He hates to tell her no, especially when a good father would say yes. He looks away from Alyssa, delaying his answer for the time being. Under the kitchen table, he rubs his hands together in a slow circular pattern before turning his gaze to his wife, Wendy, who stands in front of the kitchen sink. Apparently oblivious to his inner turmoil, she is humming and quietly rinsing the breakfast dishes—a woman in her own world.

And to Paul, this hardly seems fair. She's the one who quit her job six months earlier and threw their perilous finances into greater turmoil. Paul's thoughts are interrupted by a gust of wind that blows through the screen door, rattling it and scattering homework papers in its wake. Their younger daughter, Kirsten, to whom these papers apparently belong, screeches and bounds from her chair in hot pursuit, chasing the papers as they dance along the linoleum floor.

Hoping that this diversion will provide a reprieve, Paul spoons some bran flakes into his mouth. As he chews them, he tries to look distracted, as if he's forgotten Alyssa's question. When she asks it again, he grips his spoon more tightly and gives the soggy cereal a quick swirl around the bowl.

"We've discussed this before, haven't we?" he says, his voice sharp and condescending. Grabbing his iPhone, he begins reading emails, signaling to all that he's answered her question.

"So that's it, Paul? You're just going to ignore her?" Wendy asks. Apparently, she has been paying attention. He sets down his phone and stares at his wife, trying to gauge the level of her irritation. Wendy flicks her head toward Alyssa, who appears both disappointed and confused. He looks from Alyssa to his wife and back to Alyssa. Separated by twenty-four years, they are carbon copies of one another—dark brown hair, blue eyes, wispy bodies, and persistent.

"No, I'm not ignoring her. Nothing's changed. She knows that," Paul replies, trying to keep the frustration from his voice. What is he supposed to do—give their daughter a blow-by-blow description of their money woes? His solo law practice is a struggle—one financial crisis after the other.

"You need to repeat the message. Deliver it with patience and sympathy," Wendy says, her voice low, almost a whisper.

"What's with the whisper?" Paul asks. "The kids can hear you." As if to contradict him, a garbage truck groans in front of their home, temporarily drowning his words.

Staring unhappily at her husband, Wendy says nothing.

"Maybe you should tell her. I'm tired of being the bad guy," Paul says. He immediately regrets his churlish tone, but not his message.

Wendy bites her lower lip as she rinses a small plate under the kitchen faucet. The plate slips from her hand and bounces off the stainless-steel basin. After finding it intact, she forces it between two plates in the dishwasher.

Capitalizing on the awkward silence, Alyssa speaks again. "The other girls laugh at my teeth. One of them told me I shouldn't smile. She said it just makes me look ugly. She said that if my parents really cared about me, they'd get me braces."

"Who said that?" Paul snaps.

"Melinda Stillhouse."

"Is that Austin Stillhouse's daughter?" Paul asks, turning toward his wife. His eyes flicker with anger.

"One and the same," Wendy replies, giving him an exaggerated frown—something she hopes will lighten his mood.

"The apple doesn't fall far from the tree," he says, shaking his head.

"Yes, it's a family that spreads love wherever it goes," Wendy says, her voice sarcastic but her eyes brimming with sympathy for Paul. And just like that—confronted by a common enemy—they are allies again.

Ten years earlier, Austin Stillhouse, a local attorney, stole Paul's clients. Technically, the clients belonged to Paul's uncle, who over the years had built a flourishing law practice in Elyria, Ohio, a small city twenty-five miles west of Cleveland. When Paul graduated from law school, his uncle hired him with the expectation that the practice would be Paul's after "Uncle Jack" retired in a few years. After one year of their working together, his uncle suffered a massive heart attack and died in the emergency room. And with that, their plan for an orderly transition ended abruptly.

The sad fact was that Paul had other options when he graduated near the top of his class from Vanderbilt Law School. He received offers from Nashville's top law firms, where salaries for first-year associates often started at $150,000. Although the money was tempting, the workload was crushing and left little time for family. And the compensation system seemed like an elaborate Ponzi scheme—associates at the bottom working like indentured servants while the partners at the top reaped huge salaries and bonuses. He and Wendy favored returning to Elyria, where they'd grown up and Paul had been an all-state basketball star. The money would be good enough and Paul could lead a more balanced life.

But then his uncle died and Austin Stillhouse swooped in like a vulture. Stillhouse arranged golf games with his uncle's clients at the Elyria Country Club, took them to popular shows at Cleveland's Playhouse Square, and wined and dined them at swank restaurants in Tremont and elsewhere. In three months, Stillhouse picked the carcass clean—every business client was gone and Paul was left scrambling to pay the bills.

That was ten years ago, and Paul doesn't like to dwell on it. Although Stillhouse hurt him, he didn't run him out of town. Maybe it is just plain stubbornness, but Paul likes to think that he has the talent to succeed anywhere, including Elyria. Although he can't change what Austin Stillhouse did to him, he and his wife can make damn sure that Melinda Stillhouse does not bully their daughter.

"So tell me about Melinda Stillhouse," Paul asks his daughter. "Is she nice?"

"Not really, but she's got a lot of friends."

"Do you like her?"

"No, but I don't want her to turn everybody against me."

"How could she do that? You're smart. You're funny. You're good at everything, Alyssa," Paul says. She is very pretty, too, but he is careful not to emphasize her physical appearance.

"She just does. I don't know how."

Paul senses that Alyssa, like a reluctant witness, is holding back from him. He will tease those facts from her gently and carefully, just as he would in the courtroom. Keeping his voice casual, he asks, "Was anybody around when Melinda said those things?" He knows that bullies enjoy belittling their victims in front of an audience.

Alyssa does not answer immediately and eyes him warily. "There were a couple of kids there. Why do you want to know?"

"Because we want to understand the full picture," Wendy interjects.

"If you say anything to anybody about this, you'll only make things worse," Alyssa says, closing her eyes and shaking her head.

Ignoring her warning, Paul asks, "Did she make you cry?"

When Alyssa does not respond, Paul has his answer.

"Just stay away from her for a while," Wendy suggests. "We'll talk to your teacher about this privately. Melinda will never find out. We promise."

Paul expects an angry protest, but it does not come. Instead, Alyssa turns her head slowly from side to side, apparently weighing the ramifications of her parents' planned intervention. Finally, she nods, looking relieved. "Okay," she says, "but nobody better find out."

"I'm driving you and your sister to school today," Wendy says. "There's a big storm on its way and I don't want anyone to get drenched."

When Wendy returns, she is surprised to see Paul still sitting at the kitchen table. With his shoulders hunched and his head bowed, his six-foot-two-inch frame seem diminished, apparently burdened by his thoughts. She throws her key ring onto the counter to break his reverie. When the keys hit with a sharp pop, he glances up and then shakes his head. She offers him a bemused smile, hoping it will cheer him, but it doesn't.

"It's not your fault," she says, reading his mind.

Without replying, he shrugs and then glances away.

"Look at me," she says. When he doesn't, she places her hands on his shoulders and forces him to make eye contact with her. "You're a great father. You do all kinds of things with those girls. You help them with their homework, take them on hikes, tuck them into bed, coach their teams. You love them and they love you. Come on, snap out of it."

"If anyone would have told me that I'd be eleven years out of law school and couldn't afford to buy braces for my daughter, I wouldn't have believed it," he says.

From time to time during their marriage, Paul needs a pep talk. Wendy surmises that this is one of those occasions. "Who could have predicted that Kirsten would get sick?" she asks. "That just happened. Not your fault."

Four years earlier, their youngest daughter, Kirsten, contracted spinal meningitis and developed complications, leading to a lengthy hospitalization and almost a year of therapy. When it was all over and she was healthy again, they were left with over a hundred thousand dollars in unpaid medical bills, the result of a barebones health insurance policy that excluded much and paid little. They worked out a payment plan with the hospital rather than file for bankruptcy, but their debts remain staggering—student loans in excess of one hundred thousand dollars, a hefty home mortgage, and two car payments. Their credit cards are often maxed out, as they are now.

"When Uncle Jack died, I should have found work at a big firm," Paul says. "I'd have made steady money and we wouldn't be in this mess."

Wendy knows that this option wasn't available during that dark period. By the time Paul realized that he could not jump-start his uncle's practice, the country was in the throes of the Great Recession and large law firms were laying off their young associates. Almost all instituted hiring freezes. "It wasn't the greatest time to get a new job, remember?" she says.

"Well, yeah, but I keep asking myself if I should have done something differently."

They periodically have this conversation, always triggered by a financial difficulty. Whenever they reexamine the circumstances, they realize that they were trapped. After his uncle died, home prices dropped precipitously during the recession. They owed more on their house than it was worth, making it impossible to sell it and move elsewhere.

"We've rehashed this thing for years, haven't we? The past is the past," Wendy says. "All I know is that you're a great lawyer and people will eventually discover you."

Over the years, Wendy has witnessed Paul's dedication to his clients; he works hard regardless of what his clients eventually pay him. Last year, she slipped into a courtroom and watched him try a case in front of a jury. From her biased perspective, she thought he was magnificent, and apparently the jurors were impressed too. They awarded Paul's client a few thousand dollars more than what he'd asked for. Like his other jury trials, it unfortunately was a small case, but it showed what he could do if the stakes were higher.

"Incredible lawyers know how to make money," Paul says. "You picked the wrong guy to hitch your wagon to."

"Oh please," Wendy says, rolling her eyes. "No need to get melodramatic."

When Paul gives her a wan smile, she knows she is starting to make progress. "All you need is one big case, right?" she says. For years, Paul spouted this mantra as a cure to their money woes. However, when that big case never materialized, this solution became a standing joke between them—a remnant from a more naïve past. Unlike the bigger firms, which spent thousands of dollars on marketing, Paul spent nothing. The large firms grabbed the lucrative personal injury cases, while he received their scraps.

"Very funny," Paul says.

"Let's not worry about braces right now. Alyssa can wait another year or so," Wendy says, sounding more optimistic than she feels.

"Good. That's what I was hoping you'd say."

"And relief is just three semesters away," Wendy adds, referring to her accounting coursework at the community college.

Maybe you should have stayed at your old job, Paul thinks, but he knows that is unfair. On her last day as a substitute teacher, Wendy was menaced by a group of eighth-grade boys in the school parking lot and she saw a knife in one boy's hand. She hastily jumped into her car, locked it, and drove home. She turned in her resignation the next morning. The episode was the last straw in a series of frightening encounters that soured her on teaching forever.

"That's great," Paul says, but his voice lacks conviction.

"How about a little enthusiasm?" she asks. "That would be nice, you know."

Paul shrugs. "Sorry, I'm just caught up in our present predicament."

She's been cheerful and now she is beginning to tire of his pessimism. "What's the matter? You can't look forward to your wife making some decent money?" she asks.

Sensing her irritation for the second time that morning, Paul tries to reverse course. "Believe me, I am excited about that prospect," he says, forcing a tight smile.

Unsure of his sincerity, Wendy decides to needle him. "Watch out, I plan on becoming the breadwinner here soon."

Paul seems momentarily stunned by the suggestion but then grins. "Oh God, I can't imagine asking you for spending money. You're such a tightwad."

With that, Wendy knows that she's brought him all the way back. Grabbing a dishrag, she waves it in Paul's face. "You'll pay for that," she says.

"I don't think so," Paul says as he pins her arms to her sides and kisses her. When he relaxes the grip on her arms, Wendy wraps them around his back, the dishrag still dangling from one hand.

Suddenly, he breaks off the kiss. "Sorry, I'm supposed to be in court in half an hour."

"As I recall, you're fast," she teases, provoking a frown from him. Not wanting to hurt his pride any further, she adds, "But, I guess, you're really not that *fast*."

"Aren't you the comedienne this morning?" he responds, brushing his hand through his hair even though it isn't tousled.

She picks up his briefcase and hands it to him. "Time to get off your butt and make us some money," she says.

"Well, about that," he says, his voice still playful. "My clients paid me in advance for this morning's court appearance. And I guarantee you—we've spent their money."

Wendy pretends to look disappointed. "Well then, find something else," she says, her voice imperious.

Paul's face turns grim as he thinks about his afternoon appointment. He exhales and takes a deep breath. "I do have a husband and wife coming in after lunch to talk about a possible wrongful death case involving their teenage daughter."

Wendy's face immediately takes on a serious expression too. "I don't think you've ever handled one of those, have you?" she asks.

"No, I haven't, but I am certainly capable of it," he says, no hesitation or defensiveness in his voice. "The problem is that it's a rather questionable case on fault, but it's certainly tragic." He stops, fearing that the circumstances of the girl's death might upset Wendy. "You sure you want to hear about this?"

"I think I can handle it," Wendy says.

"Well, their daughter committed suicide and they're convinced that her psychiatrist is to blame."

Wendy closes her eyes and winces. She remembers how they almost lost Kirsten as she battled meningitis. "Oh my God. Every parent's worst nightmare," she murmurs, and then falls silent.

"I know," Paul says.

"How old was she?" Wendy asks.

"She was fifteen. I didn't talk to them over the phone. Eileen took the information. She warned me that the father seemed very angry, almost belligerent."

"People have different ways of expressing grief. I wouldn't judge him too harshly," Wendy says.

"I'll listen to them. I owe them that much. But whether there's a case, I don't know." He grabs his briefcase and turns to go out the back door.

"Wait," Wendy says. She runs to the front closet and returns with his raincoat. He drapes it over his right arm and pecks her on the cheek. As he opens the back door, the wind blows through the maple trees, straining the branches and exposing the leaves' undersides.

He walks briskly to his Honda Accord, parked as it always is—in the driveway and far from their dilapidated one-car garage. As he draws near it, a large branch breaks loose from one of the maples, flies toward him, and lands with a loud smack on the Honda's front windshield. *Please, no damage*, he thinks. He has insurance but, of course, it comes with a large deductible.

He pulls the branch away and finds the windshield intact. *Maybe that's a good omen*, he thinks. Relieved, he gets in, slams the door, hits the ignition, and shoves the Honda into reverse.

CHAPTER 2
APRIL 20, 2017
CINDY ZURCHER

As rain pummels her umbrella, Cindy Zurcher stops on the sidewalk, not more than six feet from the building's glass door. If she had her way, she would turn around, go home, and avoid the pain that the next hour will bring. As she stands frozen, her husband yanks on the door handle and lumbers in. Before the door can close, a gust of wind assaults it, holding it open. Debris swirls at her husband's feet and then skitters across the dirty linoleum floor. Beyond his bulky frame, she sees gray walls, made gloomier by the flickering of an aging fluorescent light.

Safely inside, he turns to check on her progress. When he sees that she is still outside, he looks at her in disbelief. "For Christ's sake, move your ass," he yells. Reluctantly, she takes a few steps inside and halts. As soon as the door closes, he pulls a large expandable file folder from under his raincoat and checks it for water damage. After finding it dry, he abruptly heads toward the end of the hall, where an elevator waits, its two green doors not quite touching. As if still battling the wind, she follows, her head down and her shoulders hunched.

"Why do we keep doing this to ourselves?" she asks, her voice almost a whisper.

"You just want to quit, don't you?" he says, glaring at her. "Well, let me tell you one thing: we're not stopping. We owe that to our daughter, no matter what you may think."

"I'm sorry, Dennis. It's just . . ." And then words fail her. She squeezes her umbrella with both hands as if wringing out a washcloth.

"Are you done complaining?" Dennis snaps. "You're one big loser, Cindy. You know that?"

His words sting, but she makes no reply. Throughout their marriage, he's berated her. He can call her a loser if that makes him feel better. The fact is that they've been turned down ten times, and that has nothing to do with her. Whenever they meet with attorneys, Dennis is the big shot who does all the talking. He is the loser, not her.

Near the elevator, they scan the Robinson Building's directory and find the name: *Paul Schofield, Attorney-at-Law*. For the last several days, Dennis has talked nonstop about Schofield, convinced that this young attorney is their "ticket to justice." He is sure that this home-grown lawyer will jump at their case. And then Dennis will go off on another tirade about the flashy lawyers who've already turned them down. By the time he exhausts himself with name-calling, he makes it sound as if they pursued him rather than the other way around.

To Cindy's relief, all of these lawyers firmly and politely told Dennis that they didn't want his case. Undaunted, Dennis continued to search. And now he claims to have found the perfect attorney—if only he can reel him in.

Taking the elevator to the second floor, they find themselves in another dimly lit hallway. They quickly locate Schofield's office and walk into an empty, starkly furnished waiting room. Its wooden chairs look uncomfortable, and a side table's artificial flowers are missing a few blooms. A half wall and an opaque glass window separate the waiting room from a secretarial station that appears to be empty. Cindy glances at Dennis and sees the disappointment in his eyes. Obviously, he, too, expected more. Maybe they will leave—write this off as a mistake.

Instead, he smiles and nods, as if he anticipated this all along. She suppresses a smile as he tries the handle of an interior door, only to find it locked. He prowls around the room for a minute or so before returning to the door, twisting its handle vigorously, and then cursing. Cindy is the first to spot a push bell, the type found in a hotel reception area. She rises from the bench and gingerly depresses its silver button, producing a dull ding.

"He won't hear that," Dennis says, shaking his head in disgust. He then walks over and pounds on the locked door several times. If no one responds, they can go home. And perhaps this time, Dennis will give up.

To her disappointment, the interior door opens a few seconds later. Cindy blinks in surprise as a handsome man in his mid-thirties appears in a trim gray suit without a tie. He is about six feet two inches tall, with a medium build and well-developed shoulders. His features are perfectly proportioned—a face that would make most women take a second look. His chestnut hair is cut short and seems to part naturally on the left side, where it eases its way back, away from his forehead. His smile rises above a slight dimple in his chin, revealing straight, white teeth. His gray-blue eyes seem both kind and friendly, but she dismisses the thought. He is an attorney, isn't he?

The man introduces himself as Paul Schofield and tells them he'll be back just as soon as he finishes a phone call. Pointing to the bell, he says, "Sorry about that. My secretary only works in the mornings."

Dennis gives the attorney a toothy grin. "Not a problem. We'll just read a magazine or two while we wait."

"I won't be more than ten minutes," the attorney replies before he slips out of the waiting room.

"He seems very nice," Cindy says after he leaves.

Dennis pivots quickly to face her, irritation evident in his face. "Nice is not what I'm looking for," he scoffs. "Cindy, do you listen to anything I say?" When she doesn't respond, he continues, "Is that our goal—to find some nice, namby-pamby lawyer?"

She hasn't said that and he knows it. He is baiting her again. Against her better judgment, she decides to defend herself. "I mean he makes a good first impression, that's all I'm saying." When he doesn't press the point, she exhales deeply and reaches for a worn *People* magazine.

Cindy flips through the pages, unable to focus on any of the articles. Instead, she can't stop thinking about this young attorney. He seems different.

She struggles to remember how Dennis found Schofield and then it comes back to her. He overheard two fellow employees at the dealership discussing this young attorney. Schofield won a hard-fought jury trial for one, and afterward the two celebrated with several beers at a local bar. The other respected Schofield for his honesty in handling his mother's estate. Schofield could have claimed a larger fee, basing it on a percentage of the estate's assets as most lawyers did. Instead, he charged by the hour, saving the man thousands of dollars.

When Dennis returned home, he'd dashed into his home office to do some "internet investigation." After printing every page of Schofield's website, he bolted into the kitchen, waving the papers over his head like a castaway signaling to a passing airplane. Despite the website's simplicity, it revealed several nuggets. Schofield graduated near the top of his class at Vanderbilt Law School. Under "Case Results," he reported a $550,000 medical malpractice settlement. "He may be the one," Dennis beamed.

When Dennis talked to her the next day, he was almost manic with excitement. Earlier that year, Schofield had tried to purchase a car from the dealership. After leaning on the credit manager, Dennis reviewed the credit report, discovering that the attorney's finances were a mess. He owed over $100,000 in student loans and $125,000 in outstanding medical bills. His mortgage holder reported that he was occasionally late in making his monthly payments.

"Not only is this guy smart, but he's hungry," Dennis told her as he bounced around their living room. "If I play him right, he'll take a risk where the others won't." Of course, playing people was Dennis's specialty. He routinely was the top salesman at the local Ford dealership.

Cindy is still paging through the magazine when she hears the door open and Schofield appears again. "Sorry to make you wait. My office is just down this hall," he says, his left hand pointing the way.

With his left hand in full view, Cindy impulsively looks to see if the young attorney wears a wedding band. When she spots one, she feels a pang of disappointment followed immediately by embarrassment.

Rising from her chair, she follows Dennis and the attorney down a narrow hall. After taking a few steps, Dennis stops and turns to face her. He winks and mouths the words, "Watch me." After Dennis quickens his pace to catch up with Schofield, she shakes her head in disgust. She wants this young attorney to turn them away like all the others, but she senses he is too trusting—a trait that Dennis will exploit to its fullest.

CHAPTER 3
APRIL 20, 2017
PAUL SCHOFIELD

Paul isn't quite sure what to make of the couple that sits in front of him. The wife, Cindy, seems at least fifteen years younger than her husband, Dennis. They are both well-groomed and neatly dressed: the husband in gray slacks and a navy blue blazer, the wife in a flower-print dress. Although six feet three inches tall, Dennis is a bulky man with a sizeable gut. Despite his girth, he has a ruggedly handsome face set off by piercing blue eyes. His thinning hair appears to be dyed brown, an attempt by a man in his fifties to appear much younger.

On the other hand, Cindy is a thin strawberry blonde somewhere in her late thirties. With her milky white complexion and long straight hair, she is quite pretty. Her delicate features, however, do not define her. Her sullen, subdued expression and sad brown eyes reflect a pervasive sorrow.

Paul folds his hands, places them on his desk, and clears his throat. "At the outset, I want to tell you how sorry I am for your loss. I have two children of my own. I can't even begin to understand how I would feel if I lost one of them." His offer of condolence is initially met by silence. After an awkward few moments, Dennis eventually thanks him for his words of sympathy.

As he does with most prospective clients, Paul begins by telling them about his law practice, emphasizing his commitment to service. "If you call me with a question, it's my job to get back to you within twenty-four hours. My former clients will vouch for that."

Dennis interrupts him. "It's funny that you mention former clients. Two of your former clients are my coworkers and speak very highly of you. It's the reason we're here."

"May I ask who they are?" Paul inquires.

"Oh, yes, of course," Dennis says. "Bill Mikowski and Harold Miller. They're not just coworkers; they've been my friends for a long time. And I trust their judgment."

"I was glad to help them," Paul replies, buoyed by this knowledge. Client referrals suggest that his practice is beginning to grow through its own momentum. If so, it is possible that this couple contacted him first, bypassing the heavy hitters whose personal injury ads blanket the airwaves and local billboards.

But do they have a case? He will find out. "Unfortunately, there's no easy way to begin. You've lost your teenage daughter due to an overdose and you want to sue her psychiatrist," Paul says, consciously substituting the word *overdose* for *suicide*. Paul studies the parents for their reactions. Dennis's eyes burn with an angry intensity, while Cindy stares at the floor, apparently determined to disengage from their discussion.

Paul clears his throat before continuing. "To hold a doctor accountable for malpractice, you need to show that the doctor did something wrong to cause your daughter's death, not intentionally, but carelessly. The law calls that negligence. So let's start there. How was the psychiatrist careless?"

Only Dennis holds Paul's gaze.

"Dennis, what do you think?" Paul asks.

Dennis takes a deep breath and holds out his hands in a gesture of resignation. "Believe me, neither of us want to be here talking to an attorney," he begins. "We've debated this long and hard, and at first, we weren't going to do anything." He then reaches over and grabs his wife's hand, giving it a squeeze. "But then we decided that our daughter's death was so preventable and we didn't want other parents to go through what we've experienced. It's horrible to put your child into the ground. If we can stop this from happening to just one other family, then this lawsuit will be worth it to us."

Paul has heard this explanation from other would-be clients. People often use this as an excuse for suing; no one wants to admit that they are motivated by money and a big payoff. Sometimes it is true, other times not. However, Paul studies Dennis as he speaks and the man seems sincere.

"You said this was very preventable; I need to know why you say that," Paul prods.

Before Dennis responds, he picks up an expandable folder from the floor near his chair. In his haste to bring the couple back to his office, Paul never noticed this bulging file. With a magician's flourish, Dennis retrieves a letter from a jumble of documents and wordlessly slips it into his blazer's breast pocket. Paul is immediately intrigued. What is in that letter?

As if reading Paul's mind, Dennis responds, "I'll show you the letter later. Right now, let me give you some background information, and this may take some time."

For the next ten minutes, Paul listens intently as the father tells him about his daughter Heather. She was the oldest of their three children and, for most of her life, had been a normal kid. Quiet and reserved, she had several close friends, did reasonably well in school, and showed an aptitude for art. However, when she entered high school, she changed, something Dennis calls "adjustment difficulties."

"Tell me more about these changes," Paul says, sensing that Dennis is trying to gloss over this part of the story.

Dennis does not respond immediately, apparently choosing his words carefully. "I mean, she became withdrawn and no longer spent time with her friends. I didn't think too much about it. Her best friend had gone to a Catholic high school and Heather went to North Ridgeville High School—so they became kind of distant, but I thought it had to do with a change in schools."

"Anything else?" Paul urges. "Anything happen at school, for example?"

"Well, yeah. School was a real problem for her. She didn't feel a part of it anymore. Her grades dropped and she stopped turning in assignments. You know, that kind of thing."

Out of the corner of his eye, Paul sees Cindy shaking her head ever so slightly. "Mrs. Zurcher, what did you notice?" he asks.

Like a student startled by a teacher's unsolicited question, her entire body jerks. Confused, she looks at her husband, apparently seeking some direction. He nods as if telling her to proceed.

"Well, she was very sad all the time," she says, her voice quiet and uncertain, lilted by a slight Appalachian twang.

When she says nothing more, Paul asks, "Did she cry a lot?"

"All she wanted to do was to stay in her room and listen to music," Cindy offers, not answering Paul's question.

"Let me say something here," Dennis interjects. "You asked about crying. Well, the kids at school could be mean to her and she would start crying at school. A couple of times, she couldn't stop and the school nurse called home and Cindy drove down and picked her up."

Paul thinks about his own daughter and how she has been bullied recently, and he feels a strong connection to this couple. He looks at Cindy and poses the next question to her. "How often did you have to pick Heather up from school for these crying spells?"

"Not so much at the beginning of her freshman year, but then it became more frequent," she says, her vagueness vexing Paul.

Before she can say more, Dennis steps in again. "The school nurse kept insisting that Heather needed professional help—that she needed to see a psychiatrist. Frankly, we weren't sure what to do. Taking her to a psychiatrist seemed pretty drastic when maybe all she really needed was time to mature a bit."

When Paul looks toward Cindy again, she is nodding, apparently agreeing with her husband. He can understand how parents would be reluctant to seek professional help for a child, perhaps unnecessarily stigmatizing the child. The easier course is to wait and hope that the problem resolves on its own. "At some point, you decided to take Heather to a psychiatrist. What triggered that?" Paul asks.

Dennis stares at his folded hands and then looks up to meet Paul's eyes. "She had another episode at school. According to her art teacher, Heather had just started crying in the classroom for no apparent reason. When Cindy got to the school, this teacher was waiting with Heather in the office. She had her arm around Heather, who was sobbing. The teacher gave Cindy this look, like *When are you going to do something about this?* The school nurse was there too and she took Cindy back to her little cubicle. The nurse thought that Heather needed medication and told Cindy that only a psychiatrist could prescribe that. She suggested that we call Dr. Sheldon Wright."

"Did you?" Paul asks.

"Yeah, we talked it over that night and Cindy took her the next day," Dennis says. "And that turned out to be the biggest mistake of our lives."

Although Dennis provides a basic treatment chronology, he frequently lashes out at Dr. Wright, for whom he cannot hide his animosity, calling him aloof, condescending, and arrogant. He claims that the doctor was unable "to connect with patients" and relied solely on "pushing pills" to treat them. Filtering out Dennis's criticism of Dr. Wright, Paul learns that the doctor diagnosed Heather with depression. He prescribed an antidepressant, Prozac, and sent her to counseling. When she showed little improvement after two months, Dr. Wright changed the antidepressant to Paxil and took over some of the counseling sessions himself. During the next three months, Heather continued on this plan, not improving but also not deteriorating.

Just several weeks before school ended in early June, Heather suffered another meltdown there. A fellow student had apparently seen Heather leave Dr. Wright's office two weeks earlier and told his friends about it. When they spotted Heather in the hall, they taunted her, calling her a wacko and a nut case. She came undone.

After Heather was unable to stop crying at home, Dr. Wright agreed to see her on an emergency basis that afternoon. After meeting with Heather, Dr. Wright told Cindy that Heather needed a quiet and secure environment, a new antidepressant, intensive individual psychotherapy, and group therapy. He suggested that she be admitted to the hospital's psych unit the following day.

Paul tries to digest what he's heard thus far. He hasn't learned anything that suggests that Dr. Wright has committed malpractice. Physicians can't guarantee that every treatment will be successful. It appears that Heather's depression was not responding to antidepressants and psychotherapy—the primary weapons in a psychiatrist's arsenal. What more was the doctor supposed to do?

Sensing that there is no case, Paul wants to speed things along. "Did Heather die in the hospital?" he asks.

Dennis seems irritated by the question and scowls. "You might say that, but technically, no."

Paul realizes that he should have allowed the father to tell the story in his own way. "I didn't mean to interrupt you," Paul says. "Tell me what happened."

"Well, as you might guess, Heather didn't get any better in the hospital. She was receiving a new medication and talking to lots of people in therapy sessions. After three weeks, Dr. Wright told us that we needed to do something different. If we didn't make some inroads on the depression now, it might never go away. It would become chronic. As you might guess, we were very frightened about her future."

Again, Dr. Wright's approach seems logical to Paul. "What did he suggest?"

"Electroshock therapy," Dennis says, letting the words drop like a bomb.

Paul didn't expect this turn in the story and lets his pen fall onto his legal pad. "What? I thought that treatment was abandoned years ago," he says.

Dennis gives him a rueful smile. "Not according to Dr. Wright. He called it a game changer—his exact words."

As disturbing as Dr. Wright's recommendation was, Paul is equally astonished that the parents consented to the treatment. How could any reasonable parent allow a child to undergo electroshock therapy? Trying to keep his voice neutral, Paul asks, "What did you say to that?"

"I said, 'Hell no.' I told him that he was crazy if he thought we'd allow Heather to have her brain fried," Dennis says. "I asked him, 'Isn't there something else?' And he says, 'You've got the wrong idea about electroconvulsive treatment.' He explained that it had been refined since the early days and that it was very safe. He emphasized that it posed virtually no risk to patients anymore."

Paul immediately thinks about film portrayals of shock treatment, as in *One Flew over the Cuckoo's Nest*. He visualizes Jack Nicholson's body thrashing spasmodically as electric current rips through his brain. Trying to suppress that mental picture, Paul asks tentatively, "How did Dr. Wright convince you that it was safe?"

"It was one hell of a sales job," Dennis says. "From my line of work, I should have realized it, but I didn't. You've got to remember that we were scared, we were desperate, and we trusted the doctor's superior knowledge."

The father then summarizes what Dr. Wright told them. Heather would be given a general anesthetic, rendering her unconscious and unable to feel any pain. Her heart, respiration, and brain would be carefully monitored. The electroconvulsive shock machine would stimulate her brain with just enough electrical current to trigger a slight seizure. She would not jerk or thrash about; the only movement might be some quivering in her toes. The controlled seizure would reset her brain and, in that way, fight her depression. However, it would take several weeks of shock treatments before their daughter would see any meaningful improvement.

Paul considers the doctor's explanation but remains unconvinced that shock treatments were safe, particularly for a child whose brain was still developing. After jotting down a few notes on his legal pad, Paul asks, "I'm still skeptical that electroshock treatments are appropriate for teenagers. What did Dr. Wright say about that?"

Dennis's eyes flash and he makes a fist with his right hand before he speaks. "Oh, he lied. I didn't know it then, but, after doing research on the internet, I know it now."

"Okay," Paul says, nodding his head. "Tell me what you learned."

"Well, he claimed that electroshock treatment is so safe that over a hundred thousand people receive it each year, including teenagers and the elderly. He failed to mention that many of those people experience memory loss that is permanent. And if there is any improvement from the depression, it lasts for only a few months. If he had told us of any of these risks, we would never have agreed to the treatment. No way."

Although Paul prides himself on being dispassionate as he listens to clients describe their legal problems, he feels anger. He shakes his head and grimaces. "So what happened with the shock treatments?"

"They wiped out her memory—that's what happened."

"All of it?" Paul asks incredulously.

"No, not everything. Her memories from junior high and high school were gone—so like three or four years were lost."

"What did Dr. Wright say?" Paul asks.

"Oh, he was so cavalier about it. He said, 'Sometimes this happens, but it's only temporary. We've got to stick to the program and finish all the treatments.' You can't imagine how arrogant he was."

"Did Heather finish the treatments?"

"We allowed them to continue. I know you're thinking we were bad parents or really stupid, but we trusted this guy. He had all of the degrees, not us," Dennis says.

"No, I understand your dilemma," Paul answers. "You were put in a very difficult spot."

"Exactly," Dennis says. "But we stopped it when there was no improvement and she was obviously getting worse."

"How so?"

"Sometimes she was like a zombie. Other times, she was so angry that she would barely talk to us. Several times she said, 'How could you let them do this to me?' And then she'd start shrieking and sobbing." His voice catches, and for the first time, he appears on the verge of tears.

While waiting for Dennis to regain his composure, Paul glances at Cindy. She is staring out the window, apparently trying to send her jagged recollections elsewhere.

When Dennis resumes, his voice is steady but resigned. "We'd seen enough and we made arrangements for Heather to be discharged. We decided to take her home and see about switching her treatment to a different doctor. We were finished with Dr. Wright."

"What did Dr. Wright say to that?"

"Oh, he wasn't happy with us. He wanted us to continue with the shock treatments, but when he saw that we weren't going to change our minds, he agreed to send her home with a new antidepressant and told us to follow up with him in two weeks. We didn't tell him that we'd be finding a new doctor."

"Did you ever get her to a new psychiatrist?" Paul asks.

Dennis does not answer but shakes his head instead. "We never got the chance," he says. "Heather overdosed on pills a little over a week after we got home."

Dennis maintains a stoic expression, while Cindy looks at Paul with apparent disgust—as if he's forced them to relive this final episode in their daughter's life. Her stare unnerves him. Before he can convey some compassionate words, Dennis responds. "You've got to understand that her brain was so scrambled from the shock treatments that she didn't know what she was doing. I'm convinced of that."

Paul exhales sharply. "That has to be a horrible thing to experience," he says, glancing at Cindy and then fixing his eyes on Dennis. Although Paul realizes that additional questions will only alienate Cindy further, he needs the rest of the story to evaluate the case and decide whether he should take it on. Looking at Dennis, Paul asks, "Did you have any inkling that she might do that?"

"We never left her alone in the house. She'd gone to bed early that night while the rest of us watched television. About an hour and a half later, we found her sprawled out in the hall. Well, actually our eleven-year-old son discovered her. He screamed and we all came running. She'd vomited all over the floor and collapsed into it. Her skin was gray and she was unresponsive. I couldn't tell if she was breathing or not. Cindy called 911 and I tried mouth-to-mouth resuscitation. The medics got to our house in about ten minutes, took over the treatment, and rushed her to the emergency room. We all piled into my SUV and followed the ambulance to the hospital. But it was all too late. She died in the hospital about an hour later."

It's a heart-wrenching story and Paul can't help but be moved by it. As an attorney, however, he has to put sympathy aside and analyze the facts objectively. Does this couple have a claim against Dr. Wright? Were the electroshock treatments appropriate? And if they weren't, did those things cause Heather to take her own life? He needs a medical expert to answer those questions.

To compound his uncertainty, he's only handled one medical malpractice case in his career and he was eventually overwhelmed by its complexities. When that happened, he invited a more experienced attorney to join him as co-counsel. And it was the other attorney who propelled the case to the finish line and negotiated the settlement.

He will do the same with this case if he decides to accept it. He hopes to sign the Zurchers to a representation agreement, gather the medical records, and refer it to an attorney who specializes in handling medical malpractice cases. Although the two would serve as co-counsel together, Paul, like all referring attorneys, would have a minor role in the case. The more experienced attorney would handle every important aspect of the case, while Paul would observe and help on small tasks. To encourage lawyers like him to transfer cases to their more experienced colleagues, the law allows him to receive part of the fee. He expects the division will be similar to that of his earlier case, when the fee was divided on a two-thirds/one-third basis and he received the smaller share.

As Paul considers the ramifications of this case for his struggling practice, his heart beats faster. A wrongful death case, even one involving a teenager like Heather Zurcher, could result in a settlement of several million dollars—and the attorney fee generated by it would be substantial, even the smaller share that he would receive as the referring attorney. Maybe, just maybe, this case is his way out.

"I can't tell you if you have a case," Paul says. "I will need an expert, probably a psychiatrist, to review the records and give me an opinion."

Although not angry, Dennis looks displeased. "Well, I've done months of research on the internet about electroshock," he counters. "In fact, I took it upon myself to contact a highly regarded psychiatrist about Dr. Wright's treatment."

Dennis reaches into his blazer's breast pocket and retrieves the letter he promised to share with Paul when the time was right. And that time is apparently now.

Paul senses that his luck is about to change.

CHAPTER 4
APRIL 20, 2017
CINDY ZURCHER

For the last half hour, she's tried to stay detached as Dennis and the attorney talk about Heather and Dr. Wright. But from time to time, she cannot block out Dennis's voice. Like a chain saw, it drones and pitches, demanding to be heard.

She is drawn back into the dialogue when Dennis begins talking about Heather's overdose. Her mind is fully engaged when Dennis hands the letter from the electroshock expert, Dr. Simon Masterson, to Schofield. The letter arrived just a few days earlier, and after Dennis read it, he reacted like someone who'd just won the lottery. He yelled *yes* and pounded the table with the palm of his left hand—scaring their two children. Thrusting the letter in front of her, he exclaimed, "One of the leading experts in the world confirms that the electroshock treatments killed her!"

And now, Schofield grabs the letter with an eagerness that shocks Cindy. As he reads it, his expression turns from skeptical to surprised. To her dismay, she senses that this attorney is about to be sucked in.

Dennis's lawsuit is as sick as it is wrong. Why blame Dr. Wright for a death that stemmed from a horrible home life? It was her job to protect her children from Dennis's verbal cruelty and extreme punishments. She failed at that miserably. The medical profession didn't betray Heather; she did.

"How did you get this?" Schofield asks. To Cindy, he looks like a man who's just received a top secret document.

She wonders how Dennis will explain this. When he began researching shock treatments on the internet, Dr. Masterson's name popped up early and often. Almost immediately, Dennis purchased one of Masterson's anti-ECT books from Amazon. He read it, scribbling his own comments in the margins and highlighting entire sections.

She remembers when he decided to write to Masterson, outlining Heather's treatment and seeking his opinion. He didn't really expect a reply, but Masterson answered, giving Dennis more than he could have hoped for. The letter was short and to the point. It read: "From the information provided, I believe that Dr. Wright acted recklessly in prescribing ECT to this teenage girl and that these ill-advised treatments precipitated her tragic death." He included a copy of his curriculum vitae: a paper that detailed his education, his published works, and his professional affiliations. Another document outlined his litigation fees: a $5,000 retainer to review the records, $2,500 to write a report, and $7,500 a day for testifying at trial, not including the cost of first-class airfare, travel time, and hotel expenses, all of which were extra.

"As I told you, I did extensive research on ECT after Heather died. I was really impressed by Dr. Masterson's book *Shock Treatment: The Deception Continues*. Almost on a whim, I sent him a letter that outlined Heather's treatment. Even though I figured he'd ignore me, I asked him to give me his thoughts. To my surprise, he replied just a few days ago."

Schofield stares at the letter and reads it several times. Cindy can sense that its words are knocking down whatever barriers are left in the attorney's mind.

Before Schofield can respond, Dennis hands him a packet of ten pages stapled together. Cindy doubts that Dennis has included the doctor's fee schedule in the package. "Here are Dr. Masterson's credentials."

Schofield reads the first few pages carefully and then skims through the remaining ones. He lifts his eyebrows and exhales through his mouth. "This is all pretty impressive stuff," he replies. "You wouldn't happen to have your daughter's medical records in your file, would you?"

"No. This thick file is full of medical articles that I printed off the internet and my own notes."

"So Dr. Masterson has not reviewed the medical charts or anything?" Schofield asks.

"No, I took this as far as I could go, and now I thought I'd better get an attorney involved."

"Have you talked to any attorneys before me?"

Cindy looks over at Dennis and then out the window again. She suspects that Dennis will lie outright, but perhaps he will try to sidestep the question with his well-honed evasiveness.

When Dennis met with the other attorneys, they would appear mildly interested in the case, but they'd sour when Dennis began to rant about the doctor who'd ruined his life. As Dennis became louder and more strident, interest drained from their faces.

She watches as her husband momentarily glances at the file in his lap as if the answer is somewhere buried in his stack of papers. She knows Dennis is stalling and she hopes Schofield can sense that too. Dennis clears his throat and looks directly at the attorney.

"Well, Paul, when something like this happens, you just go numb and don't do anything for months." Dennis's voice is solemn and tinged with sorrow. "You just go through the motions. Then you start wondering if somebody made a mistake. And then you wonder if this error will be repeated and other people will suffer the same way you have. You think perhaps you can do something so that this doesn't happen to somebody else. Maybe Heather's death could be turned around to save others.

"So that's when I went on the internet and started reading psychology books in my free hours—virtually everything I could discover about shock treatments. I work long hours selling cars, so it took a couple of months to complete my research."

Dennis takes a deep breath and seems to expand as he sits ramrod straight in his chair. Cindy knows that look—Dennis as the brave soldier.

"Then I didn't just go out willy-nilly looking for an attorney. Believe me, I'm not impressed by those attorneys who advertise on TV or have giant yellow-pages ads. They disgust me. Instead, I took my time, talked to the people I trust—like my close friends and coworkers.

"Well, my friends spoke very highly of you, but I didn't stop there. I also asked my buddies in the sheriff's department. You know, before I sold cars, I was a sheriff's deputy for ten years. They'd seen you in court, contesting DUI cases and such, and they had very nice things to say about you."

Cindy looks over at her husband; this is news to her. Although Dennis was a sheriff's deputy—that's how she met him, unfortunately—he never told her that he talked with any of them about Schofield. She concludes that he is lying.

Dennis continues, "And then I looked at your website. Not too many bells and whistles on it, but I saw where you went to law school at Vanderbilt. Saw where you graduated at the top of your class or close to it, I don't remember which."

"Not number one in my class, but the top five percent," Schofield volunteers, seemingly pleased by Dennis's praise.

"Yeah, that's right, and that's a damn good law school from what I hear. Then I saw where you settled a medical malpractice case for five hundred fifty thousand dollars. Now, I have a question for you, Paul.

Did you handle that case all by yourself or did you work with another law firm?"

For the first time, Schofield looks uncomfortable. At least, that's how it appears to Cindy. Leave it to Dennis—he always turns the tables on his inquisitors, deflecting attention away from himself and toward them. Dennis hasn't answered the question and now it is Schofield who seems to be on the defensive.

Schofield clears his throat. "Let me explain," he begins. "I started that case on my own and filed it. While that case was pending, I attended a medical malpractice seminar where one of the lecturing attorneys talked about a claim that he'd handled that was almost identical to mine. At the next break, we talked and he told me that he had retained some impressive experts in his lawsuit. If I wanted, he would be happy to co-counsel the case with me. We'd use the same experts and we could work it together. I thought that was a good idea."

For the first time, Cindy does not completely believe Schofield. He stared at his desktop during most of his explanation.

"But you feel comfortable handling a medical malpractice case by yourself?" Dennis asks, pressing him.

"Absolutely," Schofield replies, but Cindy hears uncertainty in his voice.

"By the way, who was this other attorney?" Dennis asks.

"Oh, he's a Cleveland attorney. His name is Scott Worthington," Schofield says.

"Really? We have an appointment to see him tomorrow," Dennis replies.

Cindy draws a sharp intake of air; they have no appointment with anyone the next day. Then she remembers: Dennis called Worthington several months ago and they met with him in a fancy office in downtown Cleveland. Like the others, he rejected the case, sending them a carefully worded turndown letter.

Schofield looks both wounded and dismayed, but he says, "Well,

Scott Worthington is a very competent attorney. I enjoyed working with him."

Cindy feels sorry for Schofield, not because of the disappointment that is evident in his face, but because she knows what is coming next.

"I really like you, Paul," Dennis begins. "It's a long drive to get into Cleveland. We'd prefer to deal with somebody local, particularly when that attorney is an up-and-comer like you. I've done my homework. It's your case if you want it."

Relief floods into Schofield's eyes. "Well, I generally like to read some medical articles on point and have an expert review the hospital chart before I accept a medical malpractice case."

"I understand," Dennis replies. "We are looking for someone who will commit now—I mean today. I'm not looking for a quitter or an excuse-maker. If I give the case to you, I want you to take it all the way —no backing out when things get tough. Our attorney will have to put it in writing that he won't withdraw from the case at any time. So if you want the case, it's yours, but with that condition."

Schofield seems stunned. "I've never done that before."

"Well, like I said, I'm looking for someone who can make a decision today. Time is running out. I've done my research and I know that a lawsuit must be filed pretty soon, before the time limit expires— that thing you attorneys call the statute of limitations."

Dennis pauses for a moment, waiting for Schofield to respond. When he doesn't, Dennis continues, "Paul, I didn't mention this, but I have a ton of unpaid medical bills associated with my daughter's hospitalization. I had an eighty/twenty plan and I have a mountain of debt. You know, when a loved one needs medical care, you get the help immediately and worry about how you'll pay for it later."

Schofield nods. "I know exactly what you mean."

Oh, you sneaky, lying bastard, Cindy thinks. Medical Mutual has paid for almost all of Heather's hospitalization. Unlike Schofield, they have no outstanding medical bills. She knows exactly what Dennis is doing. She can see it. Dennis has him.

Schofield pulls out a contingency fee contract for them to review. "I take one-third of the recovery as my fee, and this is before we take out the money I have advanced for expenses."

"That seems like a lot," Dennis says. "You'll probably settle this case before it even goes to trial."

Again, Schofield looks troubled. Finally, he says, "I'm sorry, I can't do it for any less."

Dennis stares at Cindy and exhales deeply. "Well, what do you think, honey?" he asks, his voice solicitous.

"Whatever you want to do," she says, trying to mask her disgust.

"Paul, if you add language that you will not drop this case, then we'll sign right now."

Schofield looks at the letter from Dr. Masterson again. He picks up his fee contract and begins writing on it with a pen. He places the agreement on his desk and turns it around so that they can read it. They scoot their chairs closer to the desk and read:

> *Assuming that the facts are substantially as clients have described, attorney agrees that he will not withdraw from representation in this case unless he has secured other counsel, agreeable to clients, who will take over the prosecution of this case. Nothing in this agreement shall prohibit the attorney from associating with other co-counsel to prosecute this case, provided such an association does not increase the attorney fee in this case.*

Dennis reads the language. "So you'll stay on, and if you withdraw, it's your job to get us another attorney to handle this case, is that right?"

"Yes."

"And if you get another attorney involved, the fee is still one-third, regardless of the number of attorneys handling the case? There's no increase in the fee?"

"That is correct."

"Okay, we'll sign," Dennis says, and then affixes his signature to the contract with a flourish. As he slides it across the desk's glass surface to his wife, he says, "Cindy, when we get home, will you cancel the appointment with Scott Worthington for tomorrow?"

Cindy doesn't answer him. Instead, she searches Schofield's expression, trying to discern his thoughts. When he explained the attorney-client agreement to them, his face was flushed. Now he just looks anxious and unsure of himself.

She pities him. He appears to be a good person, but he has been too trusting, and, in the end, much too gullible. She adds her signature to the attorney's contract and hands it back to him, sure that he will eventually regret tying his fate to Dennis's. She certainly does. When she linked herself to this man seventeen years ago, it was a horrible mistake—one she regrets every day of her life.

CHAPTER 5
APRIL 26, 2017
PAUL SCHOFIELD

It is only eleven thirty in the morning, but Paul's office is already unbearably hot, the temperature hovering around eighty degrees. The air-conditioning vent rattles above him, belching warm, humid air—the product of the building's ancient cooling system, which is perpetually in need of repair. On days like this, he prefers the comfort of a courtroom or the county law library. But at eleven thirty, he has an important call with a partner at one of Cleveland's leading personal injury law firms, Heidelberg and Associates. Two days earlier, he talked with one of that firm's paralegals about the Zurcher case and then sent her a summary of the facts and a copy of Dr. Masterson's letter. A few hours later, she emailed him the details for today's phone conference with Isaac Gableman, one of the firm's malpractice attorneys.

As Paul waits for the eleven thirty call, he tries to edit a custody agreement but he cannot focus. He glances at the clock on the opposite wall. It is now eleven thirty-five and still no call. He returns his attention to the custody document, scratches out a few words, and then gets up and stares out the window. Almost immediately, his phone rings and he scampers back to his chair. As he reaches for the phone, he knocks over a glass of water, the liquid quickly spreading across the desk's protective glass surface and then dripping to the carpet below.

"Hello, Paul Schofield," he answers, trying to sound unhurried.

"Oh hi, Paul. This is Izzy Gableman. Is this a good time to talk?" Gableman's voice is friendly and conversational.

"Of course. Absolutely," Paul says, his voice more eager than he intended.

For the next few minutes, Gableman dominates the conversation, touching upon the nature of his practice, lawyers that Gableman knows from Elyria, and Gableman's successful Lorain County jury trials. While Gableman talks, Paul doodles on his yellow legal pad.

Finally, Gableman clears his throat. "Paul, I wanted to talk to you personally about why we are not interested in your case. I want to make sure that you understand our reasons because I hope you'll keep us in mind if you have another malpractice case."

"Sure," Paul says, trying to stifle a sharp intake of air. He will not panic. Gableman's firm is not the only game in town. He can find somebody else.

"I want you to know that Dennis Zurcher met with us about three months ago about this case," Gableman says. Upon hearing those words, Paul drops the pen from his hand and a feeling of dread spreads from his chest to his neck.

"I obviously didn't realize that," Paul says. "I mean, I had absolutely no idea that Mr. Zurcher had consulted with another attorney."

"Oh, I think he's talked to quite a few. Some of us talk shop, and I know of at least two other law firms that have turned him down. Let's say he's made quite an impression on us."

What had Dennis said to these other attorneys? What had Paul missed when he'd talked to him?

"We've all had difficult clients," Paul says, trying to minimize Dennis's importance in the analysis. "The central question is whether the family has a good case against the psychiatrist. Shouldn't that be the focus?"

"To a point, you're right," Gableman says.

Trying to steer Gableman to the merits of the claim, Paul asks, "Haven't things changed since you met with Mr. and Mrs. Zurcher? I mean, we now have an expert report that concludes that the daughter's psychiatrist was negligent and that his negligence caused her death." As he waits for Gableman's response, Paul grips the telephone receiver tightly with his left hand and twists the telephone cord around his right one.

"I'll get to that, but I want to start at the beginning," Gableman says. For the next few minutes, Gableman tells Paul about his meeting with the Zurchers. Gableman initially was intrigued by the case and found the father likeable enough, but when Gableman asked some probing questions about their family life and the daughter's prior suicide attempt, the father became defensive, then evasive, and ultimately combative. When they discussed the daughter's overdose, Gableman asked how the daughter had accessed the antidepressant medication that killed her. Rather than answer the question, the father exploded, screaming that neither he nor his wife was to blame for their daughter's death. He then attacked Gableman personally, claiming that the attorney was insensitive to their suffering. The father's volatility convinced Gableman that he wanted no part of the case and he ended the meeting soon thereafter.

"Mr. Zurcher never lost his temper with me. He was calm and rational the entire time," Paul says, immediately regretting the statement and realizing that it has no bearing on the father's behavior toward Gableman.

"Well, he's had time to perfect his act," Gableman says, not bothering to hide his sarcasm. "My advice is to drop this case now. He's a Molotov cocktail ready to detonate in your hand. Get out while you still can."

"But what about the expert's report?" Paul asks. "Dr. Masterson will say unequivocally that ECT should never have been used and that it killed her."

"Well, we've been researching that since you called us," Gableman says. "We were willing to give this a second look."

"And . . . ?"

"Dr. Masterson is . . ." Gableman pauses as he struggles for the right words. "Paul, he's really out there—outside the norm—if you know what I mean. We can't find another psychiatrist who agrees with him. He thinks ECT should never be used under any circumstances—no way, not ever. But that's not the reality. Psychiatrists developed standards that provide for the safe use of ECT in a variety of circumstances. Without going into the details, the girl's psychiatrist followed those rules." A few minutes later, the meeting ends.

Paul doesn't want to accept Gableman's conclusions. Gableman hasn't reviewed either the hospital records or the psychiatrist's office notes. How can he be so definitive?

As he considers these things, Paul's disappointment quickly changes into desperation. What if Gableman is right? What then? What if he has to go it alone on this case? He has neither the experience nor the money to finance a medical malpractice case.

His other option is to withdraw from the case. However, if he does that, Dennis will sue him and probably win. To compound the situation, Paul has only the minimum amount of legal malpractice coverage, one hundred thousand dollars. He will be personally liable for any judgment over that limit, which could be over a million dollars.

Paul takes several deep breaths and tries to quell the crazy chatter that is overrunning his rational thoughts. As his panic subsides, he realizes that he needs to regroup and come up with a plan. After a few minutes, he decides that he'll get the hospital records and the psychiatrist's chart and see what he can develop to make the case more compelling. His sister is a nurse, and he'll enlist her to review the records and conduct some medical research. If she finds some additional medical mistakes from her review, he'll have a much stronger claim, and this time, he'll be able to hand it off to a skilled malpractice attorney who will accept the case. But he has no time to delay—the statute of limitations, the legal time limit for filing the case, will expire in a few months.

CHAPTER 6
APRIL 30, 2017
SUSIE PHILLIPS

Susie Phillips is halfway through her Zumba workout when she hears her iPhone ringing in the kitchen. After pushing the pause button on her DVD player, she tiptoes and hops about the family room floor, trying to avoid her son's Lego projects, which seem to be scattered everywhere. Tracing the sound to the counter by the microwave, she grabs the phone and sees that her brother is calling.

Great timing, Paul, she thinks. As she transfers the phone from her right hand to her left, it slips from her sweaty grip and clatters to the floor, wiggling a bit before it comes to rest on the gray tile floor. As she reaches down to pick it up, her pink T-shirt, drenched in perspiration, sticks to her back.

"Hello, Paul," Susie says, inhaling sharply.

"Is this a bad time?" Paul asks.

"You might say so," she answers.

"Oh, sorry. I can call back later," he says. "It's just a little work thing that I could use your help on."

Although her brother is trying to sound nonchalant, Susie hears anxiety in his voice. "So what's wrong?" she asks.

"Is it that obvious?"

"Sorry, Paul, but I can read you like a book," she says.

"Okay then," Paul says. "I'm in a big mess. I took a med mal case—"

"I thought you weren't going to do that again," she interrupts.

"Well, I thought I could flip it to another attorney—"

"And grab yourself one big fat referral fee," Susie interrupts again.

"Well, yes, that's how the system works," Paul says sheepishly.

"How's that working out?" she needles.

"Not so good. I kind of miscalculated," Paul replies.

While Paul tells the story, Susie occasionally rolls her eyes and fights the urge to tell him how stupid he's been. As she listens, Susie thinks about how their roles have reversed over the years. Paul was always their parents' golden boy, the high-achieving, popular kid who mastered almost anything he attempted. She, on the other hand, was the wild one, the bright child who never studied and seemed perfectly content to skate by in school. The only thing that cut through her indifference was an apparent passion for sports. Despite predictions that she'd break high school records in basketball and track, she quit all sports as a sophomore, never providing anyone with an explanation. She'd traded her sports jerseys for goth attire, hanging out with the wrong people at punk rock venues, smoking pot, and mocking everything that her parents found important.

That is, until she met Frank Phillips. Like her brother, Frank was attending Denison University and the two played a lot of basketball together when they were home on break. She joined them for a quick game of two-on-two in their driveway, and almost immediately, Frank knocked her flat while driving to the basket. He hovered over her, his handsome face and dark brown eyes overwrought with concern and shame. Who would have guessed that this would be the start of a lifelong romance? That beautiful, decent, and incredibly shy boy stole her heart and turned her life around.

Susie returns her focus to Paul as his voice grows more desperate. It pains her that he is in such distress. His once-promising legal career seems to carom from one bad break to the next. While she and her accountant husband hold steady, high-paying jobs, Paul's life has become a veritable race against the debt collectors. And now here she is, the stable and established sibling, the one being asked to rescue him yet again. His requests are almost always connected to one of his personal injury cases. Can she review medical records for him? Does she know Dr. So-and-So and, if so, can she get him to testify for him? Can she do a little medical research on a case? It never seems to end.

At first, she isn't sure how she can possibly help Paul in his current dilemma. As an emergency room nurse, she has little exposure to psychiatric patients. She treats individuals who attempt suicide or become violent or erratic when they stop taking their medication, but that's it. She's never worked in the psych ward, nor has she ever witnessed someone receiving electroshock treatment.

"Two things that I need," Paul says. "First, I need to get my hands on the records from St. Andrew's Hospital immediately. That's where the Zurcher girl was hospitalized."

"Yes, I know that," Susie says.

"And second, I need you to review them for any irregularities—something that might entice another attorney to take the case over from me."

"You can get the records yourself," Susie says. "You don't need me for that."

"Well, it's just my luck that St. Andrew's is one of the few hospitals in the United States that hasn't converted to electronic records yet. I've learned from experience that it takes forever to get their damn records."

Susie understands why. St. Andrew's is a small, independent community hospital that is still operating in the Dark Ages when it comes to its medical records (and seemingly everything else). When an attorney seeks the hospital's paper chart, suspicions are instantly aroused. The hospital's loss-prevention department springs into action and will not release the records until they have been scrutinized for mistakes, a process that can languish for weeks until someone finally looks at them. After that delay, the hospital sends the records to a third-party vendor who copies them and mails them to the attorney.

"Remind me why you can't wait four or five weeks?" Susie asks.

"Because the statute of limitations will expire in just a couple of months," Paul says. "I need to start moving on this now or I'm screwed."

"Got it," Susie says.

"Any ideas?" Paul asks.

She does have an idea, but it will require a bit of subterfuge. After she outlines her plan, they decide to meet in the hospital's lobby at eleven thirty.

As she rips off her exercise gear and dashes into the shower, she feels exhilarated. For the last decade, her life has been one unbroken string of boring and predictable events. She feels an adrenaline rush as she thinks about the risks inherent in her plan. *Not all that substantial*, she says to herself. But another part of her brain answers, *You could lose your job if things go wrong.* For some reason, this thought makes her smile. She quickly towels herself dry and heads toward the bedroom closet to grab her scrubs and a lab coat.

Oh, what she'll do for that naïve brother of hers.

CHAPTER 7
APRIL 30, 2017
PAUL SCHOFIELD

As he waits for Susie in the hospital lobby, Paul doesn't know the exact details of her plan. He understands that they are going to visit the records office together, show the custodian a medical authorization, and then review the records on site. However, she insisted that he wear casual clothes, which he finds puzzling. Nevertheless, he returned home, donned some tan pants and a golf shirt, and left his briefcase in the car (another Susie requirement). This is her show and he'll let her run it.

After waiting about ten minutes, he sees Susie burst through the revolving door. He expected her to be dressed informally too, but she is wearing a white lab coat over her dark blue scrubs. Her blond hair, still wet from a shower, is pulled into a ponytail. Her blue eyes, always dazzling, sparkle with mischief. She pulls her five-foot-six-inch frame up to him and gives him a hug. Unlike his wife, Susie is solidly built and her strong biceps seem determined to squeeze the breath out of him.

"What's with the stethoscope?" Paul asks as he pulls away from her. He felt it press against his chest as they hugged.

"I'm pretending to be on duty," she says. "You know, I want them to think it's an emergency about getting the records and all."

This seems a bit over-the-top, but Paul just shrugs. He reaches into his rear pants pocket and retrieves a folded medical authorization signed by his client. "I figured we'd need this to get the records released."

Susie snatches it from his hand, gives it a cursory glance, and hands it back to him. "We can't use that," she says. "I brought a different kind for you to sign." She reaches into her purse and pulls out a paper and pen. "What's the name of the girl?" she asks abruptly.

When Paul tells her, she begins filling out the form. When she finishes, she hands it to him and thrusts a pen at him along with it. "Now, I want you to sign the authorization as the girl's father."

"No, no, no. I can't do that," Paul protests, extending the paper and pen back in her direction. "You want me to forge a signature on that form? I could lose my license for that."

"That's only if we get caught," Susie says, refusing to take back the paper. "Look at it this way: your client signed an authorization for you to get the records. Right?"

Paul raises his eyebrows. He knows what is coming next.

"It's just a teeny, tiny step for you to sign another form on his behalf," Susie says.

"Is this some big game for you?" Paul asks indignantly. "What's wrong with using a legitimate authorization signed by my client?"

"Give me your form," Susie says. After Paul hands it to her, she reads the first line out loud. "'I, Dennis Zurcher, hereby authorize my attorney, Paul Schofield, to . . .'" She stops reading and searches Paul's face for a reaction. When she gets none, she continues, "This document identifies you as an attorney. They're never going to hand the records over to an attorney on the spot."

Paul emphatically shakes his head.

"Do you want to get this done today or not?" Susie says, arching her eyebrows in exasperation.

He does not respond.

"Paul, you need to look at this differently," she says, her voice taking on a quieter, calmer tone, as if she is speaking to a child, something that angers him even more. "You need to pretend that you are the girl's father and that we need to review the records immediately for questions about her continued care."

"But the girl is dead. There can't be any *continued care*," Paul says, as if this settles the matter.

"They don't know she's dead," Susie says.

"What if they do?" Paul counters.

"They won't. And with me there, dressed in my nurse's garb, I'll do all the talking and convince them that this is an urgent matter."

"This is ludicrous," Paul says. Why did he ask Susie for help?

"No, it's not. Just calm down. If my friend Shirley is working there, this will be easy."

"You didn't tell me you had a friend in this department," Paul says, the knot in his stomach disappearing.

"Well, maybe *friend* is an exaggeration," Susie backpedals. "I've sat with her in the cafeteria a few times."

Paul's momentary relief vanishes and his face turns grim. "I don't think the risk here is worth it. Let's just forget it."

"You told me this Zurcher guy is probably going to sue you for a gazillion dollars if you screw up his case, right?"

Paul purses his lips but doesn't answer.

"I don't think you have much of a choice," Susie insists.

Paul looks at the form again and his eyes lock on to the blank signature line. Is he overreacting? Signing his client's name under these conditions isn't really forgery, is it? These are very unusual circumstances.

Susie smiles at him. "Come on, Paulie, this is the most fun I've had with you in ages. Let's do it. Let's kick some ass."

No one has called him *Paulie* in decades. Susie looks at him just as she did when they were kids. Suddenly, they are back in their parents' basement and Susie is egging him on to toilet-paper the yard of a cheerleader who mocked Susie the day before. After he agreed, they lobbed and hurled toilet paper at an evergreen tree in the girl's front yard, turning it into the world's largest wedding cake. It was so much fun and they never got caught. Maybe he just needs to relax and give Susie's plan a try.

"Okay. Why not? What have I got to lose?" he replies.

"Your license," Susie says, giving him a wink.

"Yeah, that."

"Mine, too, you know," she says as she lightly punches his right upper arm.

They make a sharp left turn at the visitor information desk, where two senior citizens are saving the hospital a few dollars by matching patient names to room numbers. Susie walks briskly and with purpose down a hall lined on both sides with portraits of former chiefs of staff. As they pass them, Susie points from one face to the next, providing a one-word running commentary: *arrogant*, *brilliant*, *incompetent*, *caring*, *asshole*, and so on.

When they open the door to the records room, it appears abandoned. Behind a counter, four desks are a jumble of patient charts, paper clips, headphones, and rubber fingertip protectors. Beyond the desks, the huge room is filled with rows of shelving units, packed with files. Dust seems to hang in the air and Paul suppresses a sneeze.

"Lunchtime?" Paul asks.

His question is answered by a subdued laugh. They walk around the counter and follow the sound to a desk piled high with files. There, they find a very thin woman, not more than twenty years old, focused on her iPhone. Her black hair is streaked with bright green highlights and she seems delighted by whatever she is watching. Paul wonders how she can type anything with her long black fingernails. When she momentarily glances up at them, Paul is shocked to see that her lipstick matches her nails.

Susie clears her throat. "Hi, we're looking for Shirley."

The young woman doesn't respond immediately but continues typing on her iPhone. A few moments later, she stops. "Oh, Shirley. Sorry, she's on maternity leave. I'm from a temp agency and started yesterday. They left me in charge during the lunch break. Somethin' I can help you with?"

Paul immediately relaxes. Susie will charm and bamboozle this young woman and they will get what they came for. Game, set, match for Susie. His sister introduces herself as a "nurse-patient advocate" (whatever that is) and tells the temp that the man standing next to her needs to review his daughter's hospital chart immediately because the poor girl is scheduled to see an out-of-town specialist in two days.

"What's wrong with our local doctors?" the temp asks, snapping her chewing gum as if to emphasize her disapproval.

The question seems to momentarily surprise Susie. Paul can sense his sister's impatience, but Susie explains that this young girl has a rare condition and is scheduled to be examined at the Mayo Clinic in two days.

"That's a strange name for a hospital," the temp replies. "You sure you got that name right?"

Although Paul vowed to keep quiet, this young woman and her stupid questions are irritating him. He looks back at the office door, expecting to see a real employee return from lunch and derail their entire scheme. "It's a very famous hospital in Minnesota," he says, unable to hide his annoyance. "Can we just dispense with all of these pointless questions? I need these records today."

Susie grabs his forearm and pinches it hard. "You must excuse Mr. Zurcher. He's very worried about his daughter. Would it be too much for you to retrieve the records and let us review them in that little glassed-in room over there?"

With a parting glance that reveals her disdain for *Mr. Zurcher*, the employee retreats to the stacks to find the chart.

"I can't take you anywhere," Susie says, shaking her head. After

Paul apologizes for his outburst, they wait and wait for the young woman to return.

About ten minutes later, she returns with a folder that is about two inches thick. "I almost gave up," she says in a breathy, exasperated tone. "I don't know why I was thinking the last name was Barker. I kept looking in the B section. Then I remembered that the last name was Zurcher and I found it right away." Handing the file to Susie, she looks eagerly at her, like a dog expecting a treat.

After Susie thanks her, they take the file into the side room, where they plop it onto a table. Paul edges his chair next to his sister's while Susie opens the file slowly, as if she is defusing a bomb.

The records are bound with a long metal prong that pushes through two holes at the top of the pages. After Susie turns the first few pages, she sees three pages that are loose in the file.

Picking them up, she reads them once and then places two of them side by side on the table's surface. She glances from one to the next and then back again. Covering her mouth with one hand, her eyes grow wild with excitement. She grabs Paul's arm, digging into the place where she pinched him minutes earlier. "Oh my God, Paul. I can't believe this."

"What? What is it?"

"Dr. Wright changed his discharge summary. He added something that was not in the original record."

"Let me see that," Paul says, grabbing the papers from Susie's hands. Stuck to one page is a yellow sticky note with this message: *Per Dr. Wright, revise the discharge summary by adding these sentences at the end. M. Redwick, RN (11-25-2016).* The sticky note is affixed to a typewritten paper that reads:

> *I discussed with the parents that they needed to keep the antidepressant medication under lock and key. I explained that this medication has no known antidote and would be lethal if*

ingested in large quantities by their daughter. The parents voiced their understanding.

Despite Paul's lack of expertise in medical malpractice cases, he knows instantly that they have found something incredibly important. Doctors do not change the records unless they've done something wrong.

"I just want to be sure of one thing," Paul says. "I know a doctor isn't allowed to change an entry, but can a doctor add something to a record? I mean, that's what Dr. Wright did here. He added more information, but he didn't change anything else in the records per se."

Susie explains that if a doctor wants to amend the chart in that way, the new entry has to be labeled as a "late-entry addendum." It is a separate document, identified as such, and dated on the actual date that it is written. Dr. Wright did not do that. He intended for the hospital to substitute a new discharge summary for the old one, which was to be destroyed. According to Susie, this is fraudulent.

As Paul turns this information over in his mind, he tries to put himself in Dr. Wright's place. How will the doctor or his attorney attempt to defuse this? Pointing to the new discharge summary, Paul says, "You know, if I were Dr Wright, I'd say that I warned the parents, but I just forgot to include it in the discharge summary."

Susie suppresses a laugh. "Oh, just let him try that one. I'd eat him up on cross-examination."

"Well, you're not the lawyer on this case, so please educate me," Paul says.

"If it's not charted, it didn't happen," Susie says, pausing and letting the words sink in. She then explains that this is a fundamental maxim taught in both nursing and medical schools. It is drilled into would-be doctors and nurses from the moment they begin their training. "It's pretty simple," Susie continues. "If the original discharge summary did not state that he warned the parents about the antidepressant, then it is fair to conclude that he did not. End of story."

Paul nods his head in approval. However, he isn't sure why the doctor's warning is so important. "Here's another thing that troubles me. Shouldn't the parents have known to keep all drugs away from their daughter? I mean, she's chronically depressed, and if she ingests an entire bottle of just about anything, she can kill herself."

"Yes and no," Susie responds. "With a lot of drug overdoses, we can pump the stomach, get the bad stuff out, introduce an antidote, and the patient recovers. But Dr. Wright prescribed an antidepressant in the tricyclic family. Those are nasty drugs because they get into a patient's system very rapidly, leaving little time to counteract them. It's a very short window and that's why Dr. Wright needed to give them a warning."

Susie's experience in the emergency room is opening a door. He can win this case; he can feel it in his gut. However, it will all be for naught if they don't leave the hospital with those three pages.

Paul hands the documents to Susie. "Okay, how do we get these out of here?"

"Leave it to me, big brother."

Susie strides out of the side room and over to the receptionist's desk, where the new employee is once again engrossed in her smartphone. Startled, she jerks her head up when she sees Susie leaning over her.

"Finished so soon?" the employee asks.

"Well, it helps when you know what to look for. I'm really quite familiar with these charts," Susie answers evenly.

"I guess so."

"You have been so helpful to us. What is your name anyway?" Susie asks.

"Oh, I'm Cheryl, Cheryl Sadowski."

"Well, Cheryl, I just have one more small favor to ask of you and we'll be out of your hair."

"Sure, what is it?"

"Out of this huge chart, we just need you to copy three pages. Could you do that for us? And, of course, we'll pay."

"Three copies? Oh, just forget it. I think the hospital can afford that, particularly when you work for us. Anyway, I don't know how to charge for copies. Nobody's explained that to me yet."

"Thank you so much, Cheryl," Susie says as she winks at her brother.

After Cheryl makes the copies, Paul and Susie rush out of the room with their loot. Once outside, Paul sweeps his sister into his arms and hugs her.

"You're brilliant," Paul gushes as he twirls her around.

Smiling broadly, Susie says, "Now you shouldn't have any difficulty finding another attorney to take over the case."

"You know, I don't think I'm going to refer the case out," Paul replies.

Susie looks at him incredulously. "Are you the same guy who told me he was going to lose his house if he didn't refer this case to a medical malpractice specialist?"

"The very same one."

For the first time that day, Susie's face becomes serious. "I know this is good stuff, but are you sure you want to go it alone?"

Paul smiles broadly. "Every now and then, you have to bet on yourself. What you found for me is bombshell evidence. The doctor tried to cover up his mistake. Jurors can understand that without listening to a bunch of medical experts. I'll destroy the other side with it. I know it."

"But she killed herself, Paul," Susie interrupts. "Correct me if I'm wrong, but you have to prove two things. First, the doctor made a mistake. Okay, you've got that. But then you need to show that the doctor's mistake caused her death. Are you following me here?"

"I know what you're going to say," Paul replies. "There are many ways people can kill themselves. She could have jumped off a bridge or stepped in front of a truck. She didn't need this medication to kill herself. We can't prove that Dr. Wright's mistake caused her death when she had other ways to commit suicide."

"Exactly."

"Technically, that's right, but the jurors won't even look at that issue. They'll be so mad that the doctor changed his records that the case will be over."

Susie gives him a quizzical look. "I think you're making another mistake, but it's your call. You're the lawyer, not me."

Her admonition washes over him and he doesn't respond to it. Instead, he simply thanks her again. "I can't believe how much you helped me."

"Well, this time, Paul, it was fun—really fun."

As Paul walks to his car, his euphoria begins to fade, replaced by a creeping sense of guilt. The bottom line is that he gained access to a medical chart under false pretenses. A lawyer's conduct is governed by both disciplinary rules and ethical considerations. He isn't sure which particular ethical rules he violated, but he crossed the line at least once, maybe several times. He knows that when an attorney begins ignoring ethical tenets, it is a slippery slope to disaster—one that can cost him his reputation and his license, and maybe more.

CHAPTER 8
MAY 24, 2017
PAUL SCHOFIELD

Seeking privacy and quiet, Paul rises from his chair to close his office door. His secretary, Eileen Rogers, is on the phone, speaking in her loud voice, something he finds irritating but is powerless to change. He's inherited Eileen from his uncle, and Paul would be lost without her. A tall and big-boned woman in her early sixties, Eileen is his one-person support staff: receptionist, secretary, probate paralegal, and bookkeeper—jobs she completes on a part-time schedule. He hasn't intended to eavesdrop, but her grating voice seems to bounce off the hallway walls and ceiling.

"You don't jump to the head of the line just by calling three times a day," Eileen tells the caller, her voice strident and irritated.

After a brief pause, she takes another swipe at the caller. "If I wanted to listen to a temper tantrum, I'd be babysitting my three-year-old grandson right now. Just hold on to your panties, Mr. Johnson. You'll get a return phone call within twenty-four hours."

After another pause, Eileen finally says, "Have a blessed day," her voice dripping with sarcasm. He decides that he must deal with Eileen's behavior today while the encounter is still fresh. But why today? He is already on edge. Later in the day, he'll drive into Cleveland and meet with Scott Worthington and try to convince him to take over the Zurcher case.

Four weeks have passed since he and Susie discovered the "smoking gun" in the hospital records. Armed with this new development, he contacted several litigation financing firms and sought their assistance. If one of them agreed to finance the Zurcher case, it would pay the litigation expenses: experts' fees, depositions, and mock juries. Two companies turned him down outright (apparently based on his lack of experience in the malpractice arena), while the third demanded 20 percent of the settlement in return for an advance of thirty thousand dollars. He knew that Dennis would never agree to that arrangement and politely told the firm that he'd look elsewhere. And "elsewhere" turned out to be Scott Worthington, the attorney who rescued him in his one and only other medical malpractice case.

But that meeting is later this afternoon. Right now, he needs to have a talk with Eileen. As he approaches her desk, country-western music plays softly from her personal radio, placed strategically between framed photographs of her four grandchildren, all of whom seem to be missing several front teeth. Her strong perfume assails him before he speaks. He coughs, causing her to swivel in her chair to face him, her large hoop earrings swaying from the maneuver.

"Uh, Eileen, I overheard part of that conversation with Mr. Johnson," he begins.

Before he can finish, Eileen blurts, "That vile man took the Lord's name in vain. Can you believe that?"

Eileen is a devout Pentecostal; he's caught snippets of her phone conversations with her church-circle friends. From these, he's concluded that she and her churchmates are a very judgmental group, castigating gay people, transgender people, and members of other religions—which somehow also includes other Christian denominations.

"Still, Eileen, I can't have you address *our* clients in an insulting way. Promise me that you won't do that again."

Straightening in her chair, Eileen can't contain her hurt feelings. "I need this job like I need a hole in my head," she sputters. "I've stayed on this job out of respect for your uncle, but if you don't approve of the way I interact with clients, I'll quit and let you hire someone more to your liking."

Paul knows that Eileen is sensitive, but her waspish response startles him. If he weren't in such a precarious situation, he'd feel inclined to let her go. She is efficient and hardworking, but the two of them see the world in vastly different ways. Since his uncle's death, he's tolerated her politics and prejudices, convinced that her office and legal skills outweigh her personal drawbacks. However, when he replaces her, he will need her cooperation in training the new employee. He has no choice but to patch things up for now.

"Eileen, I'm sorry if I offended you. You know I appreciate your dedication," he says, backing a few inches away from her.

"Who else would take work home? Who else would continue to work in this place without a raise in seven years?" Paul can see tears form behind her large-framed eyeglasses.

"Points well taken. I know we all have bad days and sometimes regret things we've said," he replies, his head bowed as he peers down at her.

Her chin quivering, Eileen says, "Things are not great at home. Melvin is still out of work."

What else is new? Paul thinks. Eileen's husband is always getting fired, but Paul assumed that he is now old enough to receive social security benefits—gracefully erasing him from the workforce. From other phone conversations that have drifted into his office, Paul also learned that the man is a heavy drinker and an occasional gambler. "I'm sorry to hear that," he finally says. "You must be feeling a lot of stress right now."

"You might say that," Eileen responds, her indignation apparently cooling.

"Let's just forget what I said," Paul says. "I'm under some pressure, too. I need your continued good work."

Paul expects that Eileen will smile and apologize, but, instead, she grimaces and nods. *I guess that's all I'll get*, he thinks. He raises his eyebrows, turns abruptly, and walks back to his office, determined to organize his thoughts before his meeting with Scott Worthington.

When setting up the meeting, Paul disguised its purpose. He only told Scott that he needed his advice on a medical malpractice case, being deliberately cryptic about the facts. He disclosed that he'd discovered undeniable proof that a doctor changed a discharge summary by inserting a warning that he never gave. Paul explained that if the warning had been given, the patient would still be alive. Scott replied, "Oh my, I like those facts. Sounds like you've got him." From the enthusiasm in Scott's voice, he hoped that Scott would welcome a chance to handle the case. For now, Paul will play it coy.

●●●

Paul's destination is downtown Cleveland and, in particular, the eighth floor of Key Center, where Scott Worthington's firm leases its office space. Before he can take the elevator, he's been told, he needs to go to the security station in the southeast corner of the spacious lobby, which spans almost one entire city block. Once he's there, two uniformed guards check his identification and issue him a temporary card to feed an automated security gate that keeps unwanted visitors from accessing the elevators. As he approaches the elevators, his shoes click on the faux-marble floor and reflect on its polished surface.

Key Center's luxurious interior seems like an alien world to him, so different from the grit and grime of his own workplace. Regret creeps over him as he compares the two. Of course, it boils down to choices —it always does. He shunned this world upon graduation and now the decision haunts him, as it periodically does. If he'd accepted one of the many large-firm offers that came his way a decade ago, he'd be working at a prestigious law firm now—if not here, then someplace equally impressive.

After stepping into the elevator, he is joined by men and women who seem the epitome of success: crisp, proud, and driven. A pang of jealousy grips his stomach as he surveys the group. He is as intelligent as they are, maybe more so. When he finished law school, he was awarded many of the same honors that these legal stars have parlayed into high-paying jobs. They snatched the prize positions while he went home and, ultimately, was left behind. Before he can indulge in further self-pity, the elevator makes a soft ding and stops at the eighth floor. He is the only person to exit—the others will soar to higher floors where more sophisticated and rewarding work awaits them.

As Paul walks from the elevator, the modernity of the building, with its tall, tinted windows and slick corridors, makes an abrupt shift to a staid and traditional décor. Standing on the threshold of Worthington's office, Paul is dazzled by the impressive mahogany entranceway and the nameplate whose metal letters seem to be made of pure gold. Once inside, a thin, attractive brunette dressed in a stylish maroon jacket greets him with a smile that brings out matching dimples on either side of her face. No more than thirty years old, she has dark brown eyes that sparkle with intelligence and charm. The contrast between her and Eileen cannot be starker.

After Paul explains that he has an appointment with Scott Worthington, the young woman directs him to the waiting area and offers him a beverage, which he declines. Sitting on a plush sofa, Paul spots copies of *The New York Times* and *USA Today* on a nearby butler's table. He picks up the *Times* and begins scanning the articles but finds he is unable to concentrate. Setting the newspaper back on the table, he closes his eyes and listens to the soothing ticktock of a grandfather clock behind him.

"Don't fall asleep on me," a resonant baritone voice says a few minutes later.

Paul opens his eyes to see the figure of Scott Worthington towering over him. Scott is dressed casually in a pale blue cashmere sweater and navy blue dress pants. After Paul jumps to his feet and faces Scott, the circumstances are reversed. Paul is at least three to four inches taller than his host.

Scott is in his early fifties, wiry and fit, with gray hair that is combed straight back from a strong, angular face. It has been three years since the two last met and Paul thinks that Scott looks younger. After studying Scott's face for a few moments, Paul realizes that Scott no longer wears his customary thick eyeglasses. Paul considers asking him if he's had LASIK surgery but decides not to invade his privacy.

Although Scott smiles and gives him a firm handshake, Paul senses that he is intruding on the man's busy schedule. There seems to be something else lurking beneath the surface. Scott seems wary, perhaps questioning why Paul has driven all the way into Cleveland when a phone call would have sufficed. On the other hand, Paul suspects that he is simply being paranoid, uncomfortable with his planned subterfuge.

Following Scott back toward his office, Paul puts his hands in his pockets to warm them and wipes away the cold sweat. He needs to be very persuasive in the next half hour—everything depends upon it. Recalling his difficult conversation with Isaac Gableman a little over a month earlier, Paul realizes that he can be turned down again. However, this time, things will be different.

Once seated in Scott's office, Paul dispenses with pleasantries. He tells Scott how he and his sister discovered the altered discharge summary.

"I came here to get your thoughts on strategy," Paul says. "The alteration of the records is a pretty powerful weapon."

Scott nods in agreement.

"Here are my questions. When do you think I should disclose this to the other side? Does it make sense to reveal this before filing the lawsuit? You know, could it promote a settlement early on?"

Paul has no intention of providing this information to the doctor's insurance company before filing suit. Hell, any attorney with half a brain knows not to do that. A competent attorney would commence the action, take the doctor's sworn testimony in deposition, and, during the questioning, lock the doctor into a lie: namely, that the altered discharge summary was the one that he dictated immediately upon the patient's release from the hospital.

But he'll let Scott tell him the obvious and Paul can then pretend to be enlightened. From there, Paul will eventually admit that he needs someone with Scott's experience to handle the case.

As Paul expected, Scott seems startled that Paul would propose such a plan. "Uh, no. I doubt it would force a settlement pre-suit," Scott says, his tone measured and serious. "You'd be giving the doctor and his lawyers months to come up with an explanation for the alteration. And then, when you finally take the doctor's deposition, he'll admit that he changed the discharge summary but provide logical reasons for doing it. So no, it's a very bad idea. Don't do that."

Paul nods. "I should have thought of that myself. I guess I was hoping that I could sidestep all the time and expense of litigating a medical malpractice case."

Scott shakes his head as if commiserating. "Sorry, Paul. You've got to be prepared to try each and every one of these cases to a verdict. As you learned in our case, malpractice insurers will not concede anything. Even when they should pay, they dig in their heels and wait until the last minute to settle."

Paul decides that the moment has arrived to make his appeal to Scott. "Well, as you might guess, I've been struggling with whether I should handle this case on my own. I mean, am I doing my clients a disservice by not turning this over to someone more experienced?"

Scott doesn't respond to the rhetorical question but nods in encouragement.

"I brought my file with me: the medical records, my legal memoranda, my client interview notes, and Dr. Simon Masterson's initial letter criticizing the treatment. Can I leave it with you and you can call me after you've reviewed things?"

"What's the deadline for filing the case?" Scott asks.

"Two months," Paul replies.

Scott frowns. "Not much time, I'm afraid." He then holds out his hand toward Paul. "Let me look at the two discharge summaries and the sticky note now," Scott says.

Paul takes them from a file and slides them across Scott's desk. Scott spreads the two discharge summaries on his desk side by side, just as Susie did four weeks earlier. As Scott begins to read, his face takes on a quizzical expression that eventually turns into a look of dismay or disgust. Paul can't tell.

"God, I know this case," Scott says, shaking his head. "I met with the father about four months ago. I'm sorry, but I don't want any part of this."

How could Scott have met with the Zurchers? Paul scrambles to make sense of this revelation. When he first met with the Zurchers, Dennis disclosed his upcoming appointment with Scott Worthington. In fact, he indicated that it was happening the following day. After Paul and the Zurchers executed the representation agreement, Dennis specifically told his wife to cancel the meeting with Scott Worthington. That memory is seared into Paul's brain, vivid and complete. That meeting was a roller-coaster ride of emotions—first, fear that the Zurchers would select Scott, and then relief when they retained him.

Something doesn't fit. But then it does. Dennis is a liar, probably a sociopathic one. Dennis used Scott Worthington's name only to pressure Paul into accepting the case. The Zurchers had no upcoming meeting with Scott; that appointment had long passed. If the expression on Scott's face is any indicator, that meeting was a disaster.

How many attorneys has Dennis met with and then alienated? Five, ten, twenty? Does it matter? What matters is overcoming Scott's reservations about the case. Paul will not ask Scott to rehash the meeting with the Zurchers. It is unnecessary. Dennis probably became irate with Scott at some point—perhaps set off by a probing question or Scott's skepticism about the merits of his case. Again, it doesn't matter.

Unlike his conversation with Isaac Gableman, Paul will not try to sugarcoat Dennis's difficult personality. He will acknowledge it but then stress the strength of the case—the barbarity of prescribing electroshock to a teenage girl and the doctor's fraud in changing the discharge report.

For the next five minutes, Paul stays on the offensive, expressing confidence that a jury will be outraged by the doctor's conduct—enough to override a jury's dislike for the father. As Paul emphasizes the case's strong jury appeal, he makes progress with Scott, who acknowledges that the case is winnable.

"How much legal malpractice coverage do you have?" Scott asks, the question seemingly out of the blue and startling Paul.

"Well, to cut costs last year, I lowered mine to the state minimum, one hundred thousand dollars," Paul says, knowing that this admission reveals much about the state of his law practice.

"What do you think will happen if you lose this case?" Scott asks.

Paul knows where this is headed. "Mr. Zurcher will not be happy," he answers.

"Even if we try a perfect case, he'll sue us," Scott answers. "You know it and I know it. He's a litigious asshole who thinks he's always right. If we lose, he'll be convinced it was because we screwed up."

Paul can't dispute this; Scott has evaluated Dennis Zurcher fairly. Scott continues, "My firm doesn't want to be sued by Dennis Zurcher. He's a guy that is hell-bent on making someone pay for his perceived misery. When all is said and done, he'll be just as happy to receive money from our malpractice insurer as that of the doctor."

"But we can win this case. You said so yourself," Paul protests. "I don't think we should be worried about the consequences if we lose—because we won't."

Scott raises his eyebrows in disagreement. "I said the case was winnable. Yeah, that's true. But this case is also defensible. We can lose too. I'm sure of that."

Paul looks down at knees and shakes his head. "I'm kind of stuck," he says. Paul then explains how he added a provision in his representation agreement forbidding him to drop the case without securing other counsel.

"I feel like such a fool," Paul admits.

Paul thinks he sees pity in Scott's expression, either that or disbelief at his gullibility. Scott's eyes soften before he speaks. "That provision may not be enforceable. Your client wasn't truthful about several things—like meeting with me and the other attorneys."

"I don't want a jury deciding whether it's enforceable or not," Paul says. "The publicity from that trial would be disastrous for my career."

Scott nods.

"Despite everything, I feel like I can win this case," Paul says. "I just don't have a way to finance it. The litigation funding companies don't want to take a chance on me or this case." Paul retrieves the discharge summaries from Scott's desk and returns them to the file folder. He stands to leave. "Well, thanks for talking to me," Paul says. "It's my problem and I'll have to deal with it."

Scott holds up his hand in a halting gesture. "Sit down. Maybe there is another solution. Not one that meets the exact letter of our ethical rules, but one that might solve your problems." When Paul doesn't stop him, Scott continues, "What you need is money for expenses and some advice from time to time. Right?"

Paul nods and then listens as Scott proposes that his firm serve as a silent partner in the case. Scott's firm will advance up to thirty thousand dollars in expenses and, in return, receive 40 percent of the total attorney fee if Paul is successful. If Paul loses, he will owe them nothing.

So far, this is a perfectly appropriate arrangement, but then Scott adds an unethical condition. Paul is not to disclose the arrangement to his clients, nor will Scott or his firm be named on any pleadings. In essence, Scott's firm will be insulated from liability. If Dennis Zurcher is unaware of the other law firm, he cannot sue them.

Paul is no stranger to the ethical rules dealing with fee splitting.

No matter how Paul and Scott label or define their deal, they are acting as co-counsel if they are to share the fee. As such, the rules require Paul to disclose this fee-splitting arrangement to his client and obtain his approval. The rules also require both law firms to be equally responsible for any legal mistake. This, too, is being subverted.

Both men are taking a significant risk. If this arrangement ever becomes known, they'll both face disciplinary action, perhaps have their licenses suspended for a year or more. But what choice does Paul have? He is desperate.

Paul sucks in a big breath. "Okay," he says as he exhales.

Shaking hands, both men muster reluctant smiles. They will not memorialize their agreement in writing.

As he leaves Key Center, Paul replays what has just happened. It isn't what Paul wanted, but it is a solution. Technically, he violated some ethical rules, but he did so with his client's best interest at heart, didn't he? Dennis Zurcher's case against Dr. Wright can now go forward. Without this secret financial arrangement, the case would have died. Traveling the perilous road to justice, an attorney occasionally has to make some ethical sacrifices along the way.

As Paul drives back to Elyria, he plays variations of this reasoning over in his mind. As he gets closer to home, this logic becomes less and less convincing. By the time he parks his car in the driveway, he is numb with guilt.

He is trying to do the right thing, isn't he? Then why does it feel like he's losing himself in the process?

PART TWO

THE LAWSUIT

CHAPTER 9
JULY 19, 2017
ROBERT INGRAM

Robert Ingram struggles to maintain his composure as Rudy Cerruti, a brash blowhard from Defiance Mutual Insurance Company, boasts about a putt he sank on the sixteenth hole. Ingram is determined to remain congenial. His sole job is to entertain this group from Defiance Mutual, a medical malpractice insurance carrier that is one of his law firm's best clients. Every year he hosts three of the company's employees at the posh Westwood Country Club in Rocky River, where they play a round of golf, followed by drinks and dinner.

"I always perform best under pressure," Cerruti says, grabbing his beer mug and emptying it in one long gulp. "I thought the ball was slightly off course, but then it hit the edge of the hole, spun around one edge, and dropped in. Not my best putt of the day, but lady luck was with me." To emphasize his point, he wipes his mouth with his forearm and then grins.

Two of the other Defiance Mutual invitees roll their eyes and grab some nuts from a nearby bowl. Ingram forces a smile. He saw Cerruti cheat on several holes, twice reporting a score that was a stroke lower than what he'd actually shot, and once kicking his ball out of the rough and onto the fairway. In Ingram's view, people reveal their true selves on the golf course. Of course, he surreptitiously dropped a ball on the fairway when his disappeared in the rough, but, after Cerruti's behavior, he felt justified.

"Then, of course, I thought that my drive on the eighteenth fairway was hooking, but then it straightened out at about one hundred yards and just kept going after that," Cerruti says, sliding one hand over the other like a jet accelerating down a runway.

This braggard is beginning to get on Ingram's nerves. Cerruti is built like a gorilla, so, of course, he can outdrive everybody else. But the arrogant cheat has lied to beat him by two strokes. "Too bad you can't count as well as you drive," Ingram says, trying to disguise his insult with a smile.

"Hey, what's that supposed to mean?" Cerruti asks. Ingram sees menace in Cerruti's dark eyes and can envision the angry Italian taking a swing at him.

"I'm joking," Ingram says, his voice playful and calm. Before Cerruti can respond, Emily McDonald, Defiance Mutual's regional supervisor, appears in the hallway, just outside the double doors leading into the dining room. Ingram rises to greet her, hoping to catch a minute with her before taking her to their table. Looking distracted, McDonald is dressed in a navy blue business suit, and her short brown hair frames a harsh face. Her high cheekbones, thin lips, and hawkish nose give her an imposing appearance. At six feet, there is nothing delicate about this full-figured woman.

"Emily, good to see you," Ingram says as they stand. "How did your mediation go today?"

"I didn't want to settle that case, and by God, I didn't," McDonald says, grasping Ingram's right hand in a firm handshake. As she cups her left hand over their two right hands, she continues, "The judge mandated the mediation, so we had to show up, but damn if we were going to settle." McDonald keeps her hands entwined around his right hand longer than what seems normal. When Ingram studies her eyes, he thinks he sees something else. Is there something suggestive in the way she is looking at him? For the last twelve years, McDonald has always been professional when they interact—all business, never anything flirtatious or suggestive.

But tonight, she seems different. If he can read women (and he can), she seems drawn to him in a way that has nothing to do with business. And why not? Women are always attracted to him; he is handsome and charming. McDonald will be spending the night at a hotel before returning to Columbus the next morning. Of course, she will be lonely and looking for company—and he will be only too willing to oblige.

Ten years ago, Ingram would not have given McDonald a second look. But now, at sixty-nine, he is not quite so picky. Over the last ten years, he's added twenty-five pounds to his six-foot-one-inch frame. In a Brooks Brothers custom suit, he can hide his paunch, but that advantage disappears when he is naked in the bedroom.

"Emily, those plaintiffs' attorneys are no match for you," Ingram says, grinning and nodding his approval at her toughness. She never authorizes a nuisance settlement—not ever. Whenever she refuses to buckle (and that is often), she repeats her guiding mantra: "Millions for the defense but not a penny for tribute." And those are golden words to an insurance defense attorney.

But this evening, McDonald is regarding him with a warmth in her eyes, and if he wants, perhaps he can take their relationship to another level. Pretending to study her face, he asks, "Have you done something with your hair? It looks great."

"No, not really," McDonald replies, giving him an amused smile.

"Well, there's something different," Ingram says, manufacturing a mischievous grin. This middle-aged woman is decidedly plain, maybe unattractive, but she is well-endowed and that is enough for him.

Ingram has been married and divorced twice; his ex-wives are united in their disdain for him. He's never been a faithful husband, chasing after secretaries, court reporters, and deputy clerks whenever the opportunity arises. His two daughters (one from each wife) seem to like him—maybe *tolerate* is a better word. However, his three grandsons adore him. He is a super grandfather, taking them to professional ball games and showering them with electronic gadgets, autographed sports memorabilia, and science fiction books. In the end, he's somehow achieved the impossible—sleeping with an assortment of eager women while salvaging a family life that suits him.

"I'm hoping we can have some time alone, maybe after dinner," McDonald says. She looks furtively about the hallway, as if she is concerned that someone may overhear their conversation. That is all he needs for confirmation; the next move is his. However, McDonald's breath is sour, causing Ingram to move a few inches back and reconsider. But then his eyes drift to her breasts and he feels something stirring.

"I'm not doing anything tonight," Ingram replies, his voice low and conspiratorial. "What did you have in mind?" To encourage McDonald, he unleashes an alluring smile, his bleached white teeth contrasting with his deeply tanned face.

Catching his intent, McDonald laughs nervously and then stiffens. "It's about the case I just assigned to your office," she says, averting her eyes from his.

After a sharp intake of air, Ingram nods. "You know, I was hoping that we could discuss that before you drove back," he says, trying to sound nonchalant.

What the hell was he thinking? She is decidedly masculine, has never mentioned a husband or boyfriend, and wears no wedding ring. For God's sake, he's probably been trying to seduce a lesbian.

Worse yet, he was willing to jeopardize his firm's relationship with Defiance Mutual for a night's dalliance. Every year, McDonald refers about forty medical malpractice cases to his firm—each one generating a fee of fifteen to twenty-five thousand dollars. He and his partner, Ed Sparks, can't afford to lose a million-dollar revenue stream.

"Good, because I want you to handle it. Not Sparks and not one of your associates," McDonald says.

"Sure. No problem. We'll talk after dinner." Although Ingram is trying to slow down and reduce his workload, he is in no position to argue with her after his embarrassing misread.

Ingram's firm, Ingram and Sparks LLP, is comprised of seven attorneys. He and Ed Sparks broke away from a much larger firm eighteen years earlier, taking with them some of the best insurance clients and infuriating his former partners, who felt betrayed. But Ingram believed that this was just the law of the legal jungle; firms broke up all the time and clients chose attorneys who best served their needs.

It was no surprise that Defiance Mutual followed Ingram to his new firm. Throughout his career, he's demonstrated an uncanny ability to win jury trials—the ones he's supposed to win and those he isn't. As a young lawyer, he learned that once he could fake sincerity, he owned the courtroom. Like all civil defense attorneys, his job was to find the biggest weakness in his opponent's case and then exploit it. Not only did he do this well, but he accomplished it with flair, often turning his opponents' arguments or exact words against them.

And Ingram likes what he does—defending doctors. Most of the lawsuits against them are pure bullshit. Yes, personal injury attorneys parade a herd of well-paid experts in front of jurors and tell them what a doctor did wrong. But this is as unfair as it is erroneous. Everything in medicine is preventable in hindsight. The standard, however, is not hindsight but foresight. His clients are practicing medicine in the trenches and not in some ivory tower like the plaintiffs' pompous experts. His doctors are forced to make split-second decisions that seem reasonable at the time. When a jury judges a doctor in this way, it invariably find in his favor. Time and again, Ingram is proud to deliver that message and make the system work for doctors.

He understands why McDonald insists that he handle the new file. If she's already decided that this case is going to trial—no settlement offers—then she'll want him. He is the firm's marquee trial lawyer, much more skilled than the unimaginative and plodding Sparks and certainly more experienced than any of their five associates.

When he and McDonald join the others, Ingram glances at Cerruti, whose face betrays no anger, just an alcohol-induced glazed expression. The other two stand when their boss approaches the table, but neither is quick enough to pull out her chair for her before she sits down. Ingram can see that the three insurance men are on edge; two seem content to endlessly stir their drinks while another stares at a television monitor above the bar. Because their discomfort in McDonald's presence is palpable, Ingram realizes that he will have to carry the conversation and save the evening.

"How do you like the country club, Emily?" Ingram asks. "Although these guys have been here before, you're a first-timer."

"Feels like a plantation to me," Emily says as she coolly surveys the large dining room with its chandelier lighting and large picture windows.

"That's interesting," Ingram says, unsure whether McDonald's assessment is a rebuke or a compliment. "Why do you say that?"

"Oh, first you drive down that exceedingly long driveway. And then at the end of it, you see this huge building with its tall white pillars. I mean, the only things missing are the slaves and Scarlett O'Hara," Emily says, her attempt at humor generating tepid chuckles from her male subordinates.

As the dinner progresses, the mood does not improve. Although Ingram does his best to buck up the conversation, the evening is a struggle. McDonald's male co-workers seem cowed by her, abandoning the playful insults that they tossed at each other during their round of golf. Instead, they drink margaritas and Moscow mules, becoming more sullen as the evening drags on. The obnoxious Cerruti is the only exception, boring the table with tales about his sons' athletic exploits, his recently modified Harley-Davidson, and his analysis of Ohio State's new football recruits.

Apparently uncomfortable in this social setting as well, McDonald is tossing down screwdrivers at an alarming pace. Because she rarely engages in the dinner conversation, Ingram cannot tell if the alcohol has affected her. When her male colleagues finally say their goodbyes at eight thirty, Ingram feels an overpowering sense of relief. He walks the threesome to the valet stand at the club's entrance. As they wait for Cerruti's car, he tells them how much he's enjoyed the outing. As he watches them pile into the adjuster's Subaru Crosstrek, he wonders if they'll arrive safely at the Hilton in downtown Cleveland. But that isn't his problem. In fact, if that cheating Cerruti is arrested for drunk driving, well, so be it.

McDonald greets him with a wan smile when he returns to the table. She apparently reapplied her lipstick at some point after he left and has done a clumsy job, red lipstick applied unevenly on her lips. He has little doubt now that she's drunk far too much.

"This lawsuit against our psychiatrist really pisses me off," she begins. Fueled by alcohol, her voice is decidedly defiant.

Ingram is always uncomfortable talking to an inebriated woman. He can handle guys who are blitzed. Hell, most of his male friends are heavy drinkers. But women are unpredictable enough without alcohol entering the equation. How can he and McDonald have a productive conversation when she is like this? He is about to suggest that they postpone their strategy discussion for another day when he realizes that McDonald is staring at him, unable to disguise her impatience for a response. He has no choice but to pretend to be outraged too. "It's fucking ridiculous," he says, trying to match her indignation. "Sorry, I did not mean to . . ." And then his words trail off.

"No need to apologize. My feelings exactly," McDonald says, her words thick. Her eyes flutter before her next words surface. "What kind of attorney files this kind of crap?" Before Ingram can answer, McDonald continues, "I want you to crush this guy. Work him to death. Throw so much shit at him that he'll never venture into our house again."

Ingram nods, trying to hide his confusion. They've handled cases with less merit than this before and McDonald has never shown this kind of fury. She's always been tough but dispassionate. Trying to make sense of things, Ingram concludes that she is just a mean drunk.

Although she's finished her screwdriver, McDonald grabs the glass, finds the straw, and vigorously swirls the ice as if trying to create a hurricane within. When she finishes, she looks directly at Ingram. "I mean, we can't have lawyers suing psychiatrists every time one of their patients commits suicide. What's next? Oncologists being sued every time their patients die from cancer? Bad results happen every fricking day—even with the best of care." She slams her right hand on the table. "Do you see why we have to destroy this guy and his bullshit?"

Ingram winces inwardly; this woman is out of control. She is blowing this situation completely out of proportion. A psychiatrist prescribed ECT for a teenage girl and things went terribly wrong. It is a unique set of facts. Whatever happens in this case will not open the floodgates to a torrent of litigation.

"I asked you a question," McDonald says. "Is your brain in some inebriated fog?"

Her unwarranted comment angers him and he struggles to maintain his composure. After taking a deep breath, he says, "Emily, you know that I always try to beat my opponents convincingly. This case is no exception."

"And are you going to win the case for me?"

Is McDonald asking him for a guarantee? He has studied the file, and from what he's read, he feels confident of victory. Defiance Mutual hired three psychiatrists with national reputations to review the case and all concluded that Dr. Wright acted properly. They cited the electroshock standards developed by the American Psychiatric Association and found that Dr. Wright had followed them for the most part, although he'd ignored several less consequential recommendations.

How can he assure her of victory when there are a lot of things he doesn't know and can't know yet? He's not met with Dr. Wright. If the doctor is either arrogant or belligerent, a jury will not like him, and then anything can happen.

And what about the plaintiffs' attorney, Paul Schofield? Ingram has scoured Schofield's website for background information. The site's photos reveal a good-looking man in his mid-thirties, someone as handsome as he is. His academic credentials are impressive: he attended a top-twenty law school, where he graduated summa cum laude. But the guy has virtually no experience in the complex field of medical malpractice, a practice filled with its own special rules and pitfalls. On paper, Ingram should "destroy" his opponent, as McDonald wants, but this attorney is still an unknown.

"I like our chances," Ingram replies. "You've retained some impressive experts and they should carry the day."

McDonald frowns. "What do you mean, you like our chances? That obviously leaves room for defeat." He can hear the indignation in her voice. "Don't give me that bullshit that we could lose this one."

Ingram feels himself being trapped. How much should he fight back? Should he give McDonald what she wants—a guarantee of victory? But he doesn't like anyone pushing him around, particularly a woman—and a drunk one at that. For an awkward moment, he debates whether to temper her expectations with an honest appraisal. When he decides that this is the best course, his voice takes on a conciliatory tone. "Very few cases are certain winners. You know that better than anyone. There are things I still need to find out and I'll know more as we get into the case. Let's revisit this in a few months, okay?"

"Yes or no. Are you going to win this case?"

"Come on, Emily," he says. "You know my track record. No other defense attorney wins as consistently as I do."

McDonald rolls her eyes and then snorts.

"What's that supposed to mean?" Ingram asks.

"It means you have an oversized ego—like most of the attorneys I deal with," McDonald says.

She is goading him, plain and simple, but he will not lose his temper. Instead, he will speak candidly about the case and spell out the risks that they face. He'll tell her what she needs to hear, not what she wants to hear, always a dangerous tactic with clients.

Raising his hand in a placating gesture, he says, "There are some dangers and risks here. Let's not be naïve or overconfident, okay? Jurors will come into the courtroom believing that it's barbaric to subject a fifteen-year-old girl to electroshock treatments. When they learn that she committed suicide, they'll naturally attribute it to these treatments. We can call a hundred experts to dispute these things, but the jury may blame Dr. Wright and hold him responsible."

McDonald scowls and then rolls her eyes for the second time. "I really don't want to listen to your doom and gloom." Lifting her glass, she says, "I need another drink."

"Now, Emily. Just hear me out, okay?" Ingram says, his voice edgy for the first time that evening.

"I still want another drink," McDonald says. As if on cue, their waitress stops at their table. Extending her glass toward the waitress, McDonald says, "Give me another one of these but less orange juice and more vodka."

When McDonald sets down her glass, Ingram grabs her right hand and says, "Let me finish, okay?"

McDonald pulls her hand away and her head bobs.

"I'm going to win this case for you," Ingram says. "You've retained some great experts, but, besides that, I'll blame the parents. I've reviewed Dr. Wright's records. There's plenty of bad stuff about the father in them. I'll make that argument stick."

"So you'll crush them, right?" McDonald asks, Ingram's explanation apparently not registering with her.

"Yes, of course," he says, trying to keep the exasperation out of his voice. "Just don't underestimate the complexity of this case. That's all I'm saying."

"Okay. It took you long enough to get there," she says. Her smugness infuriates him, but he lets it pass.

She closes her eyes, signaling that their discussion has drained the last bit of energy from her. When she opens them again, she looks toward the bar. "Where's my drink?" she asks. Ingram can see that their waitress is servicing another table and hasn't given McDonald's order to the bartender.

"It'll be here in a few minutes," Ingram says.

McDonald places her purse on the table, opens it, and begins rummaging through it. She pulls out some crumpled bills, her wallet, and then a small package of facial tissues. "Where the hell are they?" she mutters. She becomes more and more agitated as she searches her purse.

"What are you looking for, Emily?" Ingram asks.

"What do you think? My damn car keys," McDonald says.

"They're probably with the valet," Ingram says.

"Oh yeah. I valeted the car," McDonald says, stuffing her things haphazardly back into the purse.

"Let's switch out your screwdriver for a cup of coffee," Ingram suggests.

"You think I'm drunk or something?" McDonald says, sticking out her lower lip in an act of exaggerated belligerence.

He cannot let her drive to her hotel, but she is in a combative mood and will undoubtedly resist the suggestion. "There's a Rocky River police cruiser that is routinely parked on the state route at the end of the driveway. You have to be very careful here. You should not get behind the wheel."

"You going to drive me to my hotel room, Casanova?" McDonald says, leering at him.

"No, of course not," Ingram says very quickly. "I'm going to get an Uber to drive you to the hotel, if that's all right with you."

"What about my car?" she asks.

"We'll make arrangements to get your car tomorrow."

"Will I have to pay you by the hour for that?" she asks, and then cackles at her own joke.

Ignoring her question, Ingram pulls out his iPhone and orders an Uber. "The driver will be here in ten minutes. I'll wait with you at the front door."

"I need to go to the little girls' room first," McDonald says as she stumbles and bumps into him, causing him to lose his balance. After righting himself, he watches as she lumbers down the hallway. *Just imagine, all that could have been mine*, Ingram thinks, and then shudders.

The evening has been a disaster. Tomorrow, he'll golf with a group of three Cuyahoga County bailiffs—all men who have proven extremely helpful whenever he's had a legal matter before their judges. At trial, they are routinely generous with their insights and inside information. When the bailiffs leave tomorrow night, they will be happy and full of goodwill. He shakes his head as he considers the contrast.

Just then, the Uber stops at the front entrance. Ingram looks for McDonald. She is cautiously descending the large staircase that leads from the second-floor dining area to the entrance. If he can get her safely to the car, this horrible evening will mercifully come to an end. He meets McDonald halfway on the stairs and takes her by the elbow to steady her. The move angers her and she jerks her arm free from his grasp.

"Just trying to be helpful, Emily," he says. He hopes that she won't remember much of the evening when she wakes up the next morning. However, if she does remember, he hopes that she will be embarrassed by her boorish behavior.

He's learned something tonight: adding a woman to the mix has ruined things. He'll never make that mistake again.

CHAPTER 10
AUGUST 9, 2017
TOM WILCHUCK

Tom Wilchuck, a third-year associate at Ingram and Sparks, knocks on his boss's door to discuss the upcoming meeting with Dr. Sheldon Wright.

"Come on in, Tom," Ingram calls from behind the closed door. Stepping into the office, Wilchuck is surprised to see another man sitting across from Ingram. The man is in his late fifties with a nondescript face hidden by a tightly clipped reddish-brown beard. He is probably short, around five feet eight or so, but, because he is seated, Wilchuck can only estimate. The visitor wears a brown corduroy jacket with elbow patches, giving him the air of a college professor.

"Tom, meet Dr. Sheldon Wright. He asked to move up his appointment and I guess I forgot to let you know."

Wilchuck walks over to Dr. Wright and holds out his hand. The doctor neither smiles nor stands, but grudgingly extends a limp hand to meet Wilchuck's.

The young associate is miffed by Ingram's oversight. At his boss's request, he spent the past weekend preparing a detailed timeline that chronicled Dr. Wright's treatment of Heather Zurcher. Through this tedious work, Wilchuck gained a thorough understanding of the medical issues and was excited about being part of the meeting.

The epitome of graciousness, Ingram smiles, extends his arm, and points Wilchuck toward another wing chair. "Tom is one of our bright young stars," Ingram says to Dr. Wright. "He's going to be invaluable to your defense."

Wilchuck hunches his lanky, six-foot-four-inch frame and slides into the empty chair. He nervously pushes his right hand through his shaggy brown hair. Pulling out a pen from his suit jacket, he flips his legal pad to an open page and waits for the interview to continue.

Wilchuck has a love-hate relationship with his boss. He will always be grateful to Ingram for offering him a job when no one else would. Although Wilchuck graduated in the top third of his class at Case Western Reserve University, his social awkwardness has scared away other law firms. Throughout his life, people have whispered that he is autistic, laughed at him behind his back, and routinely shunned him. Yes, he is shy and occasionally says things that are blunt and inappropriate, but he is not weird. Whatever concerns there are about his personality, he has an incredible memory and a superhuman ability to concentrate, skills that serve him well in the legal world. He is also an intuitive judge of character and can assess people quickly and accurately.

No matter how hard he toils for Ingram, it is never enough. The man runs a veritable sweatshop—a graveyard for recent law school graduates. Everyone is expected to bill seventy hours a week and be at Ingram's beck and call over the weekends. Although amiable with clients and jurors, Ingram is known for his tirades when assignments are not completed on time or are done carelessly.

No one stays more than two or three years at the firm. Why should they? There isn't even the illusion of a partner track. Robert Ingram and Edward Sparks are at the top and the five associates are destined to stay at the bottom. Associates work for the firm until they gain enough experience to find another job. Wilchuck has been circulating his résumé for the last two years but, despite his experience, has found no takers.

"Rest assured, we're not going to settle your case," Ingram says to Dr. Wright. "We've evaluated this claim thoroughly and concluded that you acted reasonably throughout. My job is to vindicate you with a jury."

Wilchuck wonders how long the two were talking before he knocked on the door. What has he missed? Has the doctor explained why he ordered electroshock treatment? He is also curious about the Zurcher family dynamics, particularly the father's behavior toward his daughter.

Wilchuck clears his throat and asks, "Uh, how much of the meeting have I missed?"

Anger momentarily flashes across Ingram's face but then he smiles. "Not much, Tom. Maybe fifteen to twenty minutes. I told the doctor a little bit about me and the firm."

Dr. Wright glances at Wilchuck and shakes his head as if to say, "Don't interrupt us." With his left hand, Wilchuck rubs the side of his pockmarked face and stares at the floor.

"Tom and I have studied your medical chart in great detail and have a few questions," Ingram continues. Dr. Wright glances disapprovingly again at Wilchuck, apparently unhappy that the young associate has reviewed the file too.

Before Ingram can ask a question, Dr. Wright reaches down and takes something from a folder at his feet. "I've got something else for you," he says, his nasal voice low and unemotional. "I didn't give this to the Zurchers' attorney when he asked for the girl's medical records. I wasn't sure he was entitled to this."

Dr. Wright hands a crinkled document, perhaps ten pages of lined notebook paper, to Ingram. "What's this?" Ingram asks.

"Heather Zurcher's autobiography. Early in my treatment I ask all of my patients to write their life story. Heather's story is filled with references about her father. She hated him. Called him a tyrant. Called him a monster. Called him all kinds of unflattering things."

Unable to hide his excitement, Ingram's face lights up. "And you say that the other attorney knows nothing about this document. Is that right?"

Dr. Wright nods. "It's not really part of the medical chart so I wasn't going to hand it over without talking to an attorney first."

"You absolutely did the right thing," Ingram says. "The other attorney, this Paul Schofield, doesn't need to know that we have this—well, not yet."

An uncomfortable feeling wells up in Wilchuck's gut and spreads into his chest—a combination of suppressed anger and guilt. It is not the first time that he's experienced these emotions while working here. Ingram is always doing things that cross the line.

The autobiography is clearly part of Dr. Wright's medical chart; it has been used to diagnose and uncover underlying issues that contributed to the patient's condition. Under Ohio law, the defense has an absolute duty to provide this since the plaintiff's attorney sought the doctor's records.

Why does Ingram consistently flout the rules? Wilchuck has watched his boss try a dozen cases. The man is a wizard in the courtroom: prepared, eloquent, nimble, and persuasive. They call him the Silver Fox, not just because of his mature good looks, but because he is charming and confident and clever. He doesn't need to cheat to win, yet he does.

"Tom, could you please go out and make a copy of this for us? I'll keep the original and give a copy back to the doctor," Ingram says.

After he copies the autobiography, Wilchuck takes a minute to scan through it. One paragraph details how the father locked his son in a closet for three hours after the boy accidentally broke his father's bowling trophy. In another part, the daughter describes how her father periodically berated her, calling her "idiotic, ugly, and worthless." In yet another paragraph, Heather describes how her father tried to hypnotize her in a futile attempt to reverse her depression. And then there are references to her father's affair with another woman. The document is a treasure trove for anyone wanting to discredit Dennis Zurcher.

When Wilchuck returns, Dr. Wright asks Ingram, "Do you think I need personal counsel in this case? I've been sued for more than my policy limit. I was talking to my business attorney, Austin Stillhouse, and he suggested that he should represent me in a personal capacity."

"That's your decision entirely," Ingram answers stiffly. "I'm paid by the insurance company, but you are my client. If you retain this Stillhouse fellow to look over my shoulder, you'll have to pay him out of your own pocket. Whether you have personal counsel or not, I will work just as hard for you —that's a solemn promise."

Wilchuck smiles inwardly. His boss hates to have personal counsel involved in a case. Ingram would be required to share strategy decisions and fend off inane suggestions from the other attorney.

"That's all well and good, but Stillhouse says that you're an out-of-town Cleveland lawyer and you're up against a local Elyria attorney. The judge will likely favor the local lawyer whenever he can. Stillhouse claims that if he's involved, that won't happen."

Ingram shakes his head and snickers. "Not true. Not true at all. I've had four or five cases in front of Judge Hardwig and he's always treated me fairly. In fact, two years ago I tried a case in his courtroom and won it." Ingram pauses and then whispers conspiratorially, "I happen to be friends with the judge's bailiff. I've golfed with him several times. Because of him, I know how to stay in the judge's good graces. Frankly, I think we have the advantage in that courtroom."

"So you think it's totally unnecessary?" Dr. Wright asks.

"Off the record, yes. It's a complete waste of your money. This guy won't do a lick of work. You're basically paying him to hold your hand and he'll charge you between ten and fifteen thousand dollars to do that. Good deal for him, not so good for you," Ingram says, raising his eyebrows.

"Okay. I'll hold off for now," Dr. Wright says.

For the next twenty minutes, they review Dr. Wright's care of Heather Zurcher, starting from his first appointment until he recommended ECT.

"Okay, we've reached the critical question," Ingram says. "Why did you recommend electroconvulsive treatment?"

Dr. Wright looks down at his hands and seems to be struggling to maintain his composure. He takes a deep breath and exhales. "You know, this is so unfair—this entire process. I have dedicated my entire life to psychiatry, thirty years of private practice and thousands of patients served. And then to have my every action scrutinized and dissected—well, it's sickening."

Ingram is quick to placate him. "I know. I know. It is unjust, particularly being sued in this case. Just bear with us on our questions. We want to help you."

"Sorry for the outburst but this lawsuit has me very upset," Dr. Wright says, shaking his head and then stroking his chin. "All right. You wanted to know why I suggested ECT."

Ingram nods.

"This was a textbook situation. The patient had failed two trials of antidepressants. She'd shown no improvement in psychotherapy. And her depression was severe. It had persisted now for over a year. The only remaining option was ECT and we had to try it. I was following well-established standards in prescribing it."

"That's exactly right," Ingram says, practically beaming. "If you can explain that to a jury just that way, we will win your case."

After Ingram's stroking, Dr. Wright ventures a slight smile and then unleashes a torrent of pent-up frustration. "That father is to blame," Dr. Wright says, his eyes full of anger. "He suffers from a narcissistic personality disorder. That much is clear. He's probably a sociopath too. And that's the person who is suing me."

Ingram and Wilchuck make no reply, their silence an invitation for the doctor to continue to vent. "Throughout the hospital stay, he kept asking me: Isn't there something more you can do? I mean, it was every day. And when I suggested ECT, he was very receptive."

Wilchuck has scoured both Dr. Wright's records and the hospital chart. Neither of them report this. "Is this documented in the records?" Wilchuck asks. Both Ingram and Dr. Wright glare at him.

"Of course it's not in the records," Dr. Wright says. "I can't write down every little detail."

Ingram gives Wilchuck a cautionary look that says *Let me ask the questions from now on.* "Yes, Tom. Dr. Wright only documents critically important conversations—you know, like his warning to keep the Tofranil under lock and key when he discharged the patient," Ingram says. "That's what makes this case so outrageous. You specifically told the parents about the drug's potency. Yet, despite this, their daughter had access to the pills and ingested the entire bottle. Unbelievable."

Dr. Wright's face tightens and he fidgets in his chair. "Well, you'd think that they'd have the common sense to do that even if I hadn't warned them."

"Right, right," Ingram says. "But the fact is that you did and I'm going to destroy them with that."

Dr. Wright forces a smile, exposing yellowed teeth.

"Anything else you want to tell us that's not evident from your records?" Ingram asks. Wilchuck suspects that Ingram has a tee time and wants to bring the meeting to a close.

The doctor turns and directs his next comment to Wilchuck. "Yes, there is, and it's not documented in the hospital record, Mr. Wilcox," Dr. Wright says, butchering the associate's last name.

Before explaining further, Dr. Wright gathers the documents that lie on the floor and slowly begins to return them to separate file folders. Ingram conveys an exaggerated look of impatience to his associate. After watching this for a few moments, Ingram asks, "So what else do you want to tell us?"

Dr. Wright jerks his head up from his sorting and his face takes on a stern expression. "This patient was discharged against my orders," he says. "Yes, I had argued with the idiot father about discontinuing the ECT, but I also fought him about an immediate discharge. He wanted her out of the hospital immediately and I insisted that she stay longer to allow me to monitor the new antidepressant. He refused."

"This is great. Noncomplying patients can hardly complain when they don't follow a doctor's orders. This argument really resonates with a jury," Ingram says. Tamping down his enthusiasm, Ingram asks in a conciliatory voice, "I don't want you to think that I'm being critical, but why didn't you document this in the chart?"

"Because health insurance companies can refuse to pay for treatment if the patient fails to comply with the doctor's orders."

"And . . . ," Ingram prods.

"And because I did not want Mr. Zurcher to get stuck with a huge hospital bill that his insurance would not pay. I was looking out for him and his family, despite how much I detested him."

"And he rewards you by suing you," Ingram says.

"That's right," Dr. Wright replies, bowing his head and taking on the air of a martyr.

"I'll weave that into our case when we do battle in the courtroom," Ingram insists. He then abruptly stands up. "Well, if there's nothing more, Dr. Wright, it's been a pleasure and we'll stay in touch. Call me if you have anything else that you want to talk about."

After Dr. Wright leaves, Ingram tells Wilchuck that he has an appointment out of the office.

"I think you'll want to read this autobiography before you go," Wilchuck says.

"Okay. Okay. I can spare a few minutes," Ingram says gruffly as he snatches the document from his desk. Ingram's expression turns from irritated to surprised to excited. "Oh my God," Ingram says as he returns the papers to his desk. "Get Bill Krantz on this," he says, his voice urgent. "Ask him to take some photographs of the father and the girlfriend together."

Krantz, an ex-cop, is the firm's private investigator. Wilchuck is confused. How is this evidence relevant? "May I ask why? It has nothing to do with the case," Wilchuck asks.

"Yeah, probably not, but it's great stuff," Ingram gushes.

"But why are we bothering with it?" Wilchuck asks.

"I might be able to get it into evidence. It explains why the daughter was so screwed up." Ingram shrugs, apparently unconvinced by his own argument. "Even if we can't, we can threaten to use it, and that may be enough to pressure them to drop the lawsuit. You never know."

Wilchuck sighs and walks out of the room. He'll make the phone call to Krantz, but this is disturbing. He didn't choose a legal career to do this.

CHAPTER 11
NOVEMBER 15, 2017
WENDY SCHOFIELD

"How could you have been so damn stupid?" Wendy yells. She doesn't care that the children are within earshot; she is beyond pretending that all is normal and good. This time, she has no sympathy for Paul, no matter how forlorn he appears. Hasn't she warned him? For years, she's offered to manage the firm's bank accounts. But no, he's dismissed her suggestions and let Eileen Rogers, his secretary, continue to write checks and balance the bank accounts. Even before she began her accounting coursework at the local community college, Wendy knew that this violated the most basic bookkeeping rule for any business, no matter how small.

Wendy has never liked Eileen, has never trusted her. She sensed that there was something corrupt under her overtly Christian veneer.

"I know. I know. I could shoot myself," Paul says. "I just never dreamed that Eileen would do this. She's worked for my uncle and me for over thirty years."

Wendy rolls her eyes and shakes her head. "I never liked that judgmental, holier-than-thou bitch," Wendy says, surprising herself with her profanity. She closes her eyes in a futile effort to subdue her anger.

"I want to go to her house, get in her face, and scream until I'm hoarse. And while I'm there, I'd like to kick that no-good Melvin in the crotch."

Wendy picks up a pillow and throws it across the room, where it strikes the wall, rattling a framed family photograph but not dislodging it. Paul winces and then picks up the pillow, carefully setting it on the family room couch as if it is an explosive.

"So, Paul, tell me—how much did Eileen steal from us?" Wendy asks.

"She admits to thirty-five thousand dollars," Paul says, raising his eyebrows.

"Well, with your slipshod accounting procedures, we'll probably never know, will we?"

Paul nods meekly.

"It's probably double that, and I bet she stole from Uncle Jack too. No wonder she never asked you for a raise. Why should she when she could embezzle from you at will?"

His head bowed, Paul continues to nod at everything Wendy says.

Once again, Paul has proven that he has no business sense. Yes, he is a very competent and caring lawyer, but he doesn't know the first thing about managing the finances of his practice. And these lapses are inexcusable.

"So, Sherlock, how did you discover that she was a thief?" Wendy asks, unwilling to end the grilling.

"I opened the escrow account bank statement when it came in the mail today. I saw that the balance was under five thousand dollars. I was holding client settlement funds in it while I worked out some closing issues. It should have held a balance of around forty thousand dollars. When she returned from an errand, I confronted her with the discrepancy."

"I bet she was really sorry," Wendy says sarcastically. "Did she start crying, get on her knees, beg for mercy? The whole sorrow show?"

"Well, she admitted to borrowing the money with the intent of paying it back and then she realized that she couldn't return the money," Paul says, taking a deep breath and looking bewildered.

"I'm sure she had a sad story ready for you, a real tearjerker," Wendy counters.

"She said that Melvin had strung together some very significant gambling debts and that they were going to lose their house if she didn't bring the payments current."

"Oh my God. You didn't buy that, did you?" Wendy interjects. "I mean, their house would have been in foreclosure if they'd been that far behind." Wendy pauses, mulling over her next thought. "Someone was going to break his legs if he didn't pay up. That's what happened."

"Whatever the reason, she says that the money is gone."

"I wish someone had broken his legs," Wendy fumes. "And Eileen's too." Wendy walks over to the couch, knocks several large pillows to the floor, and sits down, crossing her legs and bouncing them against the edge of the couch. When she sees tears well up in Paul's eyes, she realizes that she has to gain control over her anger, no matter how justified it is. Her husband is devastated. This time, they are facing a financial disaster that will probably drag them into bankruptcy—not to mention public humiliation too.

Paul paces about the family room but says nothing.

"Are you going to prosecute her?" Wendy asks.

"What's the point? She can't pay me back and, to the public, I'd look careless and incompetent."

"So, what's the plan? You've had all day to think about it before finally telling me," Wendy says, regretting her words but unable to refrain from one last cutting remark.

Paul stops in front of a wall and begins banging his head against it, not hard but not soft either.

"Okay. Okay. I'm sorry that I'm so upset with you," Wendy says, her voice softer, no longer strident. "What do we do?"

"I need thirty-five thousand dollars and I need it quickly," Paul says. He then lists and quickly eliminates the possible sources for a loan: his sister, her parents, several best friends from law school, and her spinster aunt. Some are in no position to help them. However, with those who have assets, Paul is too ashamed to ask for help. While at the office, he went on the internet, searching for banks that offer refinancing. He's found a bank headquartered in Fargo, North Dakota, that seems to court homeowners trying to stave off bankruptcy. He's spoken with a smooth, fast-talking bank representative who suggested a refinancing package that would provide funds to pay off their current loan and give them thirty-five thousand dollars for home improvements or consumer purchases.

Wendy listens expectantly, nodding as Paul replays the conversation. "The total loan would be two hundred and fifteen thousand dollars," he says. "One hundred eighty thousand dollars to pay off and then refinance our current loan with the Fargo bank, and thirty-five thousand for future consumer expenses. All secured with a mortgage on our house."

"Okay. Okay. I think this is good," Wendy says.

"It's not good," Paul says. "The interest rate is three percentage points higher than what we currently pay."

"Oh," Wendy says.

Looking at the floor, Paul says, "And the entire loan is due in two years—in one balloon payment. We either refinance before then or we lose the house."

"Oh God," Wendy says.

"Yeah, it's a huge gamble."

"Go ahead, just do it," Wendy replies, nodding her head nervously. "In two years, I should be earning money in the accounting world. If both of us are working, we should be able to get another loan."

Paul takes a deep breath. "I fired Eileen. Well, sort of fired her. She's agreed to come back one day to train the person who replaces her."

Wendy stares at Paul, anticipating the next part of his plan. "And you want me to quit my classes and run the office for you. Is that what's coming? No. No. No way, Paul."

"I can't afford to hire someone right now. You just need to take a brief leave of absence and I am hoping that this will be temporary—very temporary."

Wendy runs from the family room, bolts up the stairs, and slams the door to their bedroom. Crying, she lies down on their bed, her face buried in a pillow. How can he suggest this? She is midway through her accounting coursework. All of Paul's blunders impact her more than him. It is unfair as hell.

About a half an hour later, Paul cautiously opens the bedroom door. Taking a seat on the edge of the bed, he says, "I'm sorry. I can't think of any alternative. I can't hire some temp to do this job. Eileen wore too many hats: receptionist, typist, bookkeeper, supply purchaser, and paralegal. I need someone smart who can jump in and do this job right away."

"And someone you don't have to pay," Wendy says, sniffling.

"Well, yeah. That too," Paul agrees.

"So it's all hands on deck, is that what you're saying?" Wendy asks.

Paul nods.

"I don't see where I have a choice. I'll do this until you get things straightened out—which better be fast, buddy boy. I'll be damned, however, if I'm going to spend any time with Eileen learning this job. She can write down what she does. And if that's not enough, she can explain things to you and you can relay that information to me. I won't have anything to do with that woman."

"Okay. I agree. Very reasonable. I'll have her do those things tomorrow and perhaps you can start right after that." Wendy can hear relief in Paul's voice.

Paul rolls onto the bed and puts his arms around her. At first her body is stiff, but, after a few minutes, she relaxes from his warmth.

Eventually she raises her head from the pillow and looks at him, not making any effort to hide her weariness. "Paul, you're going to be the death of me."

"I know."

Shaking her head, she studies his face. "Lucky for you that you're so damn handsome." She gives him a peck on the cheek and pulls herself out of bed.

CHAPTER 12
MARCH 1, 2018
TOM WILCHUCK

Bill Krantz sits with Tom Wilchuck in the law firm's conference room, portraits of Robert Ingram and Edward Sparks staring down at them from the far wall. In his early sixties, Krantz has been retired from the Garfield Heights Police Department for five years. Just under six feet tall, he still maintains a fit, athletic build. Clean-shaven and red-faced, Krantz has intelligent brown eyes that peer out from aviator glasses whose yellow lenses scream "out of style." Neither man is adept at small talk; instead, they drum their fingers on the conference table, awaiting the arrival of Robert Ingram.

Wilchuck has twice watched the video that Krantz brought with him today. Krantz has caught Dennis Zurcher in a revealing conversation with a friend at the Foundry Kitchen and Bar in downtown Elyria. Zurcher has not only acknowledged his affair with Starla but bragged about the large settlement that he's expecting from the lawsuit. Dennis Zurcher's opportunism is now on full display. Any claim that he sued Dr. Wright to save another family from this type of tragedy will be torpedoed by this video.

Although Ingram has asked not to be disturbed as he prepares for an upcoming trial, Wilchuck has done just that—promising that a five-minute break to watch this video will energize him. Ingram smiled and promised to join them in just a few minutes.

"How were you able to videotape the conversation?" Wilchuck asks. "That kind of amazes me, you know."

Krantz reaches into his blue blazer and pulls out a pair of eyeglasses, with a design that is much more stylish than the pair he is wearing. "Look at the upper corners of the frames. See those little circles? One holds a video camera while the other contains a microphone," Krantz explains. He hands the glasses to Wilchuck, who stares at them, impressed by their compactness and stealthy design.

"Obviously, if someone is looking for a video camera, you know it's there. But, if your subject isn't suspicious, it works great," Krantz says.

"Who'd be expecting a video camera in a pair of glasses?" Wilchuck replies.

"They also make a sunglass model—you know, for the guy who wants to secretly videotape some hot-looking chicks at the beach," Krantz says, giving Wilchuck a knowing wink. Despite his profound shyness with women, Wilchuck finds the suggestion creepy.

"One other question," Wilchuck says. "How did you know Zurcher would be at the bar at that time?"

"Well, when I have a big budget like this one, I can hire some folks to help me," Krantz says, pride evident from his smile. "I've got a guy who can hack into computer systems. He compromised the email system for the dealership where Zurcher works. We actually thought that the girlfriend was going to show up at the bar. As you saw, she didn't, but the stuff I got was much better."

Bounding into the room, Ingram shakes Krantz's hand before sitting next to him at the conference table. "Hey, Billy, I understand that you've got something really good for us."

"Well, you can judge for yourself," Krantz says, touching the play button on his laptop computer.

The screen comes to life with the interior of a restaurant. With its high ceilings, brick walls, and exposed pipes, one can see how the large room was once part of a factory. The place is neither crowded nor noisy and the camera bounces as Krantz apparently walks toward the bar, where Zurcher and another man sit. They are an odd pair. Zurcher is dressed neatly in his work attire, a navy blue sports coat and tan slacks. His friend, a large man with a long ponytail, looks like a member of a motorcycle gang, with tattered blue jeans, cowboy boots, and a white T-shirt from which the man's stomach protrudes like he swallowed a bowling ball.

Based on the camera angle, Wilchuck surmises that Krantz sat next to the friend, someone Zurcher calls Tony. Because both men speak in loud voices, the audio is clear despite the restaurant's background noise. After some pleasantries, Tony turns the subject to Zurcher's girlfriend, Starla.

"Haven't seen you out with that fine bitch lately," Tony says, taking a swig from his beer mug.

"And you won't," Zurcher says. "We're laying low until this lawsuit is over. I mean, I still get over to her apartment and ball the shit out of her, but that's it."

Tony smiles. "That Starla is one fine piece of ass. Nice rack, too."

"Keep your fucking eyes to yourself," Zurcher says. There is anger in his voice, either real or feigned. It is difficult to tell.

"Okay, okay. Just sayin', that's all," Tony says. "Just tell her that we miss her." To placate his friend, Tony punches him lightly on his upper arm.

"Well, she keeps whining about not going out. She's driving me fucking crazy. Today, she emails me that she's coming here to surprise me. Can you believe that? I told her if she does, I'll throw her ass out of here. I'm supposed to be this devoted family man. You know, I've got to be on my best behavior because of my lawsuit."

Even though Tony's face is not visible from the camera angle, it is clear that he is laughing. His back rocks and his ponytail bobs as he holds his hand over his mouth. Suddenly, Tony's body is blocked by another patron slipping in between Krantz and his subjects. The audio of the two men is drowned out while the customer places an order with the bartender.

"That's great work, Bill," Ingram says. He stands up and begins walking toward the conference room door.

"Wait. It's not finished," Krantz says, motioning for Ingram to return.

When Krantz resumes the video, the camera again shows Tony and Zurcher. Tony is pounding his right hand against his upper thigh, and this time, it is clear that he is laughing. "Oh man, that doctor is going to shit his pants when your lawyer brings that up," Tony says.

"Yeah, the case will be over and it'll be payday for me," Zurcher says.

"Shit. My drinking buddy, Dennis Zurcher, a millionaire. Hard to believe," Tony says.

"I know," Zurcher says, smiling and looking proud. "I'm going to be set for life."

The video concludes with Tony and Zurcher giving each other a high five.

"Beautiful," Ingram says.

To Wilchuck, the video is not beautiful. Yes, they've captured their opponent in a very compromising conversation that reveals both his immorality and his opportunism. The man is unworthy of receiving a penny, but the video is not a thing of beauty. It is ugly. As Ingram's face burns with excitement, Wilchuck suddenly has a revelation. His boss is not much different from Zurcher—just a more refined version. For three years, Wilchuck has listened as Ingram demeans women and then brags about exploiting them and tossing them away.

"How will you use the video?" Krantz asks eagerly.

"My first thought was I'd send one copy anonymously to Zurcher at work and another to his wife at home. No message. No note. Just an implied threat," Ingram says.

"You think they'd drop the case?" Krantz asks.

"I don't know. That's why I'm not going to do that. I'll save it for trial and spring it on them then," Ingram says.

How can Ingram use these statements at trial? Wilchuck has his doubts. The case centers on Dr. Wright and whether he was negligent and caused this teenager to take her own life. Isn't it irrelevant if the father has a mistress? That didn't kill his daughter. As for his motivation for bringing the lawsuit, the judge might allow this evidence, but only if Ingram gives Schofield the statement prior to trial as required by the rules. That seems unlikely because Ingram seems intent on "springing" the evidence on Schofield at trial.

His right hand on his chin, Ingram takes on a thoughtful pose. "When I cross-examine the father, I can probably get him to claim that he filed this lawsuit to prevent other families from experiencing this kind of loss. If he claims this—and I'm almost certain that he will—then I'll impeach him with this video clip. It will be devastating."

Looking at his feet, Wilchuck mumbles, "Aren't we supposed to provide a copy of this video to Zurcher's attorney? I mean, he's requested copies of all statements of his clients and this certainly qualifies as one."

"Tommy, Tommy, Tommy. We are not turning this over to Paul Schofield," Ingram says, directing a mischievous grin toward Krantz.

"Then the judge won't allow us to use this at trial," Wilchuck warns. Anyone with a rudimentary knowledge of court rules knows that each side is obligated to provide the other with statements if requested. Failure to do so often results in the judge excluding the evidence.

"Let me worry about this, Tom," Ingram says. "If I read a transcript of the conversation and ask the father if he spoke those words, the jury will know that he did. Even if Schofield objects before his client answers and the judge tells the jury to disregard my question, the damage will be done. You can't unring a bell and you can't unhear a question." Ingram gives Wilchuck a disapproving look.

Like a chastened child, Wilchuck says, "Okay."

Realizing that his words have achieved their desired effect, Ingram's face takes on a paternalistic expression. "Your law school professors taught you the law, but I'm teaching you how to win. You're completing your education with me. Don't forget that."

Wilchuck nods and forces a smile.

He isn't sure how much longer he can countenance Ingram's never-ending deceits. First, Ingram has retained Heather Zurcher's autobiography when he has a clear duty to provide it to Schofield immediately. Now he is wrongfully withholding a video. If Wilchuck followed his conscience, he would send both items to Schofield, the consequences be damned. But he knows he won't, knows he can't. If he does that, he will lose his job and invite financial disaster, including an inevitable default on his student loan.

Tonight, he will send out more résumés and hope that his efforts will lead to employment with another firm. But for now, he has no choice but to stay where he is and abandon his ethical principles one by one.

CHAPTER 13
APRIL 23, 2018
CINDY ZURCHER

As soon as Cindy Zurcher steps into Schofield's waiting room, she notices the changes. The room is brighter and more vibrant. The dusty artificial plants are gone, replaced by African violets, spider plants, and an aloe vera. An attractive woman sits behind an open glass window in the secretarial/receptionist station. With shoulder-length brown hair, she appears to be in her mid-thirties. As Cindy approaches her, the woman looks up from her work, revealing a light, unblemished complexion and penetrating blue eyes. Her sleeveless dress exposes defined biceps and triceps, signs that this woman works out.

Trying to keep the nervousness from her voice, Cindy says, "Hi, I'm Cindy Zurcher. I have a ten thirty appointment with Mr. Schofield." The other woman studies Cindy's face as if she is an exotic animal. Before the secretary can acknowledge the appointment, the telephone rings. As the call progresses, Cindy admires the woman's pleasant and professional responses. After about a minute, the woman gives Cindy a bemused smile and rotates her free hand in a circular motion, silently urging the caller to wrap things up.

"You're never a bother, Mr. Milton. I'll have Mr. Schofield return your call today," the woman says, rolling her eyes as she returns the receiver to its cradle. Looking at Cindy, she says, "He calls almost as much as your husband."

Unable to hide her embarrassment, Cindy utters a sharp, "Oh."

"I shouldn't have said that," the woman says, "but he can't fire me." There is a lightness in her tone, something mischievous.

Involuntarily Cindy smiles back, but she says nothing.

The woman chuckles. "Oh, I'm Wendy Schofield, Paul's wife. Actually, I'd love it if he fired me. Then I could get back to college and finish my accounting degree. But for now, he needs me here and here I will stay." Wendy shrugs and manufactures an exaggerated frown. "Just follow me. I'll take you back to Paul's office."

After being ushered into the office, Cindy takes a seat in a wing chair in front of Schofield's desk. He is as handsome as she remembers, but he looks tired, maybe even a bit apprehensive, as he fiddles with a paperclip in his left hand.

"So you wanted to talk to me without Dennis present?" he asks with a forced smile. "What's on your mind?"

Why, indeed, did she ask for this meeting? She's been struggling with that question ever since she called for the appointment two days earlier. The easy answer is that she is responding to Schofield's letter that they received a week ago. In it, he advised them that the other side wanted to take her deposition and Dennis's too. Apparently, at the deposition, the opposing attorney will ask her questions under oath about their troubled family life, Heather's depression, Dr. Wright's treatment, and Heather's traumatic death. It will be an ordeal that she is determined to avoid. Not only is she vehemently opposed to this court case, but she is terrified that these questions will take an agonizing toll on her, second only to what she experienced immediately after Heather's death.

But there is more to it—a truth that she incessantly tries to dismiss. She liked this attorney from the moment that they met. To be more precise, she felt an attraction toward him. Since that meeting a year ago, her thoughts have frequently drifted to him, despite her best efforts to banish them. She will find herself lost in a daydream where she and Paul Schofield are married. It is a stupid and childish fantasy, but it provides a temporary escape from the ugly reality of her own marriage.

She's taken special care this morning to look her best in a casual way. She squeezed into tight-fitting jeans and donned a low-cut cotton sweater that exposes the top of her breasts. Never one to wear makeup, she's made an exception today. Likewise, she dabbed some perfume behind both ears before leaving the house.

"This deposition thing," she begins clumsily. "I don't see how I can do that, Mr. Schofield."

"It's Paul," he says quickly, his mouth tight with either a smile or a grimace, she can't tell which. He pauses for a moment before continuing. "I know this will be difficult for you, but I will prepare you for the deposition. I'll go over the questions that they'll probably ask and we'll discuss the best ways to answer them." He hesitates again and his face takes on a pained expression. "Unfortunately, this deposition is not optional. You have to comply with the defendant's request. Otherwise, the defendant has grounds to dismiss your case."

She's come here intending to talk rationally and calmly about the lawsuit, but, listening to the attorney, she feels her chest tighten, her pulse quicken, and her mind seize in a wave of agitation. "It's not *my* case," she blurts. "I don't want any part of this ridiculous lawsuit. It's just wrong." Her hands involuntarily ball into fists. She clenches and unclenches them as she waits for the attorney to respond.

Paul rocks back in his chair, his eyes reflecting confusion and panic. At first, he makes no response. When his expression finally becomes calm, he raises his hands in a placating gesture. "Well, okay. Obviously, you've got some serious misgivings about the lawsuit, but I need you to tell me why."

She is immediately struck by the contrast between this man and her husband. Dennis would have flown into a rage, while this attorney (who wants her to call him Paul) is open to a discussion.

Trying to calm herself, Cindy takes a deep breath. "I don't know what Dennis has told you about our family life, but it was like living in a war zone. We all crept around in fear of Dennis's next unpredictable outburst. When something was not to his liking, he yelled and belittled us all. He still does. He was so tough on Heather. Called her stupid, ugly, lazy—you name it. He destroyed her self-esteem. He's the reason she suffered from depression. And now this is supposedly Dr. Wright's fault. All of it. I'm sorry, but that's crazy."

Again, Paul does not respond immediately. When he speaks, his voice is soft and reassuring. "I'm aware that Heather had a difficult home life," he says, pausing for a moment. "Dr. Wright's records show that she had a troubled relationship with Dennis, who could be volatile. I agree that this contributed to her depression," Paul says.

Before he can say more, Cindy leans forward in her chair, her eyes indignant. "This is sick. You know Dennis is to blame, yet you're suing Dr. Wright? I'm sorry, but how can you do that?"

Paul does not flinch. He speaks his next words slowly and with conviction. "Because Heather would be alive today if Dr. Wright had done his job properly."

For a few moments, neither says anything. Paul finally breaks the silence. "Believe me, I do not like your husband and I don't trust anything he says. However, I agree with him on one thing—Dr. Wright was careless as hell. Heather didn't deserve to die from his malpractice. I'm fighting for her and other teens whose psychiatrists fail to do their jobs, particularly those who think ECT is an appropriate option for kids. So why am I suing Dr. Wright? It's simple: Heather deserved better from her psychiatrist—much better."

Paul's words barely register with her. Instead, she dredges up the thought that has dogged her every day since her daughter's death. "She also deserved much better from her mother," Cindy says, her voice cracking.

"You were in a difficult situation," Paul says. "You shouldn't blame yourself."

Cindy's eyes well up with tears and she brushes her forearm against them to blot them. "A mother has one job and that is to protect her children. Heather was a very sensitive child." Cindy pauses, her chin trembling. "Dennis belittled her. He was destroying her right in front of me." She pauses again and takes several deep breaths before continuing. "I should have left him—gotten the kids out of that toxic environment. I'm the one who failed her—not Dr. Wright."

When she sees tears in Paul's eyes, a wave of grief sweeps through her. Her sobs are quiet at first, but they continue to grow louder and louder. Paul hands her a box of tissues. Instead of taking one, she holds the box tightly, the cardboard collapsing on both sides.

She hears the door open behind her and the sound of approaching footsteps. A woman appears in front of her, takes the tissue box from her, drops it on the floor, and finds her hands. Through her tears, Cindy can see that this is Paul's wife, Wendy, who gently tugs on Cindy's hands, urging her to rise. When she does, Wendy envelops her in a hug. The two women stand, their arms wrapped around each other, neither wanting to let go. For the next five minutes, Wendy rubs Cindy's back while Cindy shakes, cries, and gasps for air. Eventually, Cindy relaxes her arms and they fall to her sides.

"Thank you," Cindy says. "I'm really sorry. I didn't come here to make a scene." Disoriented, Cindy turns to find her chair. Locating it, she sits down slowly. With her head slumped, she stares at the carpet, unable to look up.

Wendy drags the other wing chair next to Cindy's, sits down, and holds one of Cindy's hands. Wendy looks at Paul, who nods appreciatively. Speaking to Cindy, Wendy says, "I'll stay for the rest of this meeting and make sure that Paul doesn't make you cry again." Smiling, Wendy winks at Paul and then squeezes Cindy's hand harder. "We women have to stick together."

Through her tears, Cindy manages a fleeting smile too. She has come here with thoughts of Paul Schofield, but she will leave wishing that this woman will remain her friend.

Through the years, Dennis discouraged her from developing any friendships, insisting that she devote herself to maintaining the house and caring for the children. The infrequent times that a mother of one of her children's friends suggested that they meet for lunch or grab a cup of coffee together, Dennis would angrily insist that she stay home and tackle a time-consuming chore like washing windows, shampooing the carpet, or waxing the kitchen cabinet doors. He'd always insist that she'd ignored the task for far too long. If she tried to change his mind, he'd go from mad to furious, and she'd drop the subject.

And Cindy has no extended family. Her father abandoned her mother soon after Cindy was born. Her mom died when she was six, and afterward, Cindy's maternal grandparents raised her, finding space for her in their cramped apartment. Her alcoholic grandfather died a year after she married Dennis and her grandmother passed away several years after that. Ever since, she's had no one close who can provide guidance or emotional support. She has become accustomed to feeling isolated and alone, so much so that she's forgotten the comfort that human touch can bring.

For the next few minutes, Paul recaps for Wendy their recent conversation. When Paul recounts Cindy's feelings of guilt, Wendy squeezes Cindy's hand and gives her a sympathetic look. Eventually Paul returns to his assessment of their case against Dr. Wright.

"I've learned a lot about teen suicide since accepting this case. What struck me is that many teens do not want to take their own lives but stage an attempted suicide, expecting someone to intervene and save them. It is a dramatic cry for help and attention," Paul says.

Anticipating where Paul is headed with his analysis, Cindy draws in a deep breath and squeezes Wendy's hand.

"If Heather was determined to commit suicide, why did she leave her bedroom and crawl to the hallway? I'm convinced that she wanted to be discovered and saved. How was she to know that the medication was fast-acting and couldn't be easily reversed in the emergency room? She didn't."

Cindy's eyes fill with tears and she struggles to maintain her composure. She nods, signaling that she wants Paul to continue.

"You can see where I'm going with this. If Dr. Wright had warned you about this drug's potency and told you to keep it locked away, Heather would be alive today. He knows it and we know it. That's why he altered his discharge summary to claim that he'd warned you."

For the first time, Cindy feels a surge of anger toward Dr. Wright. She never liked the man; he was cold and condescending. However, she never questioned either his expertise or his judgment. If what Paul says is true—and she has no reason to doubt him—Dr. Wright is partly responsible for Heather's death. She is unable to excuse either Dennis or herself, but she now understands that Dr. Wright is not blameless. Their lawsuit does have merit.

"Okay, I'll give a deposition," Cindy says. "I owe that to Heather."

For the next hour, Paul reviews the questions that she'll likely be asked during her deposition. If the other attorney questions her about their home life, she'll admit that it was volatile and that Heather's relationship with her father was troubled. Despite Dennis's angry outbursts, she believes that he did love his daughter. With Paul's pressing, Cindy is able to dredge up several good memories of family outings: Sunday picnics at a local park, a father-daughter junior high dance, and trips to the zoo and a nearby amusement park.

"I know you want me to tell the defense attorney about the happy times at our home, but that was not the day-to-day reality. I'll answer his questions at the deposition but I'm not sugarcoating anything." She looks first to Paul and then to Wendy, shaking her head as she does.

When the meeting ends, both Paul and Wendy escort Cindy to the waiting room. When Cindy opens the door to leave, Wendy says, "Wait, Cindy. Let me give you my cell number."

Cindy stops and smiles. "I'd like that very much," Cindy says as she walks to Wendy's secretarial station.

As she writes her number on the back of one of Paul's business cards, Wendy says, "You can always call me at the office. I work here every day until the kids get home from school. But don't hesitate to text or phone me on my cell."

Cindy doesn't want to explain to Wendy that she can't text. The reason is too humiliating. In his never-ending efforts to isolate and control her, Dennis refuses to allow her to own a cell phone. This indignity, like so many others, is a stark reminder of her pitiful existence.

As she walks back to her car, the sense of support and connection that she felt with Wendy and Paul grows fainter—so faint that it seems like a distant memory. By the time she reaches home, it has vanished, replaced by a feeling of dread.

CHAPTER 14
AUGUST 14, 2018
PAUL SCHOFIELD

Fiddling with the radio knob inside his Honda Accord, Paul tries to suppress his apprehension about the upcoming meeting with Scott Worthington. His secret co-counsel was uncharacteristically terse when they set up this conference three days earlier. Although not panicked, Paul is unmoored by the latest developments in the Zurcher case, enough so that he's overcome his hesitancy to bother the busy attorney. His co-counsel at first begged off due to his schedule but eventually relented, suggesting a luncheon meeting at this restaurant located on his way to a Sandusky pretrial. After a ten-minute wait, Paul spots Scott's sleek BMW making a sharp turn into the Panera restaurant parking lot and sliding smoothly into a parking space.

Grabbing his briefcase, Paul exits his car and waves to Scott, who, at first, does not see him. To Paul, Scott seems anxious, a tense scowl marring his otherwise pleasant features. However, when the two make eye contact, Scott gives Paul a wide grin, one that Paul finds unconvincing.

After exchanging pleasantries and placing their orders at the counter, the men find a quiet corner table to talk. Again, Scott seems uncomfortable, fidgeting in his chair and rubbing his hands together.

"No other way to say this but I've got some bad news," Scott begins.

Bad news is not what Paul wants to hear. He's had enough of his own without Scott piling on more. Heather Zurcher's autobiography arrived in the mail just a few days earlier and her unvarnished revelations about her father are jarring. To compound the damage, the document arrived at Paul's office after both Dennis and Cindy Zurcher gave their sworn depositions, during which Ingram locked down the details of their home life.

"What kind of bad news?" Paul asks, a feeling of dread seizing his stomach.

Looking sheepish, Scott clears his throat. "I know I promised you thirty thousand dollars for your expenses in this case, but the firm has had some significant reversals and the partners are capping our line of credit to you at twenty thousand."

Paul wants to remain calm but he feels betrayed and angry. Why can't this group of ultra-wealthy attorneys keep its promise to him? They apparently don't want to tighten their own belts. Instead of reducing their office staff or eliminating perks like leased luxury cars or country club memberships, they are sacrificing him.

"We had a deal, didn't we?" Paul pleads. Then it strikes him; nothing about their agreement is in writing. Of course, it couldn't be—an undisclosed co-counsel arrangement is unethical. When deciding on how to cut costs, these attorneys conveniently decided to renege on an unenforceable agreement. Unable to hide his growing ire, Paul speaks forcefully. "I need the full *thirty thousand* to finance this case. Otherwise, I'm finished." In other circumstances, Paul would have reasoned calmly with Scott, but desperation is fostering a whole array of other emotions.

"How much have you spent so far?" Scott asks, raising his eyebrows.

Paul does not like the question. Is Scott going to niggle over expenditures? Nevertheless, Paul answers, "Close to fifteen thousand."

"Really, that much already," Scott says.

Scott's comment sounds like a rebuke—as if Paul spent the expense money frivolously. "I can't believe you're actually surprised by that number," Paul says, his voice uncharacteristically high-pitched. "Months ago, I told you that I had to pay Dr. Masterson eleven thousand dollars to review the records and write a report. He'll charge me another ten thousand dollars just to fly here and testify at trial. You, among all people, know how expensive it is to finance a medical malpractice case."

"I'm not disputing the expenses. No question that they accrue rapidly in a med mal case, but that's beside the point. The reality is that our firm just lost a class-action lawsuit and had to eat almost three hundred thousand dollars in expenses. That's what is driving all of this," Scott says, as if this justifies everything and Paul should just accept the inevitable.

Paul shakes his head and exhales loudly before responding. "Look, you made a commitment to me and I have a right to rely on it. I absolutely need money to take the deposition of the defendant's expert. That's easily five grand. And then how can I afford any focus groups to fine-tune my trial strategies?" Paul stares hard at Scott, his expression showing both desperation and anger. "Jesus, if you do this, you'll destroy any chance I have to win."

Ignoring Paul's emotional plea, Scott asks, "Can't you finance part of the case yourself?"

Scott's coolness galls Paul. He wants to yell "No, no, no!" but he bites his lower lip. How can he possibly advance any of his own money for this case? Hell, he doesn't even have enough funds to hire a new secretary, forcing his unhappy wife to fill that role without pay. To make matters worse, he has a huge balloon payment due in *fifteen months*. With that disaster looming, he is barely scraping by. He is too ashamed to disclose any of this to Scott. As these thoughts ricochet about in his head, Paul can only stare at him.

After a few moments, the silence overpowers Scott, who sighs. "The firm's decision is final—it's beyond my control," he says, spreading his arms in a gesture of futility. "But I'll tell you what I can do. I'll advance five thousand dollars of my own money to bring our support to twenty-five thousand. I know that's not perfect, but will it work?" Scott asks, a naïve hopefulness in his voice.

Paul knows that he should express gratitude but he can't find it in himself. "I guess it will have to do," he mutters. With a budget of twenty-five thousand, he will now have enough money to pay Dr. Masterson his expected trial fees and travel expenses, but that will be it. Any other major expenses will now be out of the question.

Before either man can say more, Paul spots a restaurant employee, a bedraggled teenage girl, holding a tray with their food. The girl is looking helplessly at the tables, trying to find a marker whose number matches the one on her tray. When Paul waves to her, she smiles in relief and places the tray in front of them. Almost immediately, Scott takes a spoonful of his tomato bisque soup, grimaces, and quickly takes a gulp of his iced tea. "I didn't expect it to be so hot," he complains. "I burned my tongue."

For the next few minutes, the men take bites from their sandwiches and chew wordlessly. In the uncomfortable silence, Paul realizes that he has to shake off his feeling of betrayal and move on. Plain and simple, he needs this man's advice. Setting down his sandwich, he reaches into his briefcase and pulls out Heather Zurcher's autobiography.

"I got this in the mail last week from Robert Ingram," Paul says, sliding the autobiography over the tabletop to Scott—a peace offering of sorts. Scott slips on a pair of half glasses and begins reading the document.

Scott's face registers disbelief, then irritation as he reads the autobiography. "Why doesn't this surprise me?" he says, shaking his head.

"He was very apologetic in his cover letter," Paul says sarcastically.

"Oh, he always is. He's such a snake," Scott says.

"Well, he claims that Dr. Wright just turned this document over to him *after* my clients gave their depositions," Paul explains.

"He's done the same thing to me and just about everybody else who's had a case against him," Scott replies.

"The question for us is how do we deal with it," Paul says.

"Well, you'll never prove that he knowingly withheld it from you. His client will, no doubt, back him up and claim that he just gave it over to him. Your job is to try to either minimize the girl's story or discredit it."

"As bad as that autobiography is, I think we can explain it," Paul says.

"Really?" Scott replies.

Paul relates how the wife secretly tipped him off about her husband's verbally abusive behavior toward everyone in the family, including Heather. Armed with this information, Paul convinced the father that in his deposition, he should admit to angry outbursts that he deeply regretted.

"Well, did he?" Scott asks.

"Yeah, he said he was ashamed of his flare-ups. He actually got teary-eyed when he talked about his mistakes and insisted that he loved his daughter."

"Well, that's something, but I doubt it will overcome all the damage," Scott says, pointing to the autobiography. "I mean, she called her father a monster. Let's not kid ourselves. That's pretty nasty stuff."

"It could have been a lot worse. I mean, what if the father had claimed that they had a stable, loving home life?"

"You'd have lost all credibility with the jury," Scott says. "I'm hoping the mother came across as a more sympathetic witness."

Paul explains that in her quiet way, Cindy Zurcher did her best. She carefully described their daughter, told about her fall into depression, and chronicled her treatment with Dr. Wright.

As Paul summarizes the mother's deposition testimony, Scott listens intently. When Paul pauses, Scott says, "It sounds like she was an effective witness."

"At times, yes, but at one point, she almost destroyed our case. Not on purpose, mind you, but it was close. Obviously, I'm afraid she may crumble at trial."

Paul tells Scott that the near disaster occurred when Ingram asked Cindy about Dr. Wright's warnings about the new antidepressant. She denied that he had given her a warning, but Ingram pressed her, thrusting the discharge summary under her face and asking if Dr. Wright had lied about this.

"She looked like a deer in the headlights," Paul says. "Then Ingram reminded her that she was under oath and any untruth was punishable by the crime of perjury."

"Oh shit," Scott says. "I hope you objected."

"I accused him of trying to intimidate my client and we went back and forth for a while.

Of course, I hoped this would give Cindy a breather and she'd pull herself together. When the deposition resumed, Cindy made the mistake of saying that she had no memory of Dr. Wright warning her about the drug," Paul says.

Scott groans.

"Yeah, Ingram tried to get her to admit that she'd forgotten about the warning—you know, reminding her of all the stress and chaos surrounding the sudden discharge. She looked very confused and stared at me like she wanted me to give her the answer," Paul says. "I was sure that she was going to agree with him. I could feel the case slipping away from me. If she agreed, then Dr. Wright's alteration of the discharge summary was simply an attempt to set the record straight."

Scott nods.

"When she finally answered the question, her voice was shaking and she was holding back tears," Paul says. "She said that if Dr. Wright had warned her about something that important, she would have remembered it."

"So the line was tested but it held," Scott says.

"Just barely."

"Okay. Now tell me about Dr. Wright's deposition."

Paul smiles broadly. "First of all, he's a pompous ass. When we were first introduced, he refused to shake my hand. What a jerk. Then, as I was going through the ground rules for the deposition, he scowled at me the entire time—like, how dare I sue him.

"Once I started questioning him, I just tried to tie down everything about the daughter's treatment. You know, what, when, and why. I reviewed every entry in his records to make sure I understood exactly what he'd thought and done. It was rather tedious.

"As for ECT, I wanted to know every reason behind his recommendation. I asked him to repeat exactly what he'd told the parents. Had he explained how ECT supposedly worked? What warnings had he provided? That sort of thing."

Scott holds up his hand to stop Paul. "Do you have the transcript yet?"

"I ordered it. I'll have it soon," Paul says.

"When you do, send me a copy. I'll read it in a few days and give you my feedback."

Paul can see genuine interest in Scott's eyes. After going solo for almost a year on this case, Paul is buoyed by Scott's promise to review the deposition. Finally, a more experienced lawyer will provide some much-needed reassurance and guidance.

"Here are a few takeaways from Dr. Wright's deposition," Paul says. "He doesn't treat many adolescents and teenagers—his practice is limited almost exclusively to adults. When he described the protocols for ECT, he summarized the rules that apply to adults. However, when a child or teenager is involved, the explanations and warnings are more robust; even the electrodes are attached differently. Here's the bottom line—he ignored some of these guidelines for younger patients."

Scott quietly claps his hands and smiles in approval. "Good job," he says. "Did you tie him down on the discharge summary?"

"Oh yeah. I showed him the altered discharge summary and he claimed that he dictated it on the very day Heather left the hospital."

"Well, okay then. You can nail him with that. It's not all doom and gloom here," Scott says. "Anything else you want to talk about?"

"Yes, there's a strategy decision that I've been struggling with and I'd like your input," Paul says.

Scott glances at his watch. "Sure, I've got a little time."

"Here it is: when do I disclose Dr. Wright's alteration of the discharge summary?" Paul asks. "You know, at one point, I wanted to spring it on Dr. Wright at trial, but the local court rules won't allow that. I have to give the other side a copy of all my proposed exhibits thirty days before trial. That would include the first discharge summary."

As Scott ponders his response, he plays with his napkin, folding it into a tiny rectangle. After a few moments, he says, "If I were in your shoes, I'd get it out there right now and give them something to worry about. We want to bring them to the bargaining table and this should do it."

Paul is relieved that Scott's analysis mirrors his own. "I agree. We have to shake things up," Paul says. "Right now, they think they have a very defensible case." For Paul, the sooner he can settle this case and earn his fee, the sooner he can clean up his own financial mess.

Before Paul can comment further, Scott looks at his watch for a second time and then abruptly stands. "Paul, I've got to run. I've got to be in Sandusky in a half an hour. Keep me posted, okay?"

As Paul walks to his car, he experiences a lightness in his step. They've worked out a plan and it is a good one. They are going on the offensive.

CHAPTER 15
SEPTEMBER 5, 2018
PAUL SCHOFIELD

Paul sits across the table from Mary Redwick, a registered nurse who assists Dr. Wright with his practice, and Tom Wilchuck. Paul sent a notice to take Ms. Redwick's deposition several days after meeting with Scott Worthington. Upon receiving it, Ingram called and asked why he "wanted to take this woman's deposition—of all people." Paul told him that Redwick was present at several of the psychotherapy sessions involving Heather and he wanted to discover what she remembered about them. "Suit yourself. She won't have much to say," Ingram told him. Paul knows otherwise.

"Where's your boss this afternoon?" Paul asks Wilchuck.

"He didn't tell me, but it's a Friday afternoon so he's probably at Westwood Country Club playing golf."

Paul notices that Nurse Redwick stiffens upon hearing that. She apparently does not appreciate being handed off to this awkward associate, whose uncombed hair and ill-fitting suit do not inspire confidence. Paul extends his hand to the nurse and introduces himself, something Wilchuck failed to do when Paul first entered the tiny conference room.

Mary Redwick is a severe-looking woman, scrawny and wrinkled, probably in her late sixties. She's tied her thinning gray hair into a tight bun and dressed in a dark gray business suit with a pink blouse. Her ensemble is set off by a colorful butterfly pin on her suit jacket, the vibrant insect incongruous with her mundane appearance. She looks at Paul warily, her hands folded together on top of the table. She also seems nervous, like a student waiting for the teacher to pass out the examination booklets. He surmises that during her decades of nursing, she's never been deposed.

After reciting the ground rules for the deposition, Paul begins by asking her some background questions. Redwick graduated from the M. B. Johnson School of Nursing over forty years ago. She lives with her husband not far from Paul in the University Heights area of Elyria. She spent two decades working at St. Andrew's Hospital, the last eight in the psychiatric ward, where she met Dr. Wright, who plucked her from the hospital to work for him in 1995.

As she proved herself more and more reliable over the years, he became comfortable delegating more responsibility to her, eventually entrusting her with intakes and some follow-up counseling sessions with patients. When Paul asks if she was involved in any of Heather Zurcher's treatment, she denies it.

"Are you sure of that?" Paul asks.

"Absolutely. I had no contact with that patient or her parents," Redwick answers. She smiles at Wilchuck, as if she has delivered a crushing blow to the Zurchers' case.

Paul watches as Wilchuck reaches for his briefcase, apparently convinced that the deposition is at an end. From a folder, Paul pulls three copies of a three-page exhibit. It includes a copy of the sticky note bearing Nurse Redwick's signature, the three-sentence addition to the discharge summary, and the original discharge summary without the drug warning to the family. As if dealing cards, Paul slides copies of the exhibit to the witness, Wilchuck, and the court reporter in quick succession.

"Ms. Redwick, I'm handing out a three-page exhibit that I have marked as Plaintiff's Exhibit M. The first page is a copy of a sticky note bearing your name. Can you tell me what that is, please?"

The witness's face loses all color and she blinks several times. She stares at the paper, as if by sheer willpower she can make it disappear.

"How did you get this?" she eventually mutters.

"I'm sorry, but I'm asking the questions. What is this?" Paul says, prodding her.

"It's a note I wrote to accompany a paper that I delivered to the records custodian at St. Andrew's."

"What was the sticky note affixed to?"

"Well, you have it on the other paper. It's what Dr. Wright wanted to be added to the discharge summary in Heather Zurcher's chart."

"When did you deliver this to the records department?"

"I don't know the date."

"Was it after Dennis Zurcher made an unscheduled appearance at Dr. Wright's office after his daughter's death?"

"I think so." Her voice shakes and she is close to tears.

"Ms. Redwick, there should be no uncertainty here. It was after Mr. Zurcher barged in to talk to Dr. Wright, wasn't it?"

"Yes, that's right," she says, sniffling. Mechanically, Paul hands her a tissue.

Paul knows that if Ingram were present, he would object or otherwise make a commotion, giving his witness time to regain her composure. However, his understudy, Wilchuck, looks dumbfounded and does nothing. As long as the witness remains distressed and disoriented, the truth will tumble from her. And he will take advantage of this until he has the entire story—all of it.

"Dr. Wright told you why he wanted the changes, didn't he?" Paul asks.

The witness nods.

"You need to say yes or no," he reminds her.

"Yes."

"He told you that he believed that the Zurchers were going to sue him, didn't he?"

"Yes."

"He made it clear to you that he wanted the records custodian to destroy the old discharge summary and replace it with a new one that contained three new sentences, didn't he?"

"Yes."

"Please read to me what those three new sentences were," Paul says, pushing her.

Ms. Redwick wipes her eyes before reading, "'I discussed with the parents that they needed to keep the antidepressant medication under lock and key. I explained that this new medication has no known antidote and would be lethal if ingested in large quantities by their daughter. The parents voiced their understanding.'"

"Who did you talk with at the records department when you brought this document there?" Paul asks, his voice showing just a touch of indignation.

"I can't honestly remember," Ms. Redwick says, looking helplessly at Wilchuck. He returns her gaze with an expression of indifference. He's sending her a message: she created the mess and now she'll have to deal with it.

"Was it Shirley?" Paul says, prodding her.

"I really don't know. I don't want to get anybody in trouble when I'm not sure," she says, unable to hide the panic in her eyes.

"And they would get in trouble, wouldn't they?" Paul asks. This time his voice is gentle and reassuring, like the experienced detective trying to encourage the suspect to unburden his conscience and come clean.

"Yes."

"Why would that be?" he asks.

"You're not allowed to do that," she says breathlessly. "The records are supposed to be sacred. If you want to add something to them, you must label it as a late-entry addendum and provide the actual date that the new information was added." Nurse Redwick's words are rapid and gathering a momentum on their own.

"And this was not handed to the records custodian to be filed as a late-entry addendum, was it?"

"No. It was to replace the existing record," the witness admits, her head bowed—her dejection complete.

"Anything else you want to add to your testimony?" Paul asks. This is a question he rarely asks because it gives the witness an opportunity to improve upon a previous answer. But with a distraught witness, it may add something extremely important.

Wiping tears from her cheeks, the witness looks first at the court reporter and then at Paul. "I just want to say that I am so ashamed. I knew it was wrong when he asked me to deliver this to the hospital, but I told myself that I was just the messenger. I shouldn't have been a part of this."

Paul tells her that he has no additional questions and thanks her for her honesty. As the witness and Wilchuck quickly gather their things and make a hasty departure, Paul looks at the court reporter and raises his eyebrows. He always employs her to handle his depositions and she often offers her candid thoughts when they finish.

"I hope Mr. Ingram is having a good time on the golf course," she says. "He won't like this development."

Trying not to gloat, Paul suppresses a grin. "No, not one bit."

CHAPTER 16
OCTOBER 17, 2018
PAUL SCHOFIELD

All morning Paul has been delaying the phone call to Dr. Masterson. Three days before, he received his expert's report, hoping that a strong report would push the defendant's insurer to the bargaining table. However, with each paragraph that he read, he became more and more disappointed. After he read the report for a second time, his disappointment turned into a gnawing despair. The doctor's report was highly partisan and lacked objectivity. To make matters worse, some of his opinions were just plain wrong.

Paul knows that Dr. Masterson's opinions about ECT are on the fringe, particularly his rants that ECT is wholly ineffective, should be banned, and is a fraud being perpetrated against the public. Paul has endured several long conversations with the doctor during which Dr. Masterson has railed against greedy ECT machine manufacturers, hospitals, and psychiatrists who perpetuate the fraud solely to reap insane profits.

Paul expected Dr. Masterson to lace his report with these kinds of opinions, but Dr. Masterson has gone well beyond that. He's leveled other criticisms against Dr. Wright that lack any basis. If he persists in peddling these opinions, he'll look foolish not only to the defendant's insurance company but later to the jurors at trial.

Setting aside a separation agreement that he was revising, Paul picks up the phone and dials the doctor's cell number. From the start of their relationship, the doctor has revealed a sizeable ego that Paul has tolerated and sometimes fed in trying to develop a collaborative relationship with him. Paul fears that the man's arrogance will keep him from altering any opinions, even if Paul demonstrates that their underpinnings are false. Despite this, he needs to try.

As he waits for Dr. Masterson to answer his phone, Paul stands and drums his fingers on the glass of his desk. On the fourth ring, Dr. Masterson picks up. "Yes, what is it?" His voice is harried and gruff.

"I wonder if you have a few minutes to talk about your report in the Zurcher case," Paul says.

"Well, yes and no," Dr. Masterson replies.

"Is this a bad time?"

"I'm packing a suitcase right now and will be catching a flight to Denmark in a few hours. I'm speaking at a conference there." There is impatience in the doctor's voice, tinged with a sense of self-importance.

This conversation is going to be difficult under the best circumstances. Why try to convince the doctor to make changes when he is clearly pressed for time? "I'll call you when you return," Paul suggests.

"No, that's okay. I've got five minutes. Let's talk now. So what did you think?" Dr. Masterson asks. No longer gruff, he seems expectant, eager to hear praise.

Paul will begin by feeding the man's ego and then turn to his criticisms. "I think it's a great report—succinct and definite. I would—"

"That's what I thought too," Dr. Masterson replies before Paul can finish his last sentence. "It's not often that I can so overwhelmingly demonstrate the defendant's negligence. I outlined seven departures from accepted practices and I believe my aggressiveness will ultimately cause the defendant to capitulate. Don't you agree?"

Paul takes a deep breath. "I certainly hope so," he says. "However, I'd like to make a few suggestions that I think will strengthen our position."

"Oh." Paul hears disappointment in the doctor's one-word response.

"I think some of your points are extremely strong, but others don't pack that same punch," Paul says, trying to be as gentle with his criticism as possible.

"Like what?" Dr. Masterson replies, irritation evident in his voice. "Give me some examples, if you don't mind."

"You criticize Dr. Wright for failing to provide family counseling."

"As well he should have. No doubt on that one," Dr. Masterson replies.

"The problem, as I see it, is that Dr. Wright did recommend family counseling sessions, but the father categorically refused to participate in them. I don't think you can legitimately criticize Dr. Wright for that."

"Paul, is this your first medical malpractice case?" Dr. Masterson asks. "You don't mind me calling you Paul, do you?"

Dr. Masterson's condescension galls Paul, but he tries to ignore it. "This is my second medical malpractice case," Paul says, not sure why he bothered to make that distinction.

"I don't mean to pull rank on you, Paul, but I've testified in dozens of cases. I know what I need to do to convince a jury. Leave it to me, I'll make that criticism stick. Anything else?"

"Well, you also disapproved of the patient being discharged from the hospital before Dr. Wright had adequately adjusted her new medication."

"Of course I did. That was criminal."

Paul clears his throat. "I'm afraid you will lose credibility when the defense points out that the parents insisted that their daughter be discharged immediately. Dr. Wright didn't want to release her, he just acquiesced in the parents' request."

"Don't worry about me. I can handle myself in the courtroom. I'll turn it around on them. You just have to trust me."

Paul sighs. He debates whether to continue. He is convinced that his expert will fare much better if he eliminates opinions that can easily be debunked. He decides to press on. "I would feel more comfortable if you just went with your strongest opinions, the ones that can't be countered."

"I agreed to take this call even though I am very busy right now," Dr. Masterson says, his voice both loud and snippy. "If you don't feel comfortable—as you put it—then perhaps you should find another expert."

If I could afford to pay for another one, believe me, I would, Paul thinks. Instead, he replies, "I've upset you, haven't I?"

"Nonsense." Dr. Masterson's voice is calmer now.

"Anyway, that was not my intention. I simply wanted to strategize with you about the best way to present your opinions. I won't bother you further. I know you have other things on your mind."

"Really, no offense is taken," Dr. Masterson says, apparently trying to sound magnanimous.

"I'll call you after I receive the reports of the defendant's expert. My reports are due in a week, the defendant's six weeks later."

"I'll be anxious to find out what the defendant's position will be after his team has digested my report. I have a feeling that good things will happen for us soon. Anything else?"

"No, that's it." Paul has other concerns about the report, but he realizes he is powerless to voice them. He doesn't have the resources to replace Dr. Masterson and he does not want to antagonize his sole expert any further.

"Goodbye then," Dr. Masterson says.

"Have a good trip."

After placing the phone receiver back into its cradle, Paul lowers his head onto his desk, his forearms serving as cushions. He anticipated that this conversation would be difficult, but he didn't foresee how deflated he'd feel at its conclusion. The case is challenging enough without a prima donna dictating his legal strategies.

Paul is convinced that Dr. Masterson's report would be much stronger if he included some points that Paul suggested to him several months ago. In his own medical research, Paul had learned of standards governing ECT that were developed by some of the world's most renowned psychiatrists. Many of these requirements applied solely to adolescents and teenagers, attempts to make shock treatment safer for this age group.

He'd sent those guidelines to Dr. Masterson, identified the ones that Dr. Wright had ignored, and asked him to consider including those failures in his report. To Paul's dismay, Dr. Masterson's report made no mention of these standards, nor did it criticize Dr. Wright for departures from these requirements. In today's phone call, Paul intended to ask Dr. Masterson to reconsider mentioning these departures in his report. However, after Dr. Masterson became testy and challenged him to find a new expert, Paul realized that was impossible. He's stuck with Dr. Masterson's report as written.

Paul lifts his head from his desk and takes a deep breath. His eyes fix on his children's framed artwork hanging on the opposite wall. In one, a stick figure waves to him from under a rainbow, while from another, a golden sun's jagged rays touch a purple house, beside which a mother, a father, and two children stand like giants. Staring at their primitive artwork, he is reminded that his family is what really matters, not his work and certainly not this impossible case. As this thought takes hold of him, his mood lightens.

Grabbing his sport jacket, he tosses it over his shoulder. At the reception area, he bends over and kisses his wife on the top of her head.

"What's that for?" Wendy asks.

"I thought I needed to sexually harass my one and only employee," he replies.

Wendy shakes her head. "Oh, you did, did you? Well, you've got another think coming, buddy," she says.

"Really?"

"Yeah, really," Wendy says, trying to sound indignant. "I don't care how cute you think you are." She rises from her chair and faces him. Although no one is in the waiting room, she gives it a quick look. Assured of their privacy, she tosses her hair back, throws her arms around him, and kisses him.

For a few moments, they remain locked in this embrace. When Paul pulls away, he says, "Let's close the office for the rest of the day. I think the time off would do both of us some good."

"Time off!" Wendy exclaims in mock surprise. "You're still going to pay me, right?"

"Time and a half."

Giving Paul a searching look, Wendy says, "Well, I'm guessing by your mood that your little talk with Dr. Masterson went extremely well."

"Just the opposite, but let's not talk about it," Paul says, guiding her out the door before locking it. Tomorrow, he'll figure out what to do with Dr. Masterson. Maybe a jury will believe this bizarre man with his unconventional views. Stranger things have happened.

For now, however, he'll focus on the good things in his life.

CHAPTER 17
FEBRUARY 19, 2019
PAUL SCHOFIELD

As the elevator doors opened onto the Justice Center's seventh floor, Paul spots his client in the hallway, pacing around a waste receptacle like a pit bull chained to a fire hydrant. A week earlier, they met at Paul's office to discuss what will likely happen at today's final pretrial. Dennis has repeatedly asked whether the insurance company will settle the claim, while Paul has remained steadfastly noncommittal.

As Paul approaches Dennis, he can see that his client's eyes are wild with a feverish anxiety. As the men shake hands, Dennis blurts, "They're going to make an offer today, right?"

Determined to calm his client, Paul points toward a bench and suggests that they sit. Paul takes a deep breath before repeating what he said a week earlier. They showed the insurance company their two strongest cards, one revealing Dr. Wright's alteration of the records and the other disclosing Dr. Masterson's many criticisms of Dr. Wright's care.

"I can't predict the insurance company's response any more today than I could last week," Paul says. "Neither the insurance company nor Attorney Ingram has contacted me since we last talked."

"Silence—that's a great negotiating technique. I use it all the time in my work," Dennis says, nodding his head in approval. "They'll eventually have to come to us with an offer. They can't let this case go to trial, not with all the bad publicity it will generate."

They discussed this point last week as well. Civil cases in Lorain County almost never receive any news coverage. Paul shrugs and decides not to explain this again. Instead, he tells Dennis that he will head to the judge's private chambers, where the judge will conduct the pretrial with him, Ingram, and the defendant's insurance representative. Neither Dennis nor Dr. Wright will join them in chambers.

"Why can't I go back with you?" Dennis asks, sounding like a schoolkid excluded from a playground game.

"The judge wants to talk to the attorneys and the insurance adjuster first. If he thinks he needs to talk to you, he'll bring you back," Paul responds, giving Dennis a *please be patient* look. Before Paul walks away, Dennis shakes his head in disapproval.

A few moments later, Paul follows a long hallway to a door that opens into the office of Judge John J. Hardwig and his staff. Once inside, Paul reports to the judge's civil secretary, Amy Morgan, who sits at her desk behind a half wall. Amy is a pretty woman with short-cropped blond hair, intelligent brown eyes, and a gracious smile. He has a passing acquaintance with Amy, whose daughter, Melanie, plays on his daughter's soccer team—a team that Paul has coached for the last two years. Paul enjoys coaching Melanie, who, although a timid soccer player, always gives her best effort.

Pointing to the waiting area, Amy tells him that the defense attorney and his insurance adjuster arrived a few minutes earlier and that she will let the judge know that everyone is present. Just as Paul begins to turn away, Amy says in a whisper, "When you're done with the pretrial, I need to talk to you—a little favor to ask."

Paul takes a deep breath. "Yeah, sure. As soon as this is over, we can talk," he says. He groans inwardly; he doesn't need any distractions

—not today. Amy smiles and gives him a thumbs-up before he leaves to join the others.

Ingram and a woman, who he guesses is Emily McDonald, are talking to a third man whose back faces Paul. As Paul gets closer to the group, he recognizes the other person as Frank McCloskey, the judge's bailiff—a heavyset man in his early fifties. McCloskey seems to be telling a joke or story but stops abruptly when Paul reaches the trio. Paul believes McCloskey to be a shallow gladhander, a failed businessman who seems equally inept at performing his bailiff duties. A former high school buddy of the judge, McCloskey worked tirelessly on the judge's first campaign and has been rewarded with this position. Despite his misgivings about the man, Paul treats him with respect whenever their paths cross.

"Just leaving," McCloskey says when Paul arrives.

Ingram quickly introduces Paul to Emily McDonald, the Defiance Mutual Insurance representative. Based on his conversations with Scott Worthington, Paul knows much about this woman, all of it unfavorable. McDonald is just as he imagined her. She is a tall, severe-looking woman dressed in a black business suit whose pale, sallow complexion completes her funereal appearance. Maintaining a grim expression, she perfunctorily offers him her right hand. He takes it and she responds with a short but firm handshake.

Instinctively, Paul gives her a warm smile and intends to ask her about her drive from Columbus that morning. Before Paul can say anything, she nudges Ingram in the direction of the judge's office. "Well, let's get this over with," she says.

Her comment cuts Paul, as, no doubt, she intended it to. She is here because—under the court rules—she is required to be present. Her words and manner tell Paul that she has no intention of negotiating in good faith and reaching a settlement. Although he has done his best to temper his client's expectations, he realizes that he yearns for a settlement just as much as Dennis. On his most optimistic days, he views the case as challenging and intellectually stimulating. But, when reality sets in, he sees it for what it is—a bottomless pit that is devouring him.

Taking a deep breath, Paul tells himself not to overreact to one terse comment. It is entirely possible that McDonald will extend an offer today—even a low one. How can she not recognize the risks to her insurance company? Dr. Wright blatantly altered the medical chart and ordered shock treatments to a fifteen-year-old girl. With the right jury, Paul may be able to parlay this into a verdict, something McDonald has to consider. For now, Paul will cling to hope.

A few moments later the three of them enter the judge's chambers, where Judge Hardwig sits behind a large cherry desk, studying some paperwork in front of him. His thick gray brows furrow before he glances up, revealing a ruddy, pockmarked face and his trademark turquoise eyes. With a withering stare, those eyes can destroy an unprepared attorney appearing before him.

"Please, everyone take a seat," he says, his tone uncharacteristically genial. In his third term, the fifty-eight-year-old former prosecutor and navy SEAL cuts a wiry figure. He is a no-nonsense judge, polite and reserved to those he trusts, abrupt and cutting to those he doesn't. Over the years, Paul has handled a dozen cases in his court, two progressing to jury trials. Thus far, Paul has stayed in the judge's good graces.

The judge reaches for a court file and opens it. Not wasting any time on preliminaries, he says, "We're sixty days before trial. Have we had any meaningful settlement discussions?"

"Not yet," Paul answers. "Before we talk settlement, I would like to bring you up to date on some new developments." Paul then explains how Dr. Wright altered the records to cover up his failure to warn the parents about the new antidepressant. As Paul talks, the judge seems keenly interested in the details and occasionally glances at Ingram and McDonald with raised eyebrows.

"I've seen juries punish defendants for this kind of behavior," the judge says, directing a penetrating stare at Ingram. Paul smiles inwardly; the judge is signaling to the adjuster that she, too, should appreciate this and make an offer. If Emily McDonald stonewalls him today, Judge Hardwig will not be pleased. The judge continues, "Mr. Ingram, what do you have to say about this?"

Stifling a laugh, Ingram feigns nonchalance. "Judge, to steal a phrase from the Bard, it's much ado about nothing." Ingram explains that the doctor revised the discharge summary to "set the record straight." He'd warned the parents about the drug but inadvertently omitted it from the discharge summary. There is nothing fraudulent about the doctor's insistence that the records be accurate. Finishing with a dismissive hand gesture, Ingram says, "This will all be very clear to the jury after Dr. Wright testifies."

Throughout Ingram's explanation, Judge Hardwig has appeared skeptical. Several times, he raised his eyebrows and seemed poised to interrupt Ingram but did not. When Ingram finishes, the judge asks Paul if he wants to comment further.

His heart racing and his face flushed, Paul is eager to respond to Ingram's bullshit. Controlling his emotions, Paul begins evenly. "There's an important maxim in medicine that states if it isn't charted, it didn't happen. Mrs. Zurcher met with Dr. Wright at the time of discharge and she will categorically tell the jury that Dr. Wright did not warn her. The original record and Mrs. Zurcher's testimony will align perfectly." Paul hesitates for a moment as he contemplates his next words. Knowing that Judge Hardwig enjoys an occasional salty phrase, Paul plunges forward. "What will be very clear to the jury—to borrow Mr. Ingram's phrase—is that Dr. Wright knew he'd screwed up and was covering his ass."

Judge Hardwig suppresses a smile. "Well, counselors, let's save those arguments for the jury," he says. "Right now, I want to see if we can avoid a trial. Paul, what's your settlement demand?"

"We believe our case is worth two million, but we have made a settlement demand of 1.4 million," Paul says.

The judge looks expectantly at Ingram.

Puffing out his chest, Ingram displays a solemn face. In a composed voice, he begins by reminding the judge that he's handled five cases in his court and settled three of them. However, in two cases, the parties held vastly different opinions and a jury decided these controversies. In each of those cases, the juries found in Ingram's favor. Glancing first at his adjuster and then directing his gaze back to the judge, Ingram says, "With all due respect to this court, we won't be making an offer today—or ever."

These are not the words Paul wanted to hear. Disappointment springs from his gut to his throat, but he maintains a neutral expression. He read McDonald correctly.

Shaking his head slightly, the judge sighs. Before he can say anything, McDonald coughs and then speaks. "If I may, Your Honor, I'd like to explain our decision to you."

With his right hand, the judge gestures for McDonald to proceed.

Ignoring Paul, she focuses on the judge. She explains that the case has been reviewed in committee several times, doctors from top medical institutions have weighed in, and they have found that Dr. Wright followed all accepted protocols.

Judge Hardwig's nose twitches and he shakes his head. "What about the doctor altering the records? Doesn't that concern you?"

"All it shows is poor judgment, not negligence," she shoots back, irritation in her voice.

Judge Hardwig gives her a quizzical look.

"Okay, the man panicked and did a stupid thing. Jurors can understand that. Overall, he's a good doctor and we're going to prove that," McDonald says.

"So you are telling me that this case presents absolutely no risk to your client?" the judge asks. "I know your claims committee has evaluated this claim, but I've seen many instances where these reviews were all wrong. Your people don't look at the case the same way a jury does."

"Oh no," McDonald responds. "We've been careful to do that too.

We evaluate every witness and every party for their potential jury appeal. We look at past jury verdicts in the jurisdiction where the case will be tried." She pauses and stares at Paul, indicating that her next point will be directed at him. "We look at the track records of the attorneys involved. We compare their experience and competency." She next turns her gaze toward Ingram. "And I know Bob will think that I'm jinxing him, but he almost never loses at trial."

"Thank you for your detailed response," Judge Hardwig says, and Paul hears sarcasm in his voice. "Nevertheless, I'd like to talk with both you and Mr. Ingram in private for a few moments. Paul, could you wait outside? I'll call you back after we're finished."

After Paul walks out of the judge's chambers, he takes a seat in the nearby waiting area. As he sits there, he replays the adjuster's haughty explanation, and, in particular, her dismissive statement about his courtroom experience. Although he and Scott Worthington settled his only medical malpractice case before trial, he is an effective litigator who knows how to move a jury. If she and her vaunted committee think he will stumble his way through his first medical malpractice trial, they are dead wrong.

By the time Ingram opens the judge's door a few minutes later, Paul is doing a slow burn. Not bothering to say anything, Ingram makes eye contact with him and then beckons him with his index finger, like he is his servant. As Ingram turns his back on him, Paul holds up a different finger in response.

When he reenters the room, Judge Hardwig is scowling. When Paul looks at McDonald and Ingram, they are staring straight ahead, refusing to make eye contact with him. Paul quickly concludes that the judge has not budged his intransigent opponents. The judge will not be meeting with him privately to discuss an offer.

"Paul, as you can probably surmise, the defendant is prepared to try this case to its conclusion. They're quite confident that a jury will come back with a defense verdict."

His face grim, Paul nods. This case has now become personal. It is one thing for the other side to dispute the case's merits, but it is another to doubt his trial skills.

The judge continues, "I know this case is scheduled to be tried in two months, but I currently have several criminal trials set for that same week. As you know, if the criminal case goes forward, your case will be bumped. I don't want to do that to you. I know how expensive it is to prepare a medical malpractice case for trial. Because I have ten open days beginning on September twenty-third, I would like to postpone your trial until then in order to ensure that your case will go forward. I won't schedule anything else during those days. Do I hear any objections?"

Both attorneys indicate that they are in favor of the judge's recommendation. Neither one wants to prepare for trial, show up in the courtroom, and be told to go home when a criminal defendant insists on their day in court. Paul knows that Dennis will be unhappy, but he'll deal with him. This development is for the best, particularly when he cannot afford to duplicate any expense.

Before dismissing them, Judge Hardwig says, "This trial will definitely move forward on September twenty-third. Everybody better be ready. No continuances for anything. I don't want anybody crying to me because their expert witness is not available. Understood?"

The attorneys say yes in unison.

"I'll see everyone back here in September. If settlement postures should change, I'm always willing to bring you all back for more talks. Anything else?"

Both attorneys say no in unison and then stand. To avoid shaking hands with his opponents, Paul leans over and pretends to be looking for something in his briefcase. He then follows them at a healthy distance and watches them walk toward the elevators.

Dennis is pacing outside the courtroom again. As Paul approaches, he shakes his head at Dennis. "They want to try the case."

"Damn it," Dennis roars. "That can't be. That can't be. What the fuck is the matter with them?"

"Calm down, Dennis," Paul replies, placing his hand on Dennis's forearm.

"How can I be calm?" Dennis says, waving his arms above his head. "That bastard killed my daughter and his insurance company says so fucking what."

Several attorneys walk by them slowly, obviously intent on catching as much of the show as they can without stopping.

Paul grabs Dennis by the elbow and steers him to a bench at the far end of the hall, away from any onlookers. After they sit, Paul says, "Now listen, Dennis. You need to quiet down and just listen to me. Can you do that?"

After Dennis nods, Paul explains in great detail what happened in the judge's chambers. As Paul talks, Dennis clenches and unclenches his fists but refrains from any loud outbursts. From time to time, Dennis interrupts with a question, which Paul patiently answers, no matter how inane.

When Paul finishes his summary, he looks directly into Dennis's eyes and says, "I've told you before this is a tough case, right?" After Dennis nods, Paul continues. "The defense thinks they have a sure winner." Paul pauses again, making certain that his words are sinking in. "You have my pledge that I will do everything in my power to prove the insurance company wrong. Okay?"

Dennis's agitation is gone, replaced by a quiet resignation. "Okay," Dennis mutters.

The two rise from the bench, head toward the bank of elevators, and wait for one to arrive. As they stand there, Paul remembers that Amy Morgan wanted to speak to him. He doesn't have the energy to reenter Judge Hardwig's chambers again; the disappointment and anger are still too fresh. He toys with the idea of phoning her when he returns to the office but decides he should just get it over with.

"Sorry, Dennis. I forgot that I've got another errand to run in the courthouse. I'll be around tomorrow if you want to talk more," Paul says. Before Dennis can reply, Paul touches him gently on the shoulder and walks away.

A few moments later, Paul stands before Amy Morgan, the judge's secretary, who is on the phone with someone. When she sees Paul, she raises one finger in the air, indicating that she'll end the call in a moment, which she does.

Amy brushes her blond bangs away from her forehead. "I thought you'd forgotten me," she says. "You rushed out of here looking pretty distressed."

"Oh, was it that obvious?"

"Well, I can read people pretty well, so it was to me, probably not to anyone else."

Paul nods. He wants to ask her if the judge told her anything about the pretrial but knows that would be improper. Instead, he decides to move the conversation along. "I guess you had a question for me."

"Oh yes," Amy says. "Let me begin by saying that it's okay to tell us no. I will understand."

Paul smiles. With an introduction like that, he'll probably have a difficult time saying no to this woman.

"Well, this is for Melanie, my daughter. You know her," Amy says.

"Of course I do. She's one of my favorite kids on the team," Paul says, trying to encourage Amy to relax and get to the point.

"As I said, this is about Melanie, and a school assignment. She is supposed to shadow someone for a day and then write about it. She is too shy to ask you herself, but she'd like to follow you for a day if that could be arranged."

"Oh," Paul says. He doubts that a twelve-year-old girl would gain much insight about the legal profession by spending a day with him. She cannot sit in on client conferences—no client would consent to that, nor would he ask them to. "Let me see. I've done that before but it's usually with a high school student," Paul says.

"I know she's a little young for this," Amy says, scrunching her shoulders in embarrassment. "But you know, she's convinced herself that she wants to be a lawyer. And she's a very determined little girl—so who knows?"

"When is this?" Paul asks. Maybe he can escape because of a conflict in his schedule.

"Oh, the nice thing is that the date is flexible, whenever it works for you," Amy says.

After boxing himself into a corner, he'll have to say yes. "Um, well then, I guess you should just call the office and talk to my wife, Wendy, who can schedule it."

"I didn't know Wendy worked in your office. I thought she was a substitute teacher."

"It's a long story, but she's helping me out temporarily. Just call the office. I'll tell her to choose a date when I've got a deposition or a bench trial or a preliminary hearing—something where Melanie can listen and get the flavor of being a lawyer."

Amy's eyes light up. "Oh, thank you, Paul. Melanie will be so excited. You made our day."

The irony is not lost on Paul, who, after some initial resistance, smiles reluctantly. At least he's made somebody's day.

CHAPTER 18
FEBRUARY 19, 2019
CINDY ZURCHER

One glance at her wristwatch tells Cindy Zurcher that things have not gone well at the pretrial. Three hours have passed since its start and she's heard nothing from Dennis. Although her anxiety about the case does not match his, she desperately wants the parties to settle their differences. The trial is just two months away, and if the case is not resolved out of court, she will have to testify in front of a courtroom of strangers and tell them about her daughter's life and ultimate death. She cannot imagine a more agonizing experience. It is not just reliving Heather's final day that terrifies her, it is being cross-examined about their dysfunctional family life. Dennis will be exposed as a monster while she will be vilified for her acquiescence in it all.

As the pretrial date grew closer, Dennis went berserk over the most trivial of things—an unmade bed, crayons left on the dining room table, toothpaste left uncapped, letters left in the mailbox overnight—to name a few. If the insurance company does not present Dennis with a suitable offer, she doesn't want to consider how it will affect their already tumultuous home life.

The children came home from school an hour earlier. Her twelve-year-old son, Travis, is playing a video game on a handheld device in the family room, the sounds of gunfire and explosions adding to her tension. A few feet away, nine-year-old Melissa is chattering away, providing the dialogue between two Barbie dolls. As if she does not already have enough stress, wind gusts periodically cause a maple branch to scrape against the side of the house.

At four thirty, she hears the garage door open and Dennis's SUV roars into it. A few moments later, Dennis walks into the kitchen, his overcoat folded over his arm. Spotting Cindy in the kitchen, he throws his coat to her and tells her to hang it up in the closet. Even from three feet away, she can smell liquor on his breath. His overcoat reeks of fried food and cigarettes. Who knows where he's been?

When she returns to the kitchen, Dennis is standing by the kitchen sink, looking out the window. His hands are in his pockets, where they jingle some loose coins. When he turns to look at her, his eyes are bloodshot and his entire demeanor evinces edginess and agitation. Without asking, she knows that the pretrial has been a disaster. She has seen this look countless times over their marriage and knows what is sure to follow. He'll find a pretext to verbally abuse someone. Her job is always to limit the damage and direct Dennis's fury toward herself and not one of the children.

She is uncertain of her next step. If she asks him to tell her about the pretrial, he'll criticize her for not recognizing the obvious. If she fails to ask, he'll berate her for her lack of interest and concern.

"I take it by your expression that things didn't go well this afternoon," she begins.

"Yeah, that's right," Dennis says, refusing to offer more.

Again, she is caught in the same dilemma. If she seeks more information, he'll accuse her of prying or deliberately aggravating him. Instead, she decides to rely on a stock question, one that has provided her with cover over the years.

"Do you feel like talking about it?" she asks.

"What do you think?" he says.

"I guess not."

"You guessed right."

Walking toward her children, she says, "Kids, Dad has had a tough day." This is their special code; it means they need to be quiet and stay out of his way. However, Cindy thinks that the current situation calls for greater precaution. "I think it would be best if you both went to your rooms to play."

Clutching her dolls to her chest, Melissa scampers toward her bedroom. Travis, however, voices his reluctance. "I just want to finish this game. It's almost over," he moans. He continues to focus on his game, his fingers moving feverishly over the controller.

Cindy winces as the sound of an explosion comes from Travis's device. Apparently lost in his thoughts, Dennis does not react. However, when the sounds of gunfire and squealing tires fill the quiet room, Dennis raises his head, like a predatory animal picking up a scent, and identifies the source of the noise.

"Can't a guy get any peace around here," Dennis says, directing a cold stare at his son. "Turn that damn thing off before I throw it out the fucking window."

Like a dog that has just been walloped on its rump, Travis jumps from his chair and runs out of the room.

Turning his attention to Cindy, Dennis says, "So apparently you don't want to hear about what happened at the pretrial. I suppose you don't give a shit."

Cindy's pulse quickens and a prickly unease settles in her stomach. "Of course I want to know, but that's only if you feel like discussing it," she says.

Dennis gives her an assessing glance, scrutinizing her sincerity. After she apparently passes his test, he says, "Okay, here's what happened. Those bastards made no offer. And, if that wasn't bad enough, our stupid-ass attorney agreed to a continuance. Instead of a trial in April, we have to wait until September. I don't know why he agreed to that except that he's incompetent as hell." Seeking a reaction,

Dennis stares at Cindy, whose face remains neutral as she maintains her silence.

"The guy's a loser. I know that now, but I didn't see that when I hired him. All I do is pick losers." Dennis forces a laugh and apparently expects some reaction from her—if not a laugh, then at least a smile. However, Cindy understands the comment for what it is, a jab at her, too. How many times has he called her a loser? She is tired of it. She was prepared to sympathize with him, but not now. Turning her back on him, she walks several steps toward the refrigerator.

"Don't blow me off, Cindy. I don't like to be ignored."

"I'm not ignoring you. I'm checking on dinner."

"That's bullshit. You probably haven't even started dinner yet."

Dennis is right. She hasn't.

"I was just going to start it," she replies.

"Then you lied when you said you were *checking on dinner*," he says.

She feels it all spinning away as it always does when he finds an opening. Her stomach tightens and her mind goes blank. Can she stop what is coming next?

"I misspoke," she says. "I'm sorry, Dennis."

"Oh, you misspoke. That's what politicians say when they get caught in a big, fat lie. And you were lying. Why don't you just admit it?"

"I—I don't know what you mean," Cindy stammers.

"Let me spell it out for you then. You weren't checking on dinner. You walked into the kitchen for one reason—to get away from me," Dennis says, anger filling his eyes. Pointing his finger accusingly at Cindy, he says, "After that damn pretrial, I needed a little sympathy from you and what do you do? You abandon me."

"I'm sorry, Dennis. What more can I say? I wasn't trying to be disrespectful," Cindy says, her voice both shrill and shaky.

"Well good for you. You're so skilled, you can be disrespectful without actually trying. Aren't you a clever little bitch?" he yells.

"Please, Dennis, the children will hear you."

"They can't. They're in their rooms," he shouts.

But their children aren't in their rooms. Travis stands in the hallway that leads from the bedrooms to the family room. Behind him, Melissa pokes her head.

"Please, Dad, leave Mom alone," Travis says, his voice soft and pleading.

"You stay out of it, you little shit."

"No, I want you to stop this time," Travis says. This time his voice is unsteady but louder.

Dennis moves toward his son, menace in his eyes. At twelve, Travis is big for his age, five feet six inches tall, muscular, and still growing. Although he has the body of a man, he has the chubby, unblemished face of a boy.

"So now you think you're the man of the family. Is that what you think?"

Travis shakes his head, terror now registering in his eyes. He's ventured too far and he has no idea how to retreat. As if to provide moral support, Melissa moves to her brother's side. When she sees the anger in her father's face, her mouth opens in a soundless scream.

"Here's what I'm going to do," says Dennis, jabbing his index finger into the boy's chest. "You take your best swing at me and if you knock me out, you're the man. If you don't, then this thing is coming at you full force," Dennis says, holding his right fist inches from Travis's face. "You think you can handle it, Mr. Big Shot?" The boy steps back and the movement seems to disorient Dennis, who wavers and stumbles to his right, another sign that he's had too much to drink.

Dennis has never hit the children before. Except for an occasional shove, he's never struck Cindy. He is a bluffer, an intimidator, a bully. He likes to threaten violence—scare you—but he never follows through on it. She can't picture him punching their son, but, then again, she can't be sure. There are things that she just doesn't know.

What exactly happened at the hearing today? Did the defense belittle the case? Have they been arrogant? Have they insulted him in any way?

What she does know is that he expected a large settlement offer. He's dreamed about it, counted on it, and eventually felt entitled to it. And they offered him nothing. They decided his case was worthless. To Dennis, that means they think he is worthless. They humiliated him and he was powerless to strike back.

She can assume nothing. He can do anything now. She didn't protect Heather and Heather is dead. Now he is going after Travis and she needs to act.

"No, Dennis, no," she says with as much firmness as she can muster. She nudges Melissa to the side and places herself between her husband and son. Turning her head toward her son, she says, "Travis, I want you to go to your room *now* and lock the door."

When the boy does not move, she says, "Now."

The boy takes two steps backward and then stops suddenly. "Dad, I don't want to hit you. I just want you to stop yelling at Mom."

"That's not your call. That's never your call," Dennis yells, moving so close to Cindy that the alcohol in his breath is overpowering.

"Travis, go to your room," Cindy repeats. Taking his sister's hand, the boy retreats farther into the hallway but stops, unwilling to abandon his mother.

Looking at her husband, Cindy says, "Dennis, get control of yourself before you do something you'll regret." Although her heart is pounding, her voice has remained steady.

"I am in control."

"I know you are," she says, realizing that she must placate him. She pauses, collecting her thoughts. Her next words will be critical if she hopes to defuse the situation. "I know how much you loved Heather, how disappointed you are about the case. I know you are feeling about as low as a person can feel. For your own sake, take some time to breathe and regroup. No one will think less of you if you do."

Dennis nods, considering but saying nothing. She senses that she has softened him, defused some of his anger.

"Why don't you unwind at a friend's house for a few hours? We'll be all right on our own. Then come back to us," she says. As she says these words, she pictures Dennis speeding away in his SUV, striking a utility pole, and dying at the scene, but she realizes that she could never be so lucky.

"I think I will," Dennis says, as if doing so would somehow punish them all. "In fact, don't wait up for me. I'm staying out all night."

He walks to the closet and grabs his overcoat, slings it over his shoulder, and walks out the kitchen door that leads to the garage. His SUV roars to life again, its tires squealing when it reaches the street, and then, it speeds away.

Although Cindy's hands are still shaking, she feels relief for the first time all day. Walking into the family room, she plops herself down on Dennis's La-Z-Boy. It feels good to disobey him; this recliner is supposedly for his exclusive use.

Cindy knows exactly where Dennis is headed—to his girlfriend's place. Although Cindy does not know the woman's name, she knows her perfume, Obsession. For the last two years, Cindy has smelled that scent every time she's placed his shirts in the washing machine. Strangely, Cindy feels no jealousy, no dislike for this mystery woman. Truth be told, if this woman wants Dennis to bang her, well, Cindy is all for it. Throughout their marriage, sex has been a repulsive chore—violent, quick, and deeply unsatisfying. If Dennis's girlfriend craves this, she can have him.

Cindy does, however, occasionally wonder about this woman. What is she like? What does she find attractive about her flabby, selfish husband? Do they go anywhere together or do they just hang out at her place? Beyond that, Cindy doesn't really much care. If Dennis is with her, he isn't at home.

A few minutes later, Melissa ventures out of her bedroom and joins Cindy in the family room. Cindy gets up from the recliner and hugs her daughter. As she presses her daughter close to her, Cindy kisses her on the top of her head. "This will pass, Melissa. This will pass. Daddy is upset about the case. When it's over, things will get better."

Cindy doesn't believe this. She suspects that things are only going to get worse. She needs a plan. She has to get away from Dennis and take her children with her. She has no idea how to accomplish this. Worse yet, she has no one in whom to confide. She has no family. She has no friends. She has no church. She is utterly alone.

Dennis has completely isolated her; even the internet is off-limits to her. Dennis won't allow her a smartphone, nor will he give her access to his home computer.

Since her daughter's death, only two people have demonstrated any real empathy toward her: the middle-aged emergency room nurse named Juanita who held her fiercely after the doctors stopped resuscitation efforts, comforting her when time and reality seemed suspended in another dimension. And recently, Wendy Schofield, who did the same thing when Cindy broke down in Paul's office—infusing her with a strength that only one woman can give to another.

Afterward, Wendy gave Cindy her cell phone number and invited her to call whenever she needed her. Well, tonight, she needs her.

CHAPTER 19
FEBRUARY 19, 2019
WENDY SCHOFIELD

When her iPhone rings, Wendy is slicing carrots and listening to NPR as she prepares the evening meal. In exasperation, Wendy juts out her lower lip and blows air over her forehead. Somehow the robo callers have infiltrated her cell phone and she feels betrayed and angry—by whom, she doesn't know.

"Hello," Wendy says gruffly. She doesn't recognize the voice nor the name that speeds by her from this fast-talking caller. It sounds like the woman identified herself as Sandy Zurk, but that is just a guess. As the woman continues to talk, Wendy hears the name Dennis and then a claim that Dennis has taunted and threatened their twelve-year-old son. The pieces instantly fall into place: the caller is Cindy Zurcher and she is frightened.

"Whoa, you need to slow down," Wendy says. "Are you Cindy Zurcher?"

"Yes, it's me. You told me to call if I ever needed to talk," Cindy says. "Don't you remember?"

Wendy's memory returns to that meeting months ago when Cindy fell apart in Paul's office. She held the woman and told her to call if she needed to talk, giving her this cell phone number.

"Oh yes, I remember," Wendy says. "Are you sure you don't want to talk to Paul?" When she gave Cindy her phone number, she never envisioned being thrown into a domestic dispute. Furthermore, this woman is Paul's client; she is his responsibility.

"No, I don't want to talk to your husband," Cindy says emphatically. "I'm thinking of leaving my husband and I want to talk to you, woman to woman."

Over the years, women clients in the throes of a divorce have occasionally phoned Paul at home. They are usually hysterical and require Paul's special handling. This is not Wendy's domain.

She also understands that if Cindy separates from her husband and refuses to participate in the upcoming trial, it will be a death blow to the case. It will waste all of Paul's hard work and destroy any chance for a fee that could save them from financial ruin.

Paul left for Columbus an hour earlier. Before he departed, he'd told her about the pretrial in agonizing detail. At the time, she'd thought things couldn't get much worse, but now they were. There is no way she can be objective about the situation.

Wendy's words come slowly and haltingly. "I don't think I could be of much assistance. I can't explain how divorce works—you know, talk to you about temporary alimony, custody, restraining orders—those kinds of things." She immediately regrets her response. This woman urgently needs her support and she is turning her away.

"I know you barely know me, but I need to talk. I'm not going to ask you about those legal things," Cindy says, her voice anxious and insistent. "I think I need to leave my husband. Please, just listen to me and help me sort out today's events. That's all I want you to do."

Wendy thinks about the woman on the other end of the call. She's been abused for years. Today, something has happened and she's finally summoned the courage to seek help. "Okay, I can do that," Wendy says. "Can we meet someplace where it's safe?"

Because Cindy's car is in the repair shop, they decide that Wendy will stop at the Zurcher house in North Ridgeville, where she'll pick up Cindy and her children. From there, they'll drive to the North Ridgeville Public Library, where the two women can talk while the children sit and read books. Cindy assures Wendy that Dennis has left for the evening—probably staying at his girlfriend's house overnight. She and the children will be free to leave and return without any interference from Dennis.

Around seven that evening, Wendy pulls into the Zurcher driveway in her Honda Odyssey. She is not alone. When she called her sister-in-law, Susie Phillips, to see if she could watch Wendy's girls, Susie insisted on accompanying her. Susie's husband has been left in charge of all the children, two from each household. Wendy welcomes the help. She isn't sure she has the background or experience to counsel this woman. On the other hand, Susie, an emergency room nurse, occasionally treats victims of domestic abuse.

Wendy has also been able to talk to Paul, telling him about the phone call and her response. He was on the road to Columbus, where he is spending the night before an early morning liquor control hearing the next day. She didn't know how he'd react, but she was relieved by his unambiguous response. Her job was to make sure that Cindy and her children were safe, the case be damned. "If you need to buy them a one-way bus ticket to Alaska, do it. Don't think twice."

And now, she and Susie are waiting for Cindy and her children to emerge from the front door and scramble into Wendy's van. A gust of wind hits the van broadside, rocking it sideways. With temperatures hovering in the low twenties, the wind only adds to the chill. Although it is not snowing, it is a night to stay home and stay warm.

After a minute's wait, Wendy toots the van's horn. No one appears at the door, nor does anyone flash the front porch light to signal that they'll be leaving soon. Checking her recent calls from her iPhone,

Wendy identifies Cindy's landline number and initiates a call. The phone rings six times before it goes to voicemail.

"I don't like this at all," Susie says, shaking her head. "Do you think her husband came back?"

Instead of answering Susie, Wendy hits the horn again, holding it longer and louder than the first time. She stares intently at the sheers in the front windows, hoping to see some movement behind them, but there is none. A feeling of dread engulfs her, quickening her pulse and creating more tightness in her stomach. She is tempted to back out of the driveway and go home.

"I think we need to ring the doorbell," says Susie. "She may be in trouble. You may need to dial 911."

Wendy shudders. This is not what she signed up for. This is a job for the police, not them. "I don't think that's a good idea. Maybe we should just look into the front windows, or better yet, let's just get out of here."

Susie looks at Wendy incredulously. "You can wait in the car if you want, but I'm ringing the doorbell," Susie says.

The decision to bring Susie seemed like a good idea an hour earlier, but it doesn't now. Unlike Paul, Susie is a wild one, prone to taking unnecessary risks. She seems to revel in adrenaline-inducing activities like roller-coaster rides, scuba diving, and white-water rafting—all of which she does whenever the opportunity arises.

Susie opens the door. "Are you coming?" she asks impatiently, her blue eyes reflecting the light from a nearby streetlamp.

Reluctantly, Wendy opens her door. "I think this is a very bad idea, but what the hell—I can't let you go up there alone."

Their doors slam in unison and they walk the front sidewalk side by side, their breath visible in puffs as they move quickly toward the porch. Susie reaches the doorbell first and depresses the button. When no one responds, she depresses it again. Finally, they hear the sound of someone approaching the door.

The door opens and a husky boy stares back at them. "Come on in," he says. "Mom is having trouble with Melissa. She's crying and doesn't want to leave her bedroom."

The women exchange relieved glances and enter the foyer, following the boy. As if he needs to explain further, he says, "We've had kind of a hard day."

At that moment, Wendy's eyes well with tears and she has an urge to hug this large boy who, although on the edge of adolescence, still has the face of a child. She doesn't know exactly what his father did to him, but no child should have to endure menacing from a parent. She is filled with such loathing that she could take a baseball bat to Dennis's head if he were within striking distance.

Loosening their winter coats, the women follow the boy into a kitchen that opens to the family room, the two rooms separated by a three-foot railing. In her mind, she imagined broken dishes on the floor and pictures askew on the walls. Instead, the two rooms are in perfect order, a linoleum floor shining with polish and a family room with pillows evenly distributed on the couch. The rooms seem peaceful, the hum of the dishwasher providing the only sound.

As Wendy moves into the sunken family room, she sees that it is dominated by a flat-screen television monitor on one wall and a huge brick fireplace on another. On still another wall, a large canvas photograph captures the entire Zurcher family, including Heather, smiling back at her. Dennis grins broadly while the others look at the camera with either forced or timid smiles. Wendy studies the face of the dead daughter, seeing in it a pretty girl whose vacant eyes reveal much about the family dysfunction.

It is only a few moments later that Cindy emerges from a hallway that connects the bedrooms to the family room. With one hand on her daughter's back, she urges her forward, the girl clutching two stuffed animals to her chest. The little girl's hair is disheveled and tears have not yet dried from her cheeks.

"We've had a little trouble with this one," Cindy says. "But now we're ready to head out. Sorry for the delay."

Again, Wendy is surprised by what she sees, or more precisely, what she does not see. She pictured Cindy with a split lip, a cut above her eye, or a chipped tooth—some evidence that she's been involved in a physical altercation. Wearing a long gray cardigan sweater and blue jeans, Cindy could be any housewife caught tidying up the kitchen or helping her children with their homework. How can this be? This woman appears calm and in control of her emotions.

Wendy introduces Cindy to her sister-in-law, explaining that Susie is an emergency room nurse and one of her confidants. Bundling up in winter coats and scarves, Cindy and her two children trundle after Wendy and Susie to the van.

The drive to the library takes only a few minutes, during which they struggle to make conversation. Cindy thanks them for coming, and in response, they tell her that they are glad to lend an ear. The conversation ends when Melissa starts to cry again. Her mother holds her awkwardly, their heavy winter coats creating an unwanted barrier.

Once inside the library, they sit the children on a comfortable chair, Melissa sitting on her brother's lap while he reads to her. The adults find a table not more than twenty feet away, close enough to monitor the children's activities but far enough not to be overheard.

When Cindy begins talking, her voice is composed and barely above a whisper. However, when she begins recounting the afternoon's events, it becomes shaky and then agitated. Wendy and Susie listen intently, not interrupting her. Cindy needs to tell her story in all of its disturbing details.

"I'm a passive person by nature," Cindy says. "And you can see where that's got me." She nervously twirls her right index finger around a strand of her hair, first in one direction and then in another. That movement causes Wendy to focus on Cindy's hands—fingernails chewed to nubs and cuticles that are torn and raw.

"We're not here to judge you," Susie says. Wendy nods, but she silently wishes that Susie would not interrupt Cindy in the middle of her story.

"Thank you. I just want you to listen and give me feedback," Cindy says. The two women nod their understanding and Cindy continues. "I saw something this afternoon. Clear as can be. It scared the hell out of me." Cindy's shoulders begin to shake and she struggles to maintain her composure. She bites her lower lip and starts again. "Travis is just a boy, a sweet boy who's seen a lot of awful stuff in his twelve years. He's the one who discovered Heather unconscious in the hallway, her face lying in her own vomit. Oh God." Cindy's head slumps and she begins to cry.

Wendy gets up from her chair, quickly moves behind Cindy, and puts her arms around the other woman's neck. "It's all right," Wendy says soothingly. "It's all right." As Wendy does this, Susie digs into her purse, finds a clump of tissues, and hands them to Cindy, who blows her nose. Looking to where Travis and Melissa are, Wendy sees that they are still engrossed in a book and haven't noticed their mother's breakdown.

Cindy takes several sharp gulps of air and seems to steady herself. Wendy returns to her chair and sits. Cindy starts again. "Where was I? Oh, Travis. He's a big kid for his age and he's only going to get bigger —probably will be built like Dennis when he's a teenager. I know this and I suspect Dennis knows this too. When Travis spoke out to defend me, Dennis saw his son as a threat—someone who will eventually replace him as the dominant one. That sick man sees his son as a danger to his authority.

"I can see it coming. Dennis will do anything to keep that boy in his place. Right now, he'll scare him with his words. But later, he'll physically hurt him. He'll hit him. He'll beat him. He'll do whatever it takes to stay in charge.

"The thing is—Travis isn't anything like Dennis. He's a kind boy. He never hits anyone. He never hurts anyone. I failed Heather, but I'm not failing Travis."

Wendy glances at Susie, who nods with raised eyebrows. Cindy, a woman without a high school diploma, is surprisingly insightful.

"I've thought about this for years," Cindy says.

However, before Cindy can finish her thought, Susie interrupts her. "I can make some phone calls for you. When women come into the emergency room after they've been abused, I usually start with a call to Genesis House. It's a place where women and children can stay temporarily and receive counseling. Then the counselors work out a more permanent plan for them."

Glancing at her children, Cindy frowns. "I'm not ready to do that yet," she says.

"He doesn't love you. Your husband doesn't love you," Susie interjects. "Don't confuse his abuse for love."

Cindy gives Wendy a perplexed glance—a look that says, *Why did you bring this woman along?*

"I think Cindy knows that," Wendy says, hoping that her sister-in-law will shut up and let Cindy explain herself.

Nodding, Cindy looks appreciatively at Wendy. "We haven't loved each other in years," Cindy says. "I'm under no delusions there."

Susie looks as if she is going to respond, but before she can, Wendy places a hand over Susie's right hand, signaling for her to keep quiet. In case Susie doesn't get the message, Wendy says, "I think Cindy just needs to talk right now." Chastened, Susie pulls her hand away from Wendy's and places it in her lap.

"You have no idea how many times I've dreamed of leaving Dennis. Running away with the kids somewhere. I've had a packed suitcase in the attic for years, just waiting for the right time or the courage to leave.

"I know Genesis House exists, and places like it," Cindy says, directing her gaze at Susie. "I don't want to suddenly be thrown in there and live with other traumatized women and children. I'd do it if I thought we were in real physical danger from Dennis, but we're not. I look at it as a place of last resort."

For the first time, Wendy questions Cindy's grasp of her own situation. How can she say that they aren't in any danger from Dennis?

That makes no sense. And her fear of going to a battered women's shelter seems overblown. Sure, there are drawbacks in being placed into a new environment, but there are also advantages: counselors, resources, therapy—and most important, safety.

Wendy holds out her right hand and looks at Cindy quizzically. "Cindy, you called me about an hour and a half ago and you were scared. I could hear it in your voice. There was no mistaking it. Now you're telling us that Dennis won't hurt any of you. What's changed?"

Cindy sucks in some air before responding. "I've calmed down a bit," she says. "Remember, Dennis did not strike Travis. He threatened him. He scared him."

Wendy and Susie exchange dubious glances. Threats are as damaging to the boy as physical blows. Wendy expects her sister-in-law to grab Cindy by her shoulders and shake some sense into her, but, for once, Susie shows some restraint.

"I know how much worse it's going to be for Travis, I can see that as clear as a bell. But I still have some time," Cindy says, rubbing her hands nervously over the tabletop. "We will eventually leave. It's not a question of *if* but *when*. And when we leave, it will be quick and it will be planned. But I'm not going to substitute one chaos for another."

Cindy's words deflate Wendy. She expected to help Cindy and her family escape from this man. She even had visions of harboring them in her basement for a few weeks, but not this, a woman rationalizing away the risks and returning to the status quo.

"I think you're making a big mistake," Susie says. "How can you predict when your husband will get violent—physically violent? Get out now. We'll help you."

Susie's message is much blunter than anything Wendy would have delivered. It may cause Cindy to dig in and reject it. Wendy planned to reason with Cindy, move her along gently. Once again, Susie's impetuousness is imperiling the meeting.

"That's easy for you to say," Cindy says. "You both have stable husbands, a good education, jobs, extended family to help you. I've got none of that. Understand? None of that." There is frustration, maybe anger, in her voice now.

"I hear you," Wendy says, trying to reestablish a connection with her. "What can we do to help? That's why we're here."

"Help me figure out a plan. A good plan. A plan that gives us a future," Cindy says.

Wendy stiffens, realizing that she lacks both the background and the experience to do this. The challenge is to deliver Cindy to a person who can develop a realistic plan. For over a minute, there is an awkward silence, until Susie speaks. "Okay, first thing. Do you have a high school diploma?"

"No, I dropped out in the eleventh grade," Cindy says.

"Then you need to get your GED as a starter," Susie tells her.

Wendy nods. This seems like a reasonable first step. For the next few minutes, the women discuss how Cindy might do this without Dennis's knowledge. They eventually decide that Cindy should come to Paul's office to take an online GED course on a spare computer at times when Dennis is away at work. Wendy, the former schoolteacher, will be there to tutor, if necessary. After that, they'll take Cindy to a counselor at the community college who can assess vocational interests and aptitude. From there, she can take online college courses.

Although Cindy seems excited about this prospect, Wendy remains skeptical that this woman will follow through. Wendy also worries that Dennis will escalate his threats to his family before Cindy has obtained her GED. Cindy needs to escape from Dennis if the risks become too great. "If Dennis threatens any of you again, promise me that you will leave immediately," Wendy says.

Cindy looks at Wendy warily. "Haven't I already told you that?" Wendy realizes that Cindy has evaded answering the question.

"So you will?" Wendy asks.

"If I have a better alternative," Cindy says.

Wendy expects Susie to interject and argue with Cindy, but Susie seems deep in thought, apparently not listening to their conversation.

"You are going to have to take some chances here if you leave. You can't have every little detail worked out in advance," Wendy warns.

Before Cindy can respond, Susie blurts, "Wait. Wait. I don't know why I didn't think of this before." The other two women stare at Susie, who looks like an excited schoolgirl waiting for the teacher to call on her.

Susie shifts in her seat to look directly at Wendy. "Frank's parents' house," she says, touching her right palm against her head in a *Why didn't I think of this before* gesture. Shifting back toward Cindy, she says, "My in-laws go to Florida every October and are gone for six months. Their house is vacant. Don't you see? You and your kids could stay there after you leave your husband. You'd have a good place to live while you get on your feet."

"They'd let me stay there?" Cindy asks.

"If they want me to stay married to their son, they'd better," Susie says, smiling. Then she turns more serious. "I'm sure they would. They're really good people. And it's a great house—four bedrooms, nice yard, safe neighborhood." Susie then adds after a pause, "Not to mention, fully furnished."

For the first time, Wendy is glad that she brought Susie with her. Her housing solution is brilliant. Because the house will not be available for at least seven months, it gives Cindy time to ready herself for the separation, and, once she is ready to leave, it will provide a wonderful place to live temporarily.

Over the next few minutes, Susie answers Cindy's questions about the house: the location, the school system, and the neighbors. One question, however, remains unasked: Will Cindy be safe from Dennis if she moves there? It is a question that no one can answer. It will be up to the legal system and the police to protect her, and whether they can will remain a question mark.

Soon thereafter, the meeting ends and Wendy drives Cindy and her children back to their house. When only Wendy and Susie are left in the car, Susie chatters away nonstop, rehashing all that they've discussed. This lasts until Wendy arrives at Susie's house and Wendy picks up her two daughters. By the time Wendy returns to her own home, she feels physically exhausted and mentally drained. Despite her fatigue, she needs to give Paul a detailed account of what transpired.

Paul picks up on the second ring and is anxious to hear how things went. To her surprise, she has more energy as she begins recounting the evening's events. When she's finished, she asks, "Tell me again: Why are we helping this man?" It is more of a rhetorical question than a real one.

She knows the answer. Paul is obligated by the representation agreement to prosecute the case unless he can find someone—someone stupider than himself—to take over the case. If he withdraws, he will be sued. Also, if Paul is successful in the case—and that is looking more and more doubtful—they can dig themselves out of their financial morass.

"I've been thinking about the divorce aspect of this case," he says, bypassing her question. "Cindy is entitled to her own share of any settlement or judgment, as are the children." He pauses, giving her time to digest this information. At first, she doesn't understand the importance.

"Okay. Go on," she says.

"If the parents are divorced or in the process of getting a divorce and they can't agree about the division of a wrongful death settlement, how do they divide the money?" Paul asks.

"I figure there must be some stupid statute with an arbitrary formula that comes into play," Wendy says.

"No, it's the probate judge. He hears evidence and decides which parent is most deserving of the money."

Paul's answer momentarily takes her breath away. "Really?" she asks. No probate judge in his right mind will award Dennis Zurcher anything but a token amount for his alleged losses.

"Really," Paul answers.

Unable to restrain her excitement, Wendy blurts, "Oh, Paul. You have to win this case. You just have to."

"Thanks a lot. As if I don't have enough pressure on me."

"Sorry. You know what I meant," she says. "You could actually help the people in this case who deserve to be helped."

"Every now and then, lawyers get that chance," Paul says, his voice tired and resigned. "Like the blind squirrel finding the proverbial acorn."

PART THREE

THE TRIAL

CHAPTER 20
SEPTEMBER 16, 2019
WENDY SCHOFIELD

When the door opens, Dennis Zurcher's massive body appears at the threshold. As he walks toward the open window of Wendy's secretarial station, the overpowering smell of Brut cologne accompanies him.

"Good morning, little lady," he says, a buoyancy in his voice that alarms her. She's learned from Cindy that for every one of Dennis's highs, there is a corresponding low. He leans his hairy right forearm onto the ledge of her station's sliding window and peers in. "We're here to see Paul for our prep session, not that I need it." To emphasize his point, he pops his chewing gum and grins.

Wendy somehow summons the strength to greet him with a smile. She both loathes and fears this man. Ever since that night seven months earlier, she recoils every time he appears unexpectedly at the office. At those times, she panics, certain that he's somehow learned of Cindy's decision to leave him. She imagines that Cindy, under duress, has divulged that Wendy helped devise the plan. Whenever he approaches her, her whole body tenses and she expects the worst. But mercifully nothing has ever happened. In a demanding voice, he always insists on meeting with Paul. Over the next few minutes, she'll feel her heart rate gradually slow and her breathing return to normal.

As she phones Paul to advise him of the Zurchers' arrival, Dennis steps away from her window and takes a seat in the waiting room. For the first time, Wendy sees Cindy, who has just entered the office, her head bent toward the floor as if she is searching for a lost earring. Cindy finds a seat without greeting Wendy or giving any indication that they know one another. Wendy follows Cindy's lead, ignoring her and pretending to be busy with a work project. It is quite a contrast from the easy banter and collegiality that they've developed over the last seven months.

At least twice a week, Cindy has come to the office to work on her online GED course. Beyond the coursework, they've developed a trusting friendship. Cindy keeps her apprised about her home life, while Wendy shares some funny stories about her own children. Since that fateful night seven months earlier, Dennis has not threatened their son, Travis, again. However, he continues to be both volatile and unpredictable, arbitrarily exploding whenever something in their home life is not to his liking.

A month earlier, when Cindy passed the online GED examination, Wendy treated her to lunch at the Olive Garden. Despite the noon hour, they'd celebrated with a glass of wine and talked about Cindy's future. Cindy and the children will leave Dennis sometime in mid-October, after Susie's in-laws vacate their Amherst home to spend the winter in Florida.

She and Paul decided not to tell Cindy that she (and her children) might be entitled to almost all of the proceeds if they win the case. They want Cindy to be responsible for her own future, not expecting anything or anyone to magically change her life.

After the Zurchers have been seated for less than a minute, Paul comes into the waiting room and ushers them back to his office. For the next two hours, Wendy hears them talking behind the closed door of Paul's office. Usually, their words are muted and undecipherable, but toward the end of the meeting, Dennis's voice becomes loud and angry. "Jesus, you're going to lose the damn case if you do that." She hears Paul's voice, calm and controlled, but can't make out his words. Unappeased, Dennis calls Paul an "idiot." Again, Paul's voice is low and his words remain muffled. When Paul finishes, she hears Dennis say, "If you screw this case up, I'll sue you. And then you won't be so fucking cocky."

Paul's office door opens and Dennis bolts through the waiting room like a man whose bladder is about to explode. Trailing about ten feet behind him, Cindy glances at Wendy and gives her an apologetic look. She quietly closes the door, and just like that, they are gone.

After lightly knocking on Paul's door, she enters, not waiting for a reply. Appearing exasperated and stressed, Paul is typing on his keyboard and doesn't bother to look up. Wendy takes a seat in one of his leather wing chairs, still warm from the body heat of its last occupant—hopefully Cindy.

"What the heck happened?" Wendy asks.

Paul looks up from his keyboard. "I despise that man," he says with something like venom in his voice. "I'd like to lose this case just to spite him."

"Well, you need to get over that, you know."

"I'm not serious. It's just that he has all these crazy ideas about how I should try the case."

"Like what?"

"He gave me a whole list of questions that I absolutely *have to* ask Dr. Wright—such as does he have trouble sleeping because of Heather's death, and if not, why not."

"Sounds like a great question," Wendy says, rolling her eyes.

"It's not funny," Paul says. "He also wants to testify first because he thinks he'll *connect* with the jurors and win the case right then and there."

"Sounds about right."

"Oh, Wendy, come on. I know you're trying to be humorous, but this guy is driving me nuts. He's an expert on everything. You name it, he knows what will work. And if I do things differently, well, it's all going to blow up in my face. Just ask him," Paul says, his words coming quickly.

"So how did you leave it with him?"

"I was very polite and respectful, thanking him for his suggestions," Paul says, biting his lower lip. "However, I made it very clear that I was the experienced trial lawyer, not him, and I would do it my way."

"Oh, I'm sure that went over well."

"You saw how he shot out of here," Paul says. "Fortunately, I'd already prepped them for their trial testimony before he blew up. He'll get over it. What choice does he have? Fire me?"

Wendy surveys Paul's desk. Stacked neatly in one corner sit three copies of his trial brief and jury instructions. Next to that are three huge notebooks containing Heather Zurcher's medical records and other exhibits. Leaning against the far wall, poster boards await entry into the courtroom for use as demonstrative aids.

In terms of Paul's trial preparation, these written materials are just the tip of the iceberg. Using the hospital's online medical library, Susie has obtained dozens of articles for him about ECT, teenage suicide, antidepressant drugs, and depression. He's read and reread them all, underlining paragraphs pertinent to the Zurcher case. Scott Worthington has also come through for Paul. Unable to finance a deposition of the defendant's expert witness, Scott has obtained previous depositions of this doctor by accessing the deposition banks to which his firm subscribes. Several of the depositions provide valuable nuggets that Paul can use in cross-examining the heavyweight that Ingram has hired.

"You're ready," Wendy says. "I can see it by looking around your office and I can see it in your eyes."

Paul raises his eyebrows, warning Wendy. "I know what you're going to say next. Don't go there."

"Oh, that you're going to win the case. Okay, I won't say that," Wendy says.

She knows exactly how Paul will react; she's experienced it countless times. He will recite every unfavorable fact in his case and tell her that he will likely lose. But that is just Paul. Deep inside, he always believes that he is going to win. His outward pessimism is a ploy, making his victories seem all the more remarkable. And when he loses, which is rarely, he can save face because he's predicted it. However, she'll listen and play along. She always does.

Rubbing his chin, Paul says, "Let's see. First, I have the most unlikeable client in the world, who will self-destruct in front of the jury." Wendy nods in agreement. Paul continues, "After that, his timid wife will crumble when Ingram cross-examines her. And for the coup de grâce, my expert doctor—who we both know is a pompous ass—has opinions that are so far out of the mainstream that the jury will conclude that he's a highly paid crackpot—which is not too far off the mark. Need I say more?"

"Gee, Paul, with a hand like that, why bother even showing up for trial?" she teases.

Paul doesn't respond immediately, apparently searching for a clever retort. "Because I don't have anything better to do," he says wryly.

"Because you're going to win," Wendy counters.

Like an unwelcome visitor, the balloon payment flashes through her mind and she immediately regrets her playful banter about winning. The payment is due the second week of November. If he loses the case, they plan to put their house on the market and move into an apartment—not that they have any equity in the house, but rent will be cheaper than their house payment. They will do everything in their power to avoid bankruptcy, but that looks more and more likely. She hopes that her teasing has not triggered these same thoughts for Paul.

Apparently enjoying their repartee, Paul puts an index finger in each ear and feigns indignation. "I told you not to say that. Why don't you just get out of here," Paul says, his voice playful. He points toward the open door.

"Is that how you treat your loyal wife?"

"My loyal wife *and* trusted employee," he replies.

"So tell your trusted and loyal confidant what you really think about your chances," Wendy presses.

Smiling, Paul raises his arms in surrender. "Let's just say that I have a fighting chance and leave it at that."

Wendy returns his smile, gets up, and kisses him on the top of his head. To add to the effect, she then tiptoes out of the office and gently closes the door behind her.

CHAPTER 21
SEPTEMBER 23, 2019
TOM WILCHUCK

After his second trip to his car, Tom Wilchuck deposits the last of the defendant's trial materials into the courtroom: two banker's boxes containing filings, depositions, and trial exhibits—everything Ingram will need to destroy his opponent. Taking several deep breaths, he wipes the sweat from his forehead and leans against a half wall that separates the courtroom proper from the two rows of spectator benches. The air-conditioned space contrasts sharply with the outside humid air and his body shivers as it adjusts.

Scanning his surroundings, Wilchuck realizes that he is alone in this cavernous, high-tech courtroom. Although he can't pinpoint the reason, there is something sterile and uninviting about this environment. Perhaps it is the blandness of the beige, windowless walls or the sleek, flat trial tables or the eerie, diffuse light that comes from the recessed lighting—or maybe it's just the combination of all of these things.

Monitors are positioned everywhere—on the attorney tables, at the judge's bench, on the back wall, and in the jury box—their blank screens dark and dormant. Microphones on skinny, flexible tubes seem to sprout from the trial tables, like flowers bending toward the sun.

Wilchuck cannot help but feel disappointed and angry; as usual, he'll probably have no meaningful part in this trial. He plans to ask Ingram one last time to give him some small speaking role. He'd like to question a minor witness or argue a point of law, but he knows how Ingram will respond. For more than four years now, he's been more of a lackey than a lawyer—doing nothing more than fetch and carry for his egotistical boss.

How can he ever hope to develop as a lawyer and advance in the legal world if he's always relegated to meaningless tasks? He needs real trial experience, something that must be abundantly clear to Ingram. However, his boss is apparently determined to deny him those opportunities and, as a consequence, force him to continue in his dreary employment.

Someone taps Wilchuck on his shoulder, startling him. Turning around, Wilchuck sees a grinning Ingram. Thrusting a Styrofoam cup of coffee toward him, Ingram says, "Compliments of Frank McCloskey, the judge's bailiff. He's a bit of a pain, but I take care of him and he takes care of us."

As is his custom, Ingram treated McCloskey to a round of golf a few weeks earlier. The coffee is a nice perk, but it pales in comparison to what Ingram provided—but that is Ingram. He revels in receiving preferential treatment, no matter how trivial.

Clearing his throat, Wilchuck asks, "Have you given any more thought to me questioning a few witnesses, maybe Eleanor Ranier, Heather Zurcher's former teacher?"

Ingram nervously pushes his right hand through his slicked-back silver hair, exposing perfectly manicured fingernails. "Now, Tommy, we've been through this before, haven't we? You are just too valuable to me in your current role. You know that, right?"

Wilchuck frowns. He's heard this bullshit too many times. This time he'll push back. "I've been with you for almost five years. If I don't get a chance now, then when will I?"

Shaking his head, Ingram looks perplexed, as if he was unaware of this. "Soon. Very soon. I promise you, but not in this case." Putting his right hand on his chin, Ingram manufactures a grim expression. "You know how lost I am with this new courtroom technology. I need you to work the video presenter, bring up the documents for viewing—you know, engineer everything for me. I have no idea how to do that. I know it's a thankless job, but it's critically important."

Shaking his head, Wilchuck cannot hide his frustration. Before he can continue the fight, Dr. Wright enters the courtroom. Dr. Wright is dressed in a brown suit, pale yellow shirt, and plain brown tie, colors that even Wilchuck knows are unflattering for anyone appearing before a jury. Although the doctor's reddish-brown beard hides most of his face, his exposed skin has a gray, deathly tone under the artificial light.

Holding out his hand, Ingram says, "Dr. Wright, so good to see you again. I trust you had no problem finding the courtroom. Just so you know, your insurance company has not changed its position. We're offering nothing on this case. Not a nickel. We're standing behind you one hundred percent."

If Dr. Wright is pleased by this information, he shows no indication. Ingram turns to address Wilchuck but then suddenly turns back toward Dr. Wright. "We'll get started around nine, so just make yourself comfortable until then."

Dr. Wright appears confused and slowly surveys the courtroom. "Where am I supposed to get comfortable?" he asks, the sarcasm in his voice not lost on Wilchuck.

Ingram raises his eyebrows at Wilchuck before turning to address their client. "Dr. Wright, Tom will take care of you while I attend to some last-minute details." He abruptly turns and walks briskly toward the back of the courtroom and then disappears behind the exterior double doors.

Facing Dr. Wright, Wilchuck forces a smile. Offering him his right hand, Wilchuck says, "We met several years ago when you had your first conference with Bob."

Dr. Wright extends a cold and sweaty hand to Wilchuck, who quickly pulls out of the handshake and directs Dr. Wright toward their trial table. As they walk, Wilchuck can't think of anything to say. As their silence becomes awkward, Wilchuck says, "So how are you?"

"I'm here, aren't I?" Dr. Wright says, scratching his beard and scowling.

"Well, we're glad that you are," Wilchuck says, immediately embarrassed by the inanity of his response, as if Dr. Wright's presence is some kind of honor.

Looking at him quizzically, Dr. Wright says nothing.

"I know you're not too pleased about having to spend the next week in trial," Wilchuck says, stating the obvious. "But we refuse to make a nuisance settlement. Sometimes you have to fight to achieve justice."

"Did they teach you that line in law school?" Dr. Wright replies. Up until now, Wilchuck has been willing to give Dr. Wright the benefit of the doubt, seeing him as a doctor forced to defend himself from a meritless claim. But this dour man is directing his anger at the wrong people and, in the process, alienating the individuals who are trying to help him. The doctor apparently believes that his medical degree gives him the right to be condescending and caustic.

"I learned that in the real world, not in law school," Wilchuck says, surprising himself by his own assertiveness.

"Ah, the real world. Yes, in the real world, where you learn how to bill clients for every conceivable thing," Dr. Wright says. "And your firm sends two attorneys to do the work of one. Seems to me that you and Mr. Ingram are going to rack up a pretty big bill for yourselves."

Wilchuck knows when he is being baited. He and Ingram are here to defend this man from a lawsuit. Instead of appreciating their efforts, he grouses about their attorney fees—fees that his insurance company will eventually pay, not him.

Against his better judgment, Wilchuck feels compelled to defend himself and the law firm. "Just so you know, we're very careful about our billings. We keep track of our time down to the tenth of an hour. We don't overbill, ever," Wilchuck says.

Dr. Wright snickers and shakes his head. "And why is my insurance company paying you to be here? Seems to me that you're nothing more but an overgrown cheerleader."

Wilchuck glares at Dr. Wright.

"Take it easy, counselor. I'm just teasing you," Dr. Wright says. "Where's your sense of humor?"

Wilchuck clenches his teeth as he tries to get his emotions under control.

"Looks like I struck a raw nerve with you. I didn't mean to upset you," Dr. Wright says. Although his words are conciliatory, Dr. Wright's tone suggests the opposite. He seems to be enjoying Wilchuck's discomfort.

"I happen to be an integral part of your defense team, whether you recognize it or not," Wilchuck says, his voice shaking with indignation.

"Okay, okay. I'm sure you are," Dr. Wright replies, rolling his eyes. "Just tell me which of these tables is ours. I'll sit down and get out of your hair. I'm sure you need every minute to prepare for your important role in my defense."

Wilchuck points to one of the tables. "Ours is the one closest to the jury." Wilchuck pauses for a moment and then moves closer to Dr. Wright, intent on towering over his much smaller client. "Before you settle in, here's a piece of advice. Turn off your cell phone. If it goes off during the trial, the judge will fine you two hundred and fifty dollars. Can you do that?"

Wilchuck's attempt to even the score with Dr. Wright is a resounding failure. The doctor does not react, merely shrugs and pulls a chair away from the table.

"I'm going to get some air," Wilchuck says, pivoting away from the doctor and walking toward the double doors. This exchange tells Wilchuck all that he needs to know about Dr. Wright. He is one lousy psychiatrist. It's not just that he is a cold, condescending jerk, but he lacks the compassion to develop a rapport and trust with a troubled patient. It's no wonder that he resorts to a merry-go-round of antidepressants and ECT to treat his patients. He obviously has nothing else to offer them.

Once outside the courtroom, Wilchuck enters the seventh-floor hallway, where attorneys and clients are milling about. Emerging from one of the elevators, Paul Schofield towers above the crowd as he carries his large briefcase and several posters through the hallway toward the courtroom.

Wilchuck has mixed feelings about Schofield. He admires him for his gutsiness, for being unafraid to make his own way in the legal world. However, there is also something artificial about the guy. He can charm people with his good looks, engaging smile, and affable personality. But these traits are not earned; they are simply accidents of birth that unfairly bypassed Wilchuck. He is just as intelligent as Schofield, perhaps even smarter. In terms of work ethic, no one works harder than he does. Yet despite this, Schofield will probably become a successful trial attorney, while he is destined to be a nobody, an attorney who perpetually toils in the background and is paid little for his efforts.

Laden with his trial materials, Schofield walks purposefully toward the courtroom. When Schofield spots Wilchuck, he lifts his chin in greeting and smiles. "I guess this is it."

"Yeah. Crunch time for both sides," Wilchuck replies.

"You guys wanted to roll the dice," Schofield says, referring to Defiance Mutual's refusal to make an offer. "Makes it easy for me. I've got nothing to lose by going to trial." Although there is no bitterness in Schofield's voice, his overly breezy tone betrays something else: disappointment and anxiety. Schofield can pretend all he wants, but he hoped for an out-of-court settlement, not a winner-take-all jury trial. That is obvious.

Although the case presents some risks to the defense, he and

Ingram are confident that they'll ultimately prevail. His boss will destroy the parents on cross-examination and later make the plaintiff's expert look foolish. By the time their own high-powered expert testifies, the plaintiff's case will be in shambles. However, Wilchuck is a realist. Anything can happen at trial and that is reason enough to offer some money in settlement, even a small amount. But no one asked him.

Realizing that Schofield's hands are full, Wilchuck opens the courtroom door for him. "Oh, thank you," Schofield says, obviously surprised by Wilchuck's help. "You sure you won't get in trouble for aiding the enemy?" Schofield says with a grin.

His eyes glued to the floor, Wilchuck says, "No problem."

Schofield's friendliness unnerves Wilchuck, an uneasiness that is born of guilt. Ever since their investigator secretly recorded Dennis Zurcher at the Foundry Kitchen and Bar months ago, Wilchuck knows that the law requires the defense to provide a copy to Schofield —no exceptions. However, as they prepared for trial, Ingram refused to share a copy with Schofield and, instead, devised a plan to ambush his opponent with it. What is worse, Wilchuck is an indispensable part of the scheme.

The incriminating portion of Zurcher's dialogue has been transcribed and Ingram plans to have Wilchuck, using the courtroom's video presenter, project it onto a large monitor during his cross-examination of the father. Once on the monitor, it will be visible to everyone in the courtroom, including the jury. By the time Schofield objects, the jury will have seen the statement and the damage will have been done. As he outlined the plan, Ingram bristled with excitement. Although Wilchuck was shocked, he didn't voice any objections, his need for a job overriding his ethical misgivings.

To clear his head, Wilchuck walks over to the long windows that stretch from the floor to the ceiling on the seventh floor. From here, he stares at the century-old sandstone courthouse across the street that once was a bustling center of activity before the courts moved to the

Justice Center a decade earlier. He wonders if attorneys in those bygone days were more ethical than they are today. Did they scheme to circumvent the rules like Ingram? Wilchuck doesn't know, but he hopes not.

Wilchuck's mind returns to the undisclosed video of Dennis Zurcher. Is there any way he can make Schofield aware of it without losing his job? Perhaps he can hand a thumb drive to him surreptitiously in the courthouse bathroom or, safer yet, slide it under his office door anonymously? He realizes that both ideas are ludicrous. Of course, Ingram will conclude that he was the leak. After that, his vengeful boss will do everything in his power to ruin Wilchuck's chances of finding employment elsewhere.

Wilchuck's reverie is broken by a man's loud voice. Glancing to his right, Wilchuck sees Dennis Zurcher and his wife approaching. Zurcher struts through the halls like a proud rooster while his mousy wife trails several feet behind him. "Come on, Cindy, walk faster. This is our day. We have to embrace it."

Well, that's an interesting spin on things. Wilchuck doubts that either of them will "embrace" the day after Ingram finishes with them, but that is still a few days off. Several minutes after the Zurchers enter the courtroom, Wilchuck checks his watch. It is eight forty-five, time for him to return to the trial table.

When Wilchuck enters the courtroom, he sees that Judge Hardwig has taken the bench and is addressing the attorneys. Standing, Ingram is telling the judge that he is ready to proceed. Wilchuck wonders when and how Ingram slipped by him and reentered the courtroom. Did he use the door behind the judge's bench usually reserved only for the judge and his staff? As Wilchuck quickly slides into a seat at their table, Ingram gives him a disgusted *Where the hell have you been?* look.

As the attorneys answer the judge's questions, Wilchuck quickly orients himself. Before bringing the prospective jurors into the courtroom, the judge has confirmed that no pretrial motions are pending and that the parties are not involved in any settlement talks. Schofield tells the judge that he will present seven witnesses and expects his case to be completed on the trial's third day. Ingram assures the judge that his two witnesses (his client and one expert witness) will take less than a day. The jury will have the case by the end of the week.

After a brief recess, thirty prospective jurors file into the courtroom. The bailiff directs eight of them to sit in the jury box to be questioned, while the remainder take seats on the spectator benches, ready to replace any of the eight who are excused.

Wilchuck has assisted Ingram with trials in Cleveland, but never in Lorain County, and he is curious about the types of people who'll be called. In Cleveland, Ingram always grouses about the Black people and minorities who are included in the jury pool. He is convinced that they are easily manipulated by personal injury attorneys and, once under their sway, relish punishing corporations and wealthy defendants with large verdicts. The Lorain County group is almost all Caucasian and most are over fifty, conservative demographics that favor the defense.

Wilchuck's job is to keep notes on the jurors as they are questioned, and he usually scribbles frantically trying to keep up with their answers. If Ingram later has a question about a juror's background or previous response, he'll ask Wilchuck. However, when Ingram excuses a prospective juror (and he can dismiss three for whatever reason), he never seeks Wilchuck's input. Jury selection is the exclusive domain of Ingram, the grand pooh-bah himself.

Judge Hardwig welcomes the prospective jurors and gives them a very brief introduction about the case. Until today, Wilchuck has never seen the judge, his interactions being limited to the judge's staff attorney or bailiff. Despite his diminutive size, no taller than five feet eight inches, the judge has an imposing presence. In his late fifties, he has a full head of wavy gray hair set atop a red, pockmarked face. His turquoise eyes are intimidating, seeming to bore through whomever he is addressing. He speaks in a staccato voice that is both forceful and definitive—like a football coach addressing his team before a game.

Under the law, the judge is required to ask the jurors a series of set questions. From Wilchuck's perspective, these inquiries range from the unnecessary to the ridiculous. Are any of them related to the parties? Are any subpoenaed to testify in this case? Are any of them habitual drunkards? Wilchuck always chuckles at that one. Who will admit to being a drunk in front of a courtroom of people? However, within a few minutes, the judge completes these questions and turns the jury selection process over to Schofield, who, as the plaintiff's attorney, always gets to go first.

Wilchuck has expected Schofield to be awkward, either stumbling with his questions or talking nervously about his case without engaging the prospective jurors in actual questions. But that does not happen. With an easy smile, Schofield speaks to the group in a down-to-earth, folksy way about the nature of a medical malpractice case, the difference between a civil and a criminal case, and their role in deciding the issues. When he talks to a prospective juror one-on-one, he asks open-ended questions and encourages lengthy responses—all of which reveal much about the person's beliefs and opinions. One prospective juror, who is a nurse, agrees that she will start the case slightly favoring Dr. Wright, a response that causes the judge to excuse her—saving Schofield from exercising one of his three challenges.

The more Schofield interacts with the jury, the more Wilchuck is impressed. Schofield seems as seasoned as the best trial attorneys in Cleveland. By the time Schofield has completed his first round of questioning, the judge has excused three of the jurors, all for legitimate reasons of bias.

After the judge recesses the proceedings for lunch, Ingram shakes his head at Wilchuck. "I know when I'm being homered," Ingram says, his shoulders tensing in agitation. "The judge is bending over backward to help that little shit."

Wilchuck knows better than to argue with his boss. The judge has shown no favoritism. Instead, Schofield has skillfully encouraged these people to express their actual feelings and they revealed their prejudices. In the end, the judge has simply done his job.

"You'll get your chance soon enough. Nobody questions jurors as well as you do," Wilchuck says, knowing that flattery usually mollifies his boss.

"Yeah, I know," Ingram says, taking the compliment as his due. "But it still pisses me off."

When the trial resumes, Ingram stands before the prospective jurors, self-assured and ready. After introducing himself and his client (but not Wilchuck), Ingram grabs a copy of the initial filing that commenced the lawsuit and holds it before the jury. With a slight scowl on his face, he flips through the pages. "You know, anyone can file a lawsuit. Just pay the three-hundred-dollar filing fee and it's done.

"But guess what? It's nothing more than a piece of paper. That's all it is. It's six pages of allegations—unproven allegations, I might add. And here's the thing. It doesn't mean that Dr. Wright did anything wrong. Anyone disagree with that?" From his tone, it is unclear whether Ingram is challenging the panel or making a point of clarification. After the members of the panel shake their heads, he tosses the document onto his trial table, where it races along the surface until it plummets to the floor. Smiling sheepishly, Wilchuck bends over, picks it up, and returns it to the tabletop.

For the next hour, Ingram engages each prospective juror in a friendly conversation, projecting the appearance of a sincere and caring person—the sociable uncle at the graduation party who talks to each and every guest. By the time he's finished, each of the jurors has promised that they won't make up their minds until they've listened to all of the evidence, including the defendant's witnesses. They've also agreed that they won't decide the case on sympathy.

After the afternoon break, each attorney begins exercising peremptory challenges, which then requires a new prospective juror to replace the excused one and be subject to questions by both attorneys. As this process drags on, Wilchuck finds it difficult to stay alert.

All of that changes when the judge asks Schofield if he wants to exercise his third and final peremptory challenge. When Schofield tells the judge that he is satisfied with the jury as it is currently composed, Dennis Zurcher looks at Schofield in disbelief and slams his pen onto the table. For the next minute, the two men whisper noisily at the trial table while the judge, jury, and everyone else watch and listen in amusement.

Finally, Schofield stands, his face flushed. "Your Honor, we apologize for the delay. I had to explain something to my client about the jury selection process. Thank you for your patience. We've straightened it out," Schofield says, pushing his right hand through his hair and smiling uneasily. "We are not going to exercise our third peremptory challenge."

After the jurors and the alternative juror have been selected, the judge adjourns for the day, telling the jurors to avoid all news sources about the case. As Ingram and Wilchuck walk out of the courtroom and into the hall together, they exchange glances of disbelief.

"I've practiced for over forty years and I've never seen anything like that before," Ingram says.

Wilchuck nods but says nothing.

"And our golden boy was doing so well," Ingram says, his voice dripping with sarcasm. "And then it's ruined when his client has a hissy fit in front of the jury. What a shame."

Even though his boss obviously wants him to join in the mockery, Wilchuck resists the urge. Although Wilchuck believes that he and Ingram are on the right side of this case, he is developing a growing admiration for Schofield—not so much for the person but for what he's accomplished on his own. He was flawless during jury selection. It wasn't his fault that his client sabotaged his efforts.

Wilchuck realizes that Schofield has succeeded against great odds.

He's never been apprenticed to anyone; he's received no mentoring. Yet somehow, he's developed into a skilled adversary in the courtroom.

Although Wilchuck believes that his client should win and deserves to win, he can't stomach breaking the rules to guarantee victory. It's just wrong to torpedo Schofield's case by underhanded and unethical means. If Schofield is playing by the rules, why shouldn't Ingram? And for that matter, why must he assist Ingram in his deceits? The way he's been treated, he owes Ingram nothing.

CHAPTER 22
SEPTEMBER 24, 2019
SUSIE PHILLIPS

As Susie Phillips climbs the steps outside the Lorain County Justice Center, her breathing is rapid and her heart is pounding. She's running late. As she enters the building, she sees two lines for security clearance, each with its own X-ray machine manned by a sheriff's deputy. She hasn't anticipated a security check. To make matters worse, the two deputies are more interested in gossiping with each other than doing their jobs quickly.

She makes the mistake of entering the line designated for attorneys and court personnel only. When she reaches the X-ray machine, the sheriff's deputy gives her the bad news—she is required to use the other line assigned to the general public. Joining the unprivileged and unwashed, she follows three seedy-looking men who will probably set off all kinds of alarms. But the men pass through rapidly (they apparently left their guns in their cars), and she quickly finds herself on an elevator heading for the seventh floor.

Susie has never seen Paul try a case. In fact, she's never set foot in a courthouse or a courtroom. Depending on her schedule, she plans to experience as much of the trial in person as she can. Paul has told her repeatedly that she's played a critical role at every step, not just by helping him but by aiding Cindy as she plans for a new life. She's proud of what she's done, but it's more than that. She feels incredibly invested in this case.

She desperately wants Paul to win. If he does prevail, she wants to witness firsthand how he accomplished it. On the other hand, if he loses, she needs to understand how that came to pass. To do that, she must be here and take it all in.

Finding Judge Hardwig's courtroom, Susie slips into the back row, hoping that the trial has not yet started. It hasn't; the judge and the jury have not yet entered.

She spots Paul almost immediately. He is seated at the trial table farthest from the jury and, with furrowed brow, is reading his notes on a legal pad. She guesses that he is reviewing his opening statement, something he delivered to Wendy and her several days ago in a practice session.

Dennis Zurcher sits at the table with Paul. She's never seen Dennis before, only heard about the big oaf. She can't see his face, just the back of his thick head. There is a bald spot at his crown and his attempts at a comb-over have failed. Just the sight of him fills her with loathing.

Susie searches for Cindy but doesn't see her anywhere. Other than the lawyers and their clients, no one else is in the courtroom—no reporters, no television cameras, no curious lawyers. Susie wants to talk with Cindy. Her in-laws have vacated their house and are in Florida, supervising several contractors who are working on their winter home. Once the trial has ended, Cindy will be free to move into her in-laws' Amherst home whenever she can arrange it.

At the other trial table sits a distinguished-looking man in his sixties. This has to be Robert Ingram, who is using his right index finger and thumb to clean the fingernails on his left hand. Susie is convinced that people who do this in public probably pick their noses in private. Whether this is true or not, she is happy to ascribe this behavior to Ingram, whom she has nicknamed the Villain. Sitting slouched in a chair at the other end of that table is a gangly young man who is passionately texting on his smartphone. Every villain must have a hapless sidekick, and this gawky man with unruly hair, probably Tom Wilchuck, fits the bill.

She doesn't need to resort to guesswork to identify Dr. Sheldon Wright; their paths have crossed several times in the hospital. Standing, he looks quite bored while a heavyset, middle-aged woman, probably his wife, talks to him, gesticulating nervously. If the wife is here for moral support, she seems to be more of an irritant than anything else.

A moment later, Susie is joined by Cindy Zurcher, who just entered from the double doors. "Except for the opening statements, I'm not allowed to sit in the courtroom until I've testified," she says as she slides in next to Susie.

Susie smiles and gives Cindy's left hand a squeeze.

A few minutes later the judge materializes from the back of the courtroom and takes his seat on the bench. He asks the bailiff to bring in the jury.

Susie is keenly interested in the people who make up the jury and begins studying them the moment they walk in. According to Paul, he's selected a fair, neutral jury of five men and four women, one of whom will later be designated as the alternate juror. The group includes several retired factory workers, a cashier, an auto mechanic, a school principal, a stay-at-home mom, a salesperson, and a human resource manager.

Surveying the group, Susie tries to match the faces to the occupations, but it's not easy. All are casually dressed Caucasians; per Paul, Ingram removed all minorities with his challenges. Each holds a small notebook in one hand, alert and poised to take notes. The judge, a crusty, red-faced man, tells them that they are about to hear opening statements. He explains that an opening statement is not evidence, but merely an opportunity for each attorney to outline what he believes the facts to be.

Paul rises from his chair, buttons his suit jacket, and places himself about eight feet from the panel. Although his posture is erect, he appears relaxed and poised, a stark contrast to her own feelings of nervousness and anxiety. Addressing the jury without any notes, Paul's voice is confident and friendly. Susie switches her attention to the jurors, trying to read their faces and body language. Will they be receptive to her brother's address? The uncertainty of it all only increases her angst. Who knew that watching a trial could be so stressful?

After Paul ends his introductory remarks and begins talking about the case, he has the jurors' full attention. She's heard his opening and knows that Paul wants to empower the jury from the outset and give them the confidence to judge a highly educated professional, using his "rules of the road" explanation.

"You are not here to decide whether Dr. Wright is a bad person or a bad doctor. Your job is to decide whether this doctor made a mistake, maybe a one-time mistake, that had tragic consequences," Paul says, glancing at Dr. Wright and then returning his full attention to the jury.

"My guess is that some of you may feel overwhelmed by that thought. You may think: *I don't have the experience or knowledge to do that.*

"For the moment, let's talk about driving a car, something we all do every day. There are rules of the road that govern our actions, right? If we go through a stop sign, we have violated one of the rules of the road and we are negligent. And it doesn't mean that we are bad drivers. It only means that, on this one occasion, we had a lapse.

"The same is true of doctors. They, too, are governed by rules of the road. These rules are well-established practices set by other doctors in their specialty. If they don't follow one of those rules, they are negligent. Throughout this trial, you will learn the rules of the road that governed Dr. Wright's care of my client's daughter Heather. Your job will be to see if he broke one or more of them."

Just then, Susie feels a vibration in her pants pocket from her phone. Sliding it out, she sees that the call is from work, the emergency room phone number glaring back at her.

Shit, shit, shit, she thinks. Her first impulse is to force the call into voicemail, but, instead, she gets up, slides by Cindy, and heads for the exit. Once in the hallway, she accepts the call.

"What is it?" she hisses into the phone.

"One of the patients that you saw yesterday just returned to the ER. The attending doctor wants to talk to you and compare findings. He needs to know if things are really getting worse."

"Can't he just look at the chart?" Susie says.

"If he could, we wouldn't be calling you."

Susie sighs and waits for the doctor to come on the line. Ten minutes later, an exasperated Susie returns to her seat in the courtroom.

"How's Paul doing?" she whispers to Cindy.

"Good. I think really good," Cindy whispers back.

Because she is familiar with Paul's opening, she knows that he is near its end. He's already told the jury about the altered discharge summary. A poster board–size copy of that record sits on an easel, staring accusingly at Dr. Wright.

Paul is telling the jury about Heather's autobiography, trying to defuse its impact. By bringing it up himself, rather than letting Ingram exploit it, Paul is showing the jury that he is not afraid to disclose damaging evidence and can be trusted.

"In the autobiography, Heather calls her father a monster. You'll need to look at that in its context. Her father had just recently disciplined her, and as you might expect from a teenager, she was very mad at him when she wrote that. Please keep that in mind when you decide what weight to give her story."

As Paul delivers this explanation, Susie steals glances at Cindy, who grimaces and shakes her head ever so slightly. The jurors, on the other hand, seem to hang on Paul's every word—at least from Susie's biased perspective.

After thanking the jury for its attention, Paul sits down. From what Susie has witnessed, Paul has been crisp, sincere, and committed to his cause. Because most jurors do not change their opinions about the case after opening statement, Paul has worked tirelessly on his opening, marshaling the facts to put everything in its best light.

When Ingram takes Paul's place in front of the jury, Susie knows that she will find it difficult to be objective. She despises this man even before he says one word. He begins by reminding the jurors that they promised to wait until they've heard all of the evidence before making up their minds.

"That promise is critical here, because if you are not careful, you will decide this case based on emotions and not facts. A fifteen-year-old teenager died after she underwent electroconvulsive therapy. Many of you might ask, 'What more do I have to hear? How much money should we give this poor family?'

"But that's not how our system works. You'll first have to decide if Dr. Wright did anything wrong. In other words, was he negligent?" Ingram explains that the plaintiff will call one expert witness who will say that Dr. Wright was negligent. "The defense will call someone else, a former president of the American Psychiatric Association and the author of over three hundred articles on adolescent psychology and ECT. He will tell you that Dr. Wright's actions were entirely appropriate and that he was not negligent."

The jury gives Ingram the same attention that they provided Paul. And why not? Ingram uses the same friendly and sincere tone that Paul employed. With his silver hair, handsome face, and disarming smile, he is easy to like and trust. Susie wants to scream, *Don't listen to him. He's a phony.* To her, Ingram is a huckster, no different than the aging movie stars who pitch reverse mortgages and health insurance to gullible senior citizens on television.

"You'll learn that our expert is a leader in his field and knows the standards that govern psychiatrists in this situation. To quote Mr. Schofield, he knows *the rules of the road*. He'll tell you without hesitation that Dr. Wright met all the standards. He did not run through a red light."

Ingram pauses and smiles, apparently proud of the way he's turned Paul's phrase against him. Several of the jurors return his smile, causing Susie to stare at them in disbelief.

"On the other hand, the plaintiff's expert, Dr. Simon Masterson, is on the fringe of psychiatry. His views are not shared by the majority of psychiatrists in this country." Ingram raises his eyebrows, making sure that the jurors understand the difference between his expert and Dr. Masterson.

Susie realizes how jurors might find Ingram's approach beguiling. He employs a confidential tone, as if he wants them to think that Paul has disclosed half-truths while he is giving them the full story. That becomes apparent when Ingram describes electroconvulsive therapy.

"Our expert will set the record straight on electroconvulsive therapy, otherwise known by its initials, ECT. It is mainstream medicine. If drugs and counseling fail to produce results, the next step is invariably ECT. Hundreds of thousands of patients undergo ECT with amazing results. It has been refined over the last twenty-five years and is no more dangerous than a tooth extraction. Eighty percent of the time, ECT is successful when drugs and psychotherapy fail."

Susie tenses and pushes both hands through her hair, trying to release some of her pent-up agitation. Several jurors nod, apparently accepting Ingram's assertions. From her medical research, she knows that Ingram is stretching the truth and she struggles to remember the articles that provide contrary data.

Ingram next turns his attention to Dennis Zurcher. "Heather Zurcher was a troubled girl who lived in a very dysfunctional family. Because she was so disturbed, Dr. Wright could have turned her away, but he agreed to do his best, despite her dire situation."

This last statement is almost too much for Susie to bear. Can't the jury see that Ingram is exaggerating the magnitude of Heather's illness? Her depression was no different than that of millions of other people who suffer from that disease.

Ingram quickly homes in on Dennis Zurcher. "Heather lived in a family where everyone was in fear of her father, an unpredictable man who could blow up for the most trivial of reasons. Even Heather's mother is terrified of him. Is he the monster that Heather describes in her autobiography? That's a question that you'll have to decide.

"From there, it's a short jump to answering this pivotal question: Who is responsible for Heather's death, the psychiatrist who treated her for several months or the father who terrorized her for fifteen years?"

For the first time, Susie believes that Ingram has struck a powerful blow. It's as if Ingram has been nibbling away at Paul's case and finally reached a point where the momentum has turned in his favor. A feeling of dread spreads over her.

She looks to the jury and then to her brother, searching for their reactions. Did they feel what she just experienced? The jurors, almost to a person, stare at Dennis Zurcher, who looks straight ahead, his face averted from the jury.

Susie hopes that Ingram has finished his opening statement. She's unsure how much more damage Paul's case can take at this point—certainly not much more. But Ingram is not through; he has one last salvo.

"Let's talk about this change in the discharge summary. Yes, Dr. Wright did this, and yes, it was wrong. He made a mistake and he'll admit that to you, but that's not the whole story.

"Dr. Wright only learned of Heather's death when she failed to show up for her appointment. When his receptionist called the Zurcher home, then, and only then, did they learn how she'd died. He will tell you that he was shocked that Heather had access to the new medication because he'd told Mrs. Zurcher to keep it locked away."

The jurors' eyes are fixed on Ingram. It is obvious that they want to hear the rest of this story.

"Five weeks later, Dennis Zurcher showed up in Dr. Wright's office unannounced. He demanded to see Dr. Wright immediately. He was angry and shouting in the waiting room. Dr. Wright finished with his patient and took Mr. Zurcher back into his office, where Mr. Zurcher yelled and screamed at him. He claimed that Dr. Wright had killed his daughter, blaming the ECT and the new antidepressant drug. After the father left, Dr. Wright was certain that he was going to be sued."

Susie was unaware of this story. She finds herself transfixed by Ingram's account.

"Dr. Wright pulled out Heather Zurcher's chart. He was certain that he'd provided warnings to Mrs. Zurcher but when he reviewed the discharge summary, the warning was not in it. As you might guess, he panicked. Maybe *panic* is not a strong enough word for what he experienced. What had gone wrong? Had he dictated the warning in his discharge summary and the transcriptionist failed to include it in the record? Was there a malfunction in the dictation equipment? Had he been interrupted before he'd concluded the dictation? Something had gone wrong and he wanted to correct it.

"He drafted three new sentences about his discussion with Mrs. Zurcher and had his nurse drop it off with the hospital records custodian. The nurse left instruction for the custodian to revise and replace the original discharge summary.

"Is this some devious scheme to change the facts, as Mr. Schofield claims, or is this simply an attempt by an honest doctor to set the record straight? That will be for you to decide."

Susie studies the jurors' faces, searching for some clue about whether they are accepting this explanation. None are shaking their heads in disapproval, but neither are they nodding their heads in agreement. They are inscrutable.

Ingram continues. "In the end, this civil lawsuit is about money. Who pays and who receives. That's it. In this case, Dr. Wright did nothing wrong. He provided good, competent care to a girl who was extremely sick. He did his very best, and one of the most renowned psychiatrists in the world will tell you that he should not be blamed for this tragedy. Not every treatment is successful. Not every psychiatric illness can be cured. In the end, Dr. Wright could not reverse what had been building in this poor girl for the past fifteen years.

"We are confident that when you hear all of the evidence, you will reach that decision too and find in favor of Dr. Wright."

With that, Ingram finally sits down. Not wanting to convey her concern, Susie cannot look at Cindy. Ingram has delivered a very persuasive opening statement. Did Paul's opening match his? She doesn't know.

What she does understand is that this is an incredibly difficult case. Paul has much to overcome. She hopes he can do it.

CHAPTER 23
SEPTEMBER 24, 2019
ROBERT INGRAM

After he finishes his opening statement, Robert Ingram turns away from the jury and walks slowly back to the defense table. Sensing that the jurors are watching his every move, he nonchalantly pulls his hand through his hair and straightens his tie, keeping their attention a bit longer.

He tries to maintain a neutral demeanor, but inwardly, he's buoyant. During his opening statement, he focused his efforts on three jurors whom he's identified as leaders. From his experience, he knew how to engage with them—establish eye contact and acknowledge their importance. The rest are just sheep, nobodies that he can safely ignore. Within a few minutes, the important jurors were with him: nodding, smiling, and welcoming his every point. He couldn't have had a better start.

Schofield's first witness will be Carolyn Matthews, the head records custodian at St. Andrew's Hospital. That's no surprise. She'll tell the jury that Dr. Wright violated hospital rules by destroying a record and replacing it with an updated version. Frankly, after the opening statements, this is old news. Like a sparkler on a birthday cake, this story will fizzle and then quickly sputter out. Although he's never met

Matthews, he's not worried about her testimony. Let the jurors hear it and by tomorrow, it will be insignificant.

A few minutes later, Carolyn Matthews walks into the courtroom. Several days earlier, Ingram sent Wilchuck to prepare her for her trial testimony. When Wilchuck arrived, she was a nervous wreck. Worse yet, when pressed by Wilchuck, she refused to categorize Dr. Wright's actions as inconsequential, instead labeling them "abhorrent."

As she settles herself into the witness chair, Ingram is surprised by how unattractive she is. She is in her early fifties, of average height, and very thin. With her long face and oversized teeth, she has a horse face—at least, that's what Ingram and his drinking buddies would call it. When Ingram's mind turns to sex, as it invariably does when he sees a woman for the first time, he knows he would never touch this woman, not even on his most desperate day.

After a few preliminary questions, Schofield quickly focuses on the important issues. The witness confirms that once a doctor dictates a record, it cannot be destroyed and replaced by a different version. If the doctor wants to add information or correct a misstatement, he or she must prepare a separate new document called a late-entry addendum.

"Why is that?" Schofield asks.

"Because if we allow changes to be made willy-nilly, then the records will lose their integrity."

"To be clear, if a record can be replaced at a later date, it can lose its trustworthiness, is that fair?" Schofield asks.

Matthews does not answer immediately as she apparently considers whether Schofield is trying to trick her. Finally, she replies, "Yes, it can, but not necessarily." Ingram smiles; the witness is showing some fight.

"Thank you," Schofield says. "I want to focus on what happened in this case. Five weeks after Dr. Wright dictated his discharge summary, his nurse came to your department and asked someone to destroy the old record and replace it with a new one. First question for you: Is that permissible?"

The witness responds with a sharp intake of air. "No, this is not permitted."

"The doctor claims that he needed to set the record straight by including some additional information in the discharge summary. Was he just out of luck?"

"No, Mr. Schofield, as we discussed earlier, he should have prepared a separate record with that new information, dated it, and labeled it as a late-entry addendum."

"Obviously, this begs the question. Why didn't you stop him from breaking the rules?"

The question startles the witness and she does not answer.

Capitalizing on her silence, Schofield asks, "His nurse came to you, didn't she?"

"Let me make one thing perfectly clear: I had absolutely nothing to do with this switch," Matthews says, her voice shrill and her eyes burning with indignation. "I am the head of hospital records and I would never be a party to this."

Don't be so sanctimonious, you old biddy, Ingram thinks.

"In your eighteen years at St. Andrew's, have you ever destroyed and replaced a hospital record?"

"Never," Matthews replies.

"Never ever?"

"Never, never, never," Matthews says, each *never* spoken louder than its predecessor.

Through sheer willpower, Ingram forces his expression to remain neutral. However, he's lost all patience with Matthews. This self-righteous bitch is allowing Schofield to manipulate her.

"Who then is the culprit in your department who aided and abetted Dr. Wright in this scheme?" Schofield asks.

Ingram jumps to his feet and yells, "Objection!"

"The grounds?" Judge Hardwig asks.

"The words *culprit* and *aided and abetted*. Mr. Schofield is treating this innocent mistake as if it were a crime," Ingram says, and immediately regrets his objection. Schofield baited him, and by objecting, he's only causing the jury to pay more attention to the witness's answer.

Although Judge Hardwig seems unimpressed by the objection, he asks Schofield to rephrase the question.

"Which one of your employees allowed this to happen?" Schofield asks.

The witness shakes her head. "I don't know. We've had a lot of turnover in my department. We've even had some temporary employees."

"You can't narrow it down to a few suspects—I mean a few people?" Schofield asks, turning to the jury and smiling.

"No," Matthews answers, irritation evident in her voice.

"And once this infraction came to light, no one at the hospital cared to investigate?" Schofield asks.

Ingram is tempted to object again. Schofield is milking this incident for all it's worth. However, if he objects, he'll look like he is trying to hide something from the jury. He says nothing.

For the first time, Matthews appears contrite. "No. There was no investigation. It just happened and I'm really sorry that it happened on my watch."

"No further questions."

When the judge looks to Ingram, he shakes his head. "No questions."

The next witness will be his client, Dr. Wright, whom the plaintiff will call "as if upon cross-examination." Under the rules, Schofield is allowed to cross-examine Dr. Wright to prove parts of his own case. When Schofield concludes his questioning of Dr. Wright, Ingram will not be allowed to ask follow-up questions until the defense presents its case several days later. Under this arrangement, Schofield can develop a distorted, one-sided version of the facts. That is, unless Dr. Wright clarifies his answers rather than just responds with a yes or no.

Trying to gauge his client's demeanor, Ingram studies Dr. Wright as he takes his seat in the witness chair. Dr. Wright's face is locked in a serious and determined expression, and as the doctor adjusts the microphone, his movements are confident and deliberate.

Schofield's first questions are routine background questions that develop Dr. Wright's treatment of Heather Zurcher. Although not friendly, Schofield's manner is polite and businesslike. No longer appearing confident, Ingram's client answers warily, like a man who expects a trapdoor to open and swallow him whole.

As the questioning progresses, Dr. Wright outlines Heather's diagnosis, her treatment, her hospitalization, his decision to order ECT, her discharge, and her death from ingesting the recently prescribed Tofranil. Gradually, Dr. Wright appears more relaxed and answers more quickly. *Don't let down your guard*, Ingram thinks.

When Schofield turns his questions to the altered discharge summary, Dr. Wright's body noticeably jerks. *Good, stay on high alert here*, Ingram thinks. As he's been coached, Dr. Wright becomes more measured, pausing before responding, as if he is repeating the question in his head before answering. After responding to several questions about the discharge summary, he admits that it was his idea to alter it, a mistake for which he takes full responsibility. *Keep on course*, Ingram says inwardly.

"And this mistake—as you call it—was a clear violation of the hospital rules, was it not?"

For the first time, Dr. Wright scowls. "Sometimes it's not," he says somewhat defiantly.

"Oh, when is that?" Schofield asks.

Ingram has coached Dr. Wright not to fence with Schofield, advice his client apparently is now ignoring.

Dr. Wright shrugs. "If a doctor reads a dictated summary and finds that a word is missing or misspelled, the doctor simply corrects it. There's no late-entry addendum."

Schofield walks away from the podium and stands a few feet from the jurors, facing them. He stares at the jury as he directs his next question to the witness.

"But that's not what happened in this case, is it? There weren't any misspelled words to correct."

"No," Dr. Wright replies. "I just wanted the jury to understand the nuances here."

Schofield returns to the podium and flips a page on his yellow pad. "You know, some people might say that you changed this record to bolster your defense if you got sued. What do you say to that?"

Dr. Wright looks down before he speaks. "I was setting the record straight. Everything I added to the record was the truth."

"So help you God?" Schofield says mockingly.

"Yes."

"Since you brought it up, let's talk about truth for a moment. You raised your right hand just a few minutes ago and swore to tell the truth, didn't you."

"Yes."

"And on August 15, 2018, before I began questioning you in your deposition, you did the same thing—raised your right hand and gave your solemn oath to answer truthfully. Right?"

Dr. Wright nods, his face taut with anticipation.

"You have to say yes or no for the court reporter," Schofield reminds him.

"Uh, yes."

"In your deposition, I handed you the altered discharge summary. Do you remember that?" Schofield asks.

Dr. Wright nods, then remembers that he must give an oral response and says, "Yes."

"And I asked you: 'When did you dictate everything in that summary?' And you said: 'The very day that Heather Zurcher was discharged from the hospital.' Do you remember saying that?"

"I guess."

"I don't want you to guess. I have your deposition right here and I have the pages marked where you said that. Do you want to see it?"

"No, that's not necessary. I said it."

"And what you said in your deposition was not true?"

"It was not."

Schofield shifts his gaze from the witness to Ingram. "In your attorney's opening statement, Mr. Ingram claimed that you were panicked when you changed the discharge summary. Is that right?"

"Yes, it is."

"During your deposition, were you panicked at any time when I questioned you?" Schofield asks, turning again toward the jurors and raising his eyebrows conspiratorially.

"I was nervous," Dr. Wright says.

"Oh, okay. Nervous but not panicked, right."

Dr. Wright nods and murmurs, "I suppose not panicked."

Ingram purses his lips as he awaits Schofield's next question.

"You chose to lie to me under oath in your deposition. That was a deliberate decision, not something induced by panic. Do I have that right?" Schofield's voice is authoritative but not angry.

"I admitted that I made a mistake when I changed the record," Dr. Wright says, sounding like a schoolboy pleading to avoid a paddling from the principal.

"Please just answer the question," Schofield says.

"Objection, badgering the witness," Ingram says, hoping to give his client time to regroup.

"Overruled."

"What was the question again?" Dr. Wright asks, his feigned confusion fooling no one.

Nodding and smiling at the jury, Schofield asks, "Did you make a deliberate decision to lie in your deposition? Yes or no?"

Dr. Wright does not answer immediately. Instead, he looks like a man about to swallow a spoonful of cod liver oil. "Yes, and I regret it very much," he finally responds, but his words lack conviction.

"What do you regret—lying or getting caught?" Schofield presses.

"Objection." Several of the jurors titter at this exchange, including one of Ingram's leaders.

"Sustained."

"Do you know what the crime of perjury is?" Schofield asks.

"Objection!" Ingram shouts.

Turning to face Ingram, Schofield gives him an irritated look. "I'll withdraw the question. I have a lot more ground to cover."

Schofield's gratuitous comment infuriates Ingram. How dare Schofield suggest that he is being magnanimous by moving on?

Schofield looks at his yellow pad, taking a few moments before asking his next question. Finally, he says, "There's a rule in medicine about documenting your actions in the records, isn't there?"

"There are many rules or guidelines," Dr. Wright replies.

"How about this one: 'If it's not charted, it didn't happen.' Is that one that doctors, nurses, physical therapists, everybody is taught early in their training?"

"Yes, I'm aware of that maxim," Dr. Wright says.

"And what does it mean?" Schofield presses.

"It means that a practitioner is supposed to document the important things that are happening with a patient in the medical chart," Dr. Wright says.

"And if something important is not documented, one can conclude that it didn't happen. Is that right?"

"Theoretically," Dr. Wright says.

"Just to be clear, the warnings that you supposedly gave Mrs. Zurcher about the Tofranil were important, right?" Schofield asks.

"Yes," Dr. Wright says.

"And these important warnings were not documented in your original discharge summary, right?"

"Yes, but I warned her about the Tofranil," Dr. Wright.

"Mrs. Zurcher says you didn't. Do you know that?" Schofield says, looking from the witness to the jury and back again.

"That's what she says."

"Okay, let's talk about something else, the standards set by the

American Academy of Child and Adolescent Psychiatry," Schofield begins.

Ingram clutches his pen tightly. Dr. Wright's answers to these questions will be critical. In preparing Dr. Wright for his trial testimony, Ingram impressed upon his client that he needed to disavow his deposition testimony in which he conceded that these standards were *authoritative*. If that stands, Schofield will be allowed to cross-examine Dr. Wright using these standards. If his client claims today that they are not authoritative (but only helpful), the rules of evidence forbid Schofield from introducing or even mentioning them.

"When I took your deposition back in August of 2018, you agreed with me that these standards were authoritative for your practice. Do you remember saying that?"

Dr. Wright glances at Ingram as if seeking guidance. Knowing that the jury is watching them, Ingram pretends not to notice.

When Dr. Wright does not answer the question, Schofield asks again, "Do you remember saying that?"

"Yes, but I—"

Schofield interrupts him. "And you were under oath at your deposition, weren't you? You're not going to change your testimony, are you?"

Dr. Wright looks flummoxed and seems reluctant to answer, apparently afraid that he will lose all credibility with the jury if he strays from his earlier deposition testimony. Before Ingram can pose an objection, Dr. Wright says, "No, I am not changing my deposition testimony."

"So they're still authoritative?" Schofield asks.

"Yes."

What the hell did you just do? Ingram lets his pen drop from his hand and onto his legal pad. *You just opened Pandora's box, you fucking idiot.* Ingram has the impulse to rush the witness stand, grab his client by his shoulders, and shake him senseless. Instead, he sits quietly and awaits the debacle that is sure to follow.

Through his questions, Schofield establishes that a committee of renowned psychiatrists drafted these standards, had them vetted during a period of public comment, and then published the final version in a leading medical journal. Schofield turns the questioning to Tofranil, the antidepressant that Dr. Wright prescribed after Heather was discharged from the hospital. Again, Schofield's questions provide background about the drug: that it was one of the first antidepressants developed, came into the market in the 1960s, and is part of the tricyclic family.

"Are you aware that these standards say that Tofranil and other tricyclics should not be prescribed for the suicidal child or adolescent?" Schofield asks.

"The key words there are *should not*," Dr. Wright replies. "It's not absolutely forbidden."

"Thank you for that clarification," Schofield says. Ingram hears a hint of sarcasm in Schofield's voice. "And Heather Zurcher did admit to suicidal thoughts during counseling sessions while in the hospital?"

"Yes."

"Let's read the next part of the standard: 'They are potentially lethal, because of the small difference between therapeutic and toxic levels of the drug, and have not been proven to be effective in children or adolescents.' Did I read that accurately?"

"Yes."

"And this standard was written by the very best in your profession? Right?"

"Supposedly," Dr. Wright says.

"The best and the brightest in psychiatry say: 'Don't use it. There's little difference between a safe dosage and a deadly dosage. It's not effective with kids.' Have I paraphrased that correctly?" Schofield asks.

Dr. Wright shrugs.

"Despite this, you decided that you'd give it a try?" Schofield asks, looking slightly incredulous.

"I've had good results with it," Dr. Wright protests.

"With adults or children?" Schofield presses.

"Both," Dr. Wright says. Ingram hears uncertainty in Dr. Wright's voice.

"Oh," Schofield says with a touch of mock surprise. "Are you certified in child and adolescent psychiatry like the doctors who wrote these standards?"

"No, I am not."

"In fact, eighty percent of your patients are adults, right?"

"Something like that."

"So how many times have you prescribed Tofranil for children?"

Dr. Wright scowls. "How can I give you an exact number? I've treated thousands of people."

Schofield shakes his head as he approaches the jury. "Before I brought this standard to your attention at your deposition, did you even know that you weren't supposed to prescribe this medicine to a teenager, particularly one who had attempted suicide once before?"

"Of course I was aware," Dr. Wright says. Ingram watches the jurors; several of them look skeptical.

"Well, Tofranil wasn't your only choice for a new antidepressant. There are over fifty other antidepressants on the market that you could have tried, am I correct?" Schofield asks.

"I thought this one was the best under the circumstances," Dr. Wright says.

"Well, we'll let the jury decide that one," Schofield says.

For the next thirty minutes, Schofield directs Dr. Wright to four additional standards that he disregarded. Schofield establishes that Dr. Wright failed to get a second opinion before starting ECT, failed to warn the parents that ECT can cause significant memory loss, failed to properly space the ECT treatments, and improperly placed electrodes to both sides of the brain, increasing the chance of memory loss.

By the time Schofield finishes his questioning about these standards, Ingram senses a dramatic shift in the trial's momentum. In attempting to explain his omissions, Dr. Wright has sounded like a foolish bumbler.

Around noon, the judge asks, "Mr. Schofield, we are approaching the lunch recess. How much longer do you have?"

Ingram hopes Schofield is mercifully finished.

Schofield looks at the jury and then at his legal pad. "I had several more areas of inquiry, but I think I will end my examination now."

After the judge dismisses the jury, Ingram stares at his client, who still sits in the witness chair. To his left, Dennis Zurcher is pounding Schofield on the back, obviously congratulating him on the way he's just bludgeoned Dr. Wright on the witness stand. Ingram beckons Dr. Wright to join him at the trial table.

Dr. Wright slowly rises and makes his way toward Ingram. Chastened, he takes a seat at their table, his head bowed.

"Why the hell did you say the standards were authoritative? I told you repeatedly that you couldn't do that. You needed to say that you misspoke at your deposition," Ingram says, his finger jabbing toward Dr. Wright's face.

"I was in a tough place," Dr. Wright says. "I didn't want to look like my word couldn't be trusted."

Ingram shakes his head. "If you'd followed my instructions, this would all have been avoided. You know that, right?"

Dr. Wright sits motionless.

"You dug us a big hole. That's what you did," Ingram says.

"I'm sorry," Dr. Wright says. "Did I just lose the case for us?"

"No, I'll win it," Ingram replies, still angry with his client. "Although the jury may believe that you screwed up, fortunately for you, that's not enough. The other side must prove that your negligence caused the girl's death. Whatever you did, you didn't kill her. That distinction belongs to her father."

Dr. Wright recoils. Ingram knows the doctor is offended by the insinuation that he was negligent.

"Do you think I was negligent?" Dr. Wright asks.

"No, I don't. However, this jury may believe that you were," Ingram says, and then gives Dr. Wright a reassuring smile. "Don't worry, I'm on your side all the way."

Looking defeated, Dr. Wright stands with his shoulders hunched.

Pointing to the chair recently vacated by Dennis Zurcher, Ingram says, "By the time I'm through with that guy, the jury will despise him and you'll be off the hook."

Still appearing anxious, Dr. Wright looks doubtful.

"I'm very confident of that," Ingram says, nodding encouragingly. "I really am. In the end, everything will turn out fine."

Ingram sees gratitude in Dr. Wright's eyes. For the first time, Dr. Wright views him as his rescuer, the one who will pull him out of the murky and turbulent waters. *It's about time*, Ingram thinks.

He turns to walk away but then pivots back to face his client. "Just one more thing. Don't ever ignore my instructions again."

"I won't."

CHAPTER 24
SEPTEMBER 24, 2019
CINDY ZURCHER

As Cindy Zurcher walks to the witness stand, dread seizes her body. She shivers as a blast of air-conditioned air buffets her chest and arms. Immediately after she sits, the bailiff adjusts the microphone an inch from her mouth, locking her in place. The moment has arrived; she must testify about Heather and her death.

Before the questioning begins, the judge addresses the jury and apologizes for the delayed start for the afternoon's session. He explains that he was forced to interrupt the trial for several criminal sentencings. As the judge speaks, Cindy tries to slow both her breathing and her heart rate, all to no avail. Her fear is so great that she finds it difficult to concentrate on the judge's words.

Inside her head, she sees only failure. Will she be able to utter a single word when asked a question? Will her voice shake if she does speak? Will she be able to get through this ordeal without breaking down?

Then it begins. Paul smiles at her and asks her to recite her name. She finds that she can talk, and, with the help of the microphone, her soft, quavering voice is amplified so that everyone can hear her. As she fixes her eyes on her attorney and answers his questions, she feels detached, almost as if she is in a dream. She hears herself talk about her daughter, describing the first twelve years of her life. Because she and Paul have rehearsed her examination several times, her words spill out quietly and efficiently.

Paul's eyes are encouraging; his voice is gentle and sympathetic. She feels like she is talking to a friend, someone she trusts. Then his questions turn to family dynamics and she freezes. They've rehearsed this too, but for a moment her mind goes blank and she's unable to recall the words and phrases that they've decided upon to describe her rocky marriage.

"Did you and Dennis argue?" Paul asks.

She tells him that they did, sometimes in front of the children. And she acknowledges much more—that Dennis could be volatile, belittle those around him, and insist that he be strictly obeyed. She counterbalances this with several stories about Dennis and the children that show how funny he could be. She insists that he is a good provider and wants his children to excel; she admits that he can become very angry when the children don't give their best efforts.

"We weren't perfect parents—far from that—but we loved Heather. We made many mistakes. There are so many things we would do differently, and . . ." Cindy's voice trails off and she does not finish her sentence. For the first time, Cindy ventures a glance at the jurors. Their stares unnerve her. They're studying her face, trying to decide what to make of her. From their looks, they probably despise her.

She returns her attention to Paul, someone who accepts her despite her flaws. She decides never to look at the jurors again.

Paul asks her about the onset of Heather's depression. She describes the changes in her daughter's behavior in high school: the crying spells, her isolation in her bedroom, and her loss of interest in almost everything. Like most parents, she and Dennis hoped that this behavior would eventually pass, but they finally realized that Heather needed professional help.

She chronicles Heather's treatment and lack of progress, leading to the hospitalization and Dr. Wright's strong recommendation that they authorize electroshock treatments.

"We opposed it at first, but he warned us that Heather would probably never get well unless she had the treatments," Cindy says. "What do you do when the doctor tells you that? He made it seem like we had no choice."

She claims that Dr. Wright minimized the risks. "If he'd warned us about permanent memory loss or decreased brain function, we'd never have agreed to it," she says.

Cindy provides the jury with graphic descriptions of Heather after the ECT treatments: periods of zombie-like behavior followed by violent, angry outbursts. "She was so upset that she'd lost three or four years of her memory. She didn't blame the doctor; she blamed us," Cindy says, biting her lower lip.

Although Dr. Wright wanted to continue with more shock treatments, she and Dennis had seen enough after ten. "She was getting worse, not better. We wanted her out of there. We'd lost confidence in Dr. Wright," she says, stealing a glance at the defense table and Dr. Wright.

Cindy explains that Dr. Wright did not want to release Heather but agreed after Dennis insisted during a heated argument. They were to pick her up the next morning, but, when it was time to go to the hospital, only she was free to get her.

"What did Dr. Wright tell you when you met with him?"

"First off, he did not warn me to keep the new medicine locked up. I'm certain of that," Cindy says, fidgeting in her chair.

"What else?"

"He was very short and curt with me. It was obvious that he was angry that we were overruling him. He said something like, 'I only have a minute, I have other patients to care for.' He wanted to see Heather in two weeks and he told us not to leave her alone in the house. That was it," Cindy says.

"This leaving alone, how did you understand that?" Paul asks.

"That there should always be an adult in the house with her. We weren't to go out and leave her there by herself," Cindy says.

"Did he tell you anything else about the new drug? Whether it was more dangerous than the others that he'd prescribed?"

"No, he did not," Cindy says, shaking her head for emphasis.

"Did you plan to keep the appointment with Dr. Wright in two weeks?"

"Yes, but we were going to research and find a new psychiatrist. I figured the upcoming appointment would be our last one with him."

"Your witness," Paul says, and then turns to walk back to the trial table.

Robert Ingram stands and walks to the podium, a yellow pad in hand. He smiles but Cindy sees only menace. Before he asks a question, he expresses his sorrow for the loss of her daughter. She's not fooled by his supposed compassion, but the jury probably is.

"I will ask you some difficult questions that I would rather not ask. However, I need to ask them to defend my client. Will you forgive me in advance if you believe that the questions are insensitive or hurtful?" His tone is fatherly and kind.

A year earlier, when Ingram deposed her, he pried, pushed, and tried to trick her with his questions. The memories are still vivid and raw. *And he wants me to forgive him in advance?*

She replies, "I'll answer your questions as best as I can."

He begins by asking if she and Dennis insisted on Heather's release from the hospital against Dr. Wright's advice. She agrees that they did.

"Dr. Wright wanted to monitor and assess the new antidepressant in the safe hospital setting, didn't he?" he asks.

She's never understood why Dr. Wright wanted to keep Heather in the hospital after they discontinued shock treatments. "I don't know," she says. "I really don't. I think he wanted to continue with counseling sessions."

"Well, for whatever reason, Heather was safe in the hospital, wasn't she?"

"I suppose," Cindy answers warily.

"My question is: Wouldn't Heather be alive today if she had remained in the hospital?"

Cindy looks to Paul; this is a question that they've never discussed. She knows Paul cannot help her and returns her gaze to Ingram. While her mind swirls with indecision, Ingram repeats the question.

"I don't know," she finally says.

"Well, they have safeguards in the hospital. She couldn't have swallowed a bottle of pills there, right?"

"I suppose so."

"Safeguards you did *not* have in your home?" he presses.

Ingram has cornered her. She will look stupid if she denies this. Defeated, she replies, "Apparently not."

His voice no longer fatherly, Ingram asks, "And Heather was suicidal, wasn't she?"

This is not a question but, instead, an accusation. She is the one who allowed her suicidal daughter to have access to a lethal drug. Although her eyes are trained on Ingram, she senses that the jurors' eyes are boring into her, judgmental and unforgiving. She needs to give context. It is not as simple as Ingram is implying.

"Can I explain something?" she asks.

She sees a flicker of hesitation cross Ingram's face, but then it vanishes, replaced by a smile. "Of course."

"Before Heather was a patient of Dr. Wright, she told me that she'd ingested ten aspirin tablets. She said that she knew they wouldn't kill her, but she wanted to see what they would do." Cindy pauses and studies Ingram's face. He looks impatient. "It's one of the reasons we decided that she should see a psychiatrist."

"But there's more than that, isn't there?" Ingram interrupts.

"I wasn't through," Cindy says. "When she was in the hospital, one of the nurses apparently overheard Heather and another patient talking about suicide. I don't know what was said. But that's it. That's her history regarding suicide."

"Thank you for that explanation," Ingram says in a tone Cindy believes mocks her. "Regardless of your explanation, when Heather came home, she was at risk for committing suicide."

Cindy looks down at her hands and does not answer.

"You had to be on guard for that, right?" Ingram presses.

"Yes," Cindy says, her voice soft, barely audible despite the microphone.

Ingram gives her a sympathetic look, but Cindy is not fooled. She knows he is gearing up for another strike. He begins slowly, confirming that she decided to store the Tofranil in a kitchen cupboard along with spices and a bottle of aspirin. He also has her admit that other prescription drugs were kept in the master bathroom's medicine cabinet, a more secluded location.

"Again, I apologize in advance for this question," Ingram says, looking at the jury and not at Cindy. "If you had locked the Tofranil away or hidden it securely, Heather would be alive today, wouldn't she?"

Despite anticipating this question during her prep session with Paul, she is unmoored by it. Paul suggested that she respond with this answer: if Dr. Wright had told her to lock up the medication, she would have done so. However, at this moment, she doesn't want to deflect blame away from herself. She wants to be brutally honest. She will own it—in front of everybody.

"I ask myself that question every day," she says, her voice trembling. "Don't think that I don't. It keeps me awake at night. It's always there—always." She closes her eyes and lowers her head.

Ingram lets her answer linger in the courtroom before posing his next question.

After a lengthy pause, he asks, "You're not in favor of this lawsuit, are you?"

This question startles her. How could he know this? Did she inadvertently reveal this during her deposition? Even today, after Dr. Wright's mistakes and cover-up are in plain view, she is still a reluctant participant.

"I—I don't know what you mean," she stammers.

Ingram pretends to look surprised by her response. "You just told the jury that you blame yourself, didn't you?"

"Yes."

"And I assume you also blame your husband, too?"

"No, I don't," Cindy says quickly.

"Do you deny that your husband was abusive toward Heather?" Ingram asks, his voice loud and forceful.

"He never hit her," Cindy says.

"There are other kinds of abuse," Ingram says, not hiding his impatience. "What about verbal abuse?"

"I testified that he could get very angry and call her names. We both made mistakes."

"Let's talk about one of your husband's *mistakes*," Ingram says, opening a document and flipping to a page. "You are aware that Heather provided Dr. Wright with an autobiography as part of her treatment, aren't you?"

"Yes."

"Let me read you this paragraph from it and then I'll ask you if it is true. She wrote: 'I forgot to make my bed one day last week. To punish me, my dad took my watercolor that had won first prize in the scholastic art contest and burned it in the fireplace.' First of all, did that happen?"

"It did," Cindy says, offering no explanation.

"Is that the kind of *mistake* your husband made with Heather?"

She can't defend him. It was one of the most terrible things he did to her. "Yes," Cindy replies. She can only imagine what the jurors are thinking.

"She also writes that he tried to hypnotize her to banish her depression. Is that true?"

"Yes." She feels herself falling into an abyss, her body spinning head over heels, awaiting the thud when it hits solid rock.

"Did you try to stop him?" he asks.

"Yes," Cindy says, offering no details. She should expand her answer, but she simply wants the examination to end. If that means offering no resistance to Ingram's questions, then that is what she will do.

Cindy's thoughts are interrupted by the sound of coughing in the courtroom. She glances in the direction of the sound and spots Susie sitting in the back row. When their eyes meet for a second, Susie silently mouths one word to her: *fight*. *Leave me alone*, Cindy thinks. But Susie's message distracts Cindy and she misses Ingram's next question.

"I'm sorry, what was your question?" Cindy asks.

"Did he call her a loser?" Ingram presses.

"Yes, he called her names when he was angry," she answers. "We know that was wrong."

"It sounds like a miserable home life for Heather," Ingram says.

"Objection," Paul says. "Is there a question there or is Mr. Ingram just testifying?"

"Sustained," Judge Hardwig says. "Ask a question."

"My last one, Your Honor, and then I'll be done," Ingram says as he flips through several pages of his legal pad. "I don't mean to be insensitive," Ingram begins, "but wouldn't you agree that if Heather wanted to take her own life, she could have done so in countless ways?"

"Meaning . . . ?" Cindy asks.

"Even if you had locked up or hidden the Tofranil, she would have found another method to commit suicide. Don't you agree?"

She and Paul discussed this potential question and she understands why Ingram asked it. If Heather was determined to kill herself, whether Dr. Wright warned them about the Tofranil becomes moot.

Heather would have accomplished this some other way and Dr. Wright would be blameless.

Ignoring his question, Cindy responds. "She left the empty pill bottle in the bathroom sink. She crawled fifteen feet into the hallway from the bedroom. What does that tell you?" Answering her own question, Cindy says, "It tells me that she wanted to be found—that she wanted to be saved." For only the second time during her examination, she turns and looks at the jurors, slowly scanning each of their faces. "She wanted to live. I have no doubt about that."

Ingram scowls. "I would ask that the witness's answer be stricken as being unresponsive to my question."

Judge Hardwig holds up his hand. "I want the court reporter to reread the question and answer." Ingram's eyes bulge in exasperation, but he says nothing.

After the court reporter reads the last two exchanges, the judge nods his head as he thinks. Finally, he says, "Overruled. I'll let that response stand. You opened the door to that answer, Mr. Ingram. Mrs. Zurcher did not agree with the proposition that you posed. She just took a roundabout way of telling you no.

"Now, if you don't have any additional questions, we will adjourn for the day."

CHAPTER 25
SEPTEMBER 25, 2019
PAUL SCHOFIELD

As Dr. Simon Masterson waddles to the witness stand, Paul's eyes are drawn to the doctor's bright tie, which ends several inches short of his belt. His expert sits down heavily in the witness chair and energetically scans the courtroom, like a pet hamster surveying his surroundings after being released from his cage. He adjusts the microphone and twists in his seat, eventually finding a comfortable angle. "There," he says, loud enough for everyone in the courtroom to hear.

Paul hopes that the jury will focus on the doctor's words and not his gnomelike appearance. For the first five minutes, Paul develops Dr. Masterson's qualifications: his degree from Harvard Medical School, his many academic articles, and his two books on electroconvulsive therapy. The doctor speaks in a choppy but sonorous voice, pronouncing his words distinctly and with a slight British accent. Paul knows that the accent is an affectation; Dr. Masterson was born and bred in a Kansas farming community.

Paul asks Dr. Masterson to provide the jury with a quick history about shock therapy (the doctor will refuse to call it ECT throughout his examination). He starts with its introduction by two Italian doctors in 1938 to treat schizophrenia, its widespread use before antidepressant medications were developed, its notoriety in a number of films in the 1970s, its disuse, and finally its reemergence after general anesthesia and muscle relaxers were implemented to eliminate the thrashing that otherwise made the procedure seem barbaric. While reciting this history, Dr. Masterson speaks in a condescending and dismissive tone.

"What is the scientific evidence that shock treatments actually work in treating depression?" Paul asks.

"There is none," Dr. Masterson says, raising his eyebrows as he looks at the jurors.

"Shock treatments have been used now for over eighty years," Paul says. "How can that be?"

"Well, they've had a few studies where one group of patients receives shock treatments while the other group receives what they call 'sham treatments.' Now, the shocked patients do slightly better while receiving the treatment, but here's the big takeaway: after the treatment ends, both groups do about the same."

Dr. Masterson explains that most psychiatrists don't use shock treatment anymore and those who do are either ill-informed or greedy.

"What do you mean 'greedy'?" Paul asks.

As if addressing a child, Dr. Masterson fixes his eyes upon Paul. "Mr. Schofield, shock treatments are a billion-and-a-half-dollar industry—that's revenue generated every year by this procedure. It is a huge moneymaker for hospitals, psychiatrists, and anesthesiologists alike. Who would want to shut down this cash cow? Not this group, I daresay."

Waving his pudgy fingers to emphasize his words, Dr. Masterson becomes agitated as he focuses on the cold economics of shock treatments. "Let's face it, we're not talking about one shock treatment and it's over. No, not at all. When shock treatments are ordered, this means a dozen or so sessions over a period of weeks, and for some unfortunate souls, a lifetime of maintenance shock treatments." Dr. Masterson looks away from the jury and turns to the judge, trying to bring him within his orbit. "It's a gift that keeps on giving," he says with a smile. Maintaining his neutrality, the judge does not react.

After Dr. Masterson discloses the materials that he's reviewed regarding Heather Zurcher, Paul is ready to ask the ultimate questions for which he's hired this expert. "Did Dr. Wright meet the standard of care of a reasonably careful psychiatrist in his treatment of Heather Zurcher?" Paul asks.

Like a racehorse at the starting gate, Dr. Masterson is eager to respond. His eyes intense, Dr. Masterson says, "He was negligent. He did not meet the standard of a reasonably careful psychiatrist in his treatment of Heather Zurcher."

To hold Dr. Wright accountable, Paul must also show a connection between Dr. Wright's carelessness and Heather's death. "Was Dr. Wright's negligence a proximate cause of Heather Zurcher's death?"

"Unfortunately, it was. Dr. Wright's acts and failures to act led directly to her death," Dr. Masterson says solemnly.

When Paul asks Dr. Masterson to explain, his expert is adamant that Dr. Wright should never have recommended shock treatments for a fifteen-year-old, adding that in some states, it is illegal to administer ECT to anyone under the age of sixteen. He also criticizes Dr. Wright's tragic choice of Tofranil. Because the drug gets into the bloodstream very quickly, its "lethal effect can't be reversed when too many tablets are ingested."

Although Dr. Masterson's opinions have checked the boxes on negligence and causation, Paul needs more to motivate the jury to find in his favor. The jury must believe that Dr. Wright set something in motion that would inevitably lead to Heather's death. Can Dr. Masterson deliver that kind of narrative?

"The jurors have heard your opinions about Dr. Wright's care. However, can't we assume that Heather was ultimately going to take her own life—if not from a Tofranil overdose, then from something else? What do you say about that?" Paul looks at the jurors. Several have their trial notebooks open with pens poised above the paper.

Dr. Masterson nods thoughtfully before answering. "The shock treatments caused a brain dysfunction that led to Heather's extreme confusion. Not only did this increase her depression, but it caused a number of cognitive deficits that prevented her from thinking properly." The doctor pauses and studies the jury, making sure that they are listening to him. Dr. Masterson has captured the attention of several of the jurors, who stare at him intently. "Now, after Dr. Wright prescribed the dangerous antidepressant, the stage was set for tragedy. With Tofranil in the home, Dr. Wright might as well have handed Heather a loaded gun."

It is a bold answer. Paul fears that his expert has gone too far and that the jury will reject him as being too partisan. But Paul has no alternative; it is Dr. Masterson or bust. He will ask one final question and hope that the jurors will be swayed by this strange little man.

"Doctor, you know the circumstances surrounding Heather's death?"

Dr. Masterson nods.

"From your experience as a psychiatrist who has treated thousands of depressed patients, did Heather want to take her own life on October 7, 2016?" Paul asks, trying to build on Cindy Zurcher's moving testimony on this point.

Ingram jumps to his feet. "Objection. This is highly speculative. It requires this expert to look into the mind of the deceased on the day that she died."

Paul expected this objection and is ready. "There are facts and circumstances surrounding her death that this expert, through his decades of experience, can interpret for the jury. This will be helpful, not speculative."

"Overruled," Judge Hardwig says. "I'll allow it."

Like Cindy Zurcher, Dr. Masterson focuses on the empty pill bottle in the sink and Heather's attempt to crawl from her bedroom to the family room, where her family was watching television. "I've seen this hundreds of times in my practice. I can say unequivocally that this young teenager did not want to die. She desperately wanted to be saved. That is the tragedy here. The effects of the drug could not be reversed and Dr. Wright has to take responsibility for that."

As Paul walks away, Ingram practically leaps from his seat and takes his place behind the lectern, dropping a yellow pad and deposition on its surface with a loud plop. Dr. Masterson observes Ingram's eagerness and raises his eyebrows, almost mockingly—or so it seems to Paul. In their prep session, Dr. Masterson assured Paul that he could hold his own against the best malpractice defense attorneys in the country. Paul will soon find out.

Ingram smiles at Dr. Masterson. "So only incompetent and greedy physicians employ ECT, did I get that right?"

"That is the unfortunate truth, sir," Dr. Masterson replies. "But it's mainly greed."

"Since we're on the topic of greed, how much are you charging Mr. Schofield for your testimony today?" Ingram asks, his tone smug.

Paul flinches; he realizes that he should have asked questions about fees when he questioned his expert. It would have softened the blow. An objection here will be futile; the defense is permitted to inquire about fees to establish the expert's bias.

Dr. Masterson studies Ingram for a moment and returns his smile. "Mr. Ingram, I am not being paid for my testimony. You know better than that. I am being paid for my time." Dr. Masterson then explains that, when he testifies, he cannot see patients for at least two days and he must be compensated for that lost income.

"So how much is that?" Ingram asks.

"I haven't computed my bill yet. I don't know how long I will be here. I mean, it depends on how many questions you have for me," Dr. Masterson says, turning to the jury to see if any appreciate his humor.

Ingram does not smile but reaches for a document on the lectern. After explaining that he's obtained a copy of the doctor's fee schedule from his website, Ingram lists Dr. Masterson's charges for a trial appearance: $7,500 a day in trial, $500 an hour for preparation time, first-class airline tickets, and reimbursement for meals and hotel expenses.

"Very standard," Dr. Masterson says, looking unconcerned.

"Apparently you've conducted a survey of medical experts to know this," Ingram says. Several jurors titter; they apparently like this line of questioning. Ingram then confirms that Dr. Masterson has also charged separately for the initial review of the medical records and the preparation of his report, another $7,500.

Drumming his fingers on his thigh, Dr. Masterson nods.

"Seems to me that you'll rack up fees of fifteen to twenty thousand dollars for your *help* in this case. Right?"

"It's possible. I haven't worked out the math," Dr. Masterson says, protruding his lower lip.

For the next few minutes, Ingram asks a series of questions that aim to isolate Dr. Masterson from the mainstream of medicine. The expert must concede that the finest hospitals in the United States still provide ECT to their psychiatric patients. He also admits that the most important psychiatric organizations have published findings that ECT is effective in treating adolescents and can be used when two trials of antidepressants have failed.

"Everywhere in the developed world, doctors employ ECT—the United Kingdom, New Zealand, Italy, almost everywhere?" Ingram presses, his voice louder and tinged with anger. "Despite your crusade against shock treatments, it is not banned anywhere in the world, isn't that right?"

"No, that's not true," Dr. Masterson says. "The World Health Organization has issued directives banning its use on children." The doctor's voice is indignant, an implied invitation for Ingram to debate him.

Ingram rolls his eyes and looks impatiently at the jury. "Now you want to throw standards about children into the case. Heather Zurcher was not a child. She was an adolescent who'd gone through puberty, weighed one hundred and ten pounds, and was five feet three inches tall."

Dr. Masterson scowls. "Do you have a question for me?"

"How can you bootstrap standards about children and apply them to this case?" Ingram asks, his body leaning over the lectern and his hands squeezing its sides.

"I will tell you," Dr. Masterson replies coolly. "Teenagers may be physically as strong as adults, but their minds are still very much developing, and, in particular, they are unable to fully evaluate risky behavior until their mid-twenties. Psychiatry is the treatment of the *mind*. Heather Zurcher's mind was closer to that of a child."

As Ingram shakes his head, Paul realizes that his opponent is frustrated. In contrast, Dr. Masterson seems calm and in control. Maybe his expert can handle a vigorous cross-examination.

"Even though the best psychiatrists in the United States have issued standards for the safe use of ECT on children and adolescents, you categorically reject their findings. Am I right? You know more than they do."

Sidestepping his questions, Dr. Masterson says, "Let's be clear: I wouldn't recommend shock treatments for adults either." Pointing his finger at Ingram, Dr. Masterson says, "Would you want to receive four hundred fifty volts to your brain, Mr. Ingram? You know, you could stick your finger into that electrical socket over there and see if it benefits you."

Several jurors laugh, while others look amused. They signed on for jury duty expecting it to be boring, but these exchanges are anything but.

"Your Honor, would you instruct the witness to answer my question?"

"Dr. Masterson, your answer was not responsive to the question. Please answer it."

Dr. Masterson sighs. "Yes, I reject the recommendations of that panel of psychiatrists—absolutely and completely."

"And to be abundantly clear, you are telling this jury that ECT has no benefit in the treatment of any psychiatric condition. Is that correct?"

"Yes, you understand me completely," Dr. Masterson says, unable to suppress a smile.

"Whether the treatment is for severe depression, mania, catatonia, or severe autism. It is wholly ineffective. Is that your position?"

"Well, it's mainly used to treat depression, rarely for those other conditions that you mentioned," Dr. Masterson says.

"Please humor me, Dr. Masterson. Is ECT a waste of time in treating all of these conditions?"

Dr. Masterson shakes his head and gives Ingram a condescending look. "Yes, it is a waste of time—totally ineffective in the long term. All of these conditions return in full force several weeks after the shock therapy is completed."

Paul is suspicious of this line of questioning. Why has Ingram spent so much time forcing his expert to commit to this proposition? Is he setting a trap? If so, Ingram is saving it for later. He veers away from it and ventures into another line of questioning—proximate cause.

Ingram restates Dr. Masterson's testimony on this point, zeroing in on his opinion that Dr. Masterson's negligence was *a* cause of Heather's death, not *the* cause of her death.

"You know this begs the question. Were there other causes that led to her death?" Ingram asks.

At first, Dr. Masterson claims that he doesn't understand the question, forcing Ingram to restate it. Paul realizes that his expert is merely stalling for time, trying to sidestep this damning question. If he admits to other causes, then it weakens their case against Dr. Wright. If he denies other causes, the expert loses credibility with the jury. There is no right answer.

"If you mean that the parents are also to blame, I disagree," Dr. Masterson says.

"Wait a minute," Ingram says. "The parents insist on her discharge against the doctor's orders. They fail to keep the antidepressant out of their daughter's hands. And, even though they are never supposed to leave her alone, they watch television for over an hour while their daughter overdoses on Tofranil in her bedroom. Are you really asking this jury to disregard these things? You still maintain that the parents are blameless?"

It's as if Ingram has loaded his entire closing argument into this one question. Paul believes that his expert is trapped.

Dr. Masterson puts his right hand under his chin, mimicking the pose of the Thinker. After a few moments, he responds. He tells the jury that he has scoured the hospital chart and nowhere does he see where Dr. Wright documented that the patient was leaving against his orders.

"You know, if he went to so much trouble changing the discharge summary, he should have added something about this in the chart, too," Dr. Masterson says, glancing at the jury to gauge the effect of his little salvo.

When Ingram begins to ask another question, Dr. Masterson tells him that he hasn't finished answering his question. He reinforces that if Dr. Wright had warned the parents about the drug, they would have kept it away from their daughter. Finally, he insists that the parents acted reasonably in allowing Heather to go to her bedroom for a nap and not interrupt her.

Although Dr. Masterson seems to have a ready response for all of Ingram's questions, Paul worries that his expert is too smooth and too glib for the jurors to trust him.

Paul senses that Ingram is struggling to end his cross-examination on a strong point. Finally, he asks Dr. Masterson if any parent exercising common sense would keep all medicines away from a suicidal teenager.

"I don't disagree with that statement," Dr. Masterson says. "However, in the Zurchers' situation, they might let their guard down a bit if they thought their daughter was improving at home."

Apparently ignoring the last part of Dr. Masterson's answer, Ingram says, "We finally agree on something. Thank you. No further questions."

Paul decides that he won't ask any additional questions of his expert on redirect. Either the jurors are going to accept Dr. Masterson's testimony or they will not. A few extra questions and answers will not change their impressions.

When the trial resumes this afternoon, he will call Dennis and two lay witnesses before resting his case. If Dennis self-destructs, all will be lost. As he thinks about all the ways Dennis is vulnerable, he is too nervous to eat lunch. The afternoon session cannot come soon enough.

CHAPTER 26
SEPTEMBER 25, 2019
WENDY SCHOFIELD

"Scoot over, you're hogging the bench," Wendy says as she leans her shoulder against her sister-in-law, who is sitting in the courtroom's back row.

"Who let you loose?" Susie replies. "Aren't you supposed to be holding down the fort?"

Smiling, Wendy says, "I can't stand it in the office. I had to find out how Paul is doing."

"What, you guys don't talk at night?" Susie says.

"You know Paul. He's Mr. Doom and Gloom during a trial. He's getting killed by this witness or that ruling. He's never going to win."

Susie laughs. "That's my brother."

"So tell me, how is he really doing?"

"I've been here every day and I think he's doing great," Susie says. "I've been studying the jurors and they're with him. I can feel it."

Before they can talk more, the bailiff leads the jurors into the courtroom and they take their seats. The judge asks Paul to announce his next witness and Paul calls Dennis Zurcher to the stand.

Dennis Zurcher rises slowly from his chair, stands erect, and walks resolutely to the witness stand. He wears a navy blue blazer over a pale blue dress shirt, accented by a red and white striped tie. Through Wendy's eyes, he's an overweight car salesman whose patriotic attire is simply part of his showy façade.

Susie leans over and whispers, "Paul says he's going to keep his examination short. The less the jury is exposed to this guy, the better."

Paul does just that. He quickly develops Dennis's background: his military service, including a deployment in Afghanistan; his years as a sheriff's deputy; and his reliable and steady work as a car salesman that has provided a comfortable life for his family. As he answers these questions, Dennis maintains an erect posture and speaks with authority, occasionally making eye contact with individual jurors.

"How would you describe your relationship with Heather?" Paul asks.

"Well, that's complicated," Dennis says. "It really is." His shoulders slump and he becomes a different person. The man with the military bearing is replaced by someone who looks vulnerable and troubled. Wendy is not fooled. She studies the jurors to gauge their reaction but cannot read their expressions.

"How so?" Paul asks.

"In this courtroom, I know I've been depicted as some kind of monster," Dennis says. He turns his gaze from Paul to Ingram and lets his eyes linger there. "But I loved Heather. I love all my children. Things just went off the tracks with Heather. A lot of that was my fault, some of it wasn't."

Paul leads Dennis through his life with Heather, from the little girl who followed him around the house incessantly to the troubled teenager who grew more and more distant. He admits to many mistakes, most of them caused by his penchant for discipline and his hair-trigger temper. He regrets his outbursts and wishes he had been more understanding, something he claims he has become with his two remaining children.

With her elbow, Susie delivers a soft poke to Wendy's ribs. "Tell that to his son," Susie whispers.

Dennis chronicles Heather's treatment with Dr. Wright. He claims that he initially opposed almost all of Dr. Wright's recommendations: first, the trial of antidepressants; second, the admission to the hospital's psychiatric ward; and, finally, the use of shock treatments. In each instance, he deferred to the "man with the degrees." After Heather's depression worsened with shock treatments, Dennis put a halt to them and insisted that his daughter come home.

Dennis claims that Heather improved once she was home. On the morning that she died, Heather and Cindy had discussed going shopping the next day. Around seven thirty that evening, Heather claimed that she was tired and wanted to lie down for a while in her bedroom. After she left, the rest of the family watched television in the family room. About an hour and a half later, his son, Travis, went to get something from his bedroom. It was then that he discovered his sister, unconscious in the hallway, lying in a pool of her own vomit.

"I'll never forget his scream," Dennis says, his eyes locked with Paul's. "It was awful, like a terrified animal. We all came running to see what had happened. I saw Heather on the floor, her skin gray, and obviously just clinging to life. At first, it didn't seem real, but then I knew it was. And I needed to act fast.

"I immediately dropped to the floor, rolled her over, and checked her breathing, which was shallow and raspy. I knew she was just barely hanging on. My other daughter, Melissa, was wailing by now and Cindy ran to call 911 on the kitchen phone. I used my hand to clean the vomit from her mouth and then began mouth-to-mouth resuscitation."

But then Dennis falters. His words will not come and he begins to cry. "I promised myself I wouldn't do this," Dennis says.

Despite her loathing for this man, Wendy, at this moment, feels his agony. It's as if he has transported her back to his house on that fateful night. If she feels this way, it must also seem real and immediate to the jurors.

Dennis finishes his story—their SUV speeding after the ambulance on its way to the hospital, the grim-faced emergency room doctor delivering the tragic news, and the guilt that has plagued them ever since. He tells the jury that he began researching ECT a few days after his daughter's death, first on the internet and later at the library. Five weeks later, he confronted Dr. Wright in his office, asking him pointed questions about his treatment. He denies that he was agitated when they talked. Instead, he insists that Dr. Wright became very defensive, and when Dennis continued to press him, Dr. Wright ordered him out of his office.

"Why did you file this lawsuit?" Paul asks. Wendy knows that Dennis proposed this question. Paul is against it, convinced that the answer will seem contrived and convince no one. However, Dennis insisted and Paul acquiesced.

"Because no child, no teenager, should ever undergo shock treatment. It's dangerous and it's wrong. Cindy and I want to send a message to psychiatrists everywhere that they cannot do this to teenagers."

"Anything else?"

"I'm also very angry with Dr. Wright for not giving us all the facts about ECT. If he had, we'd never have agreed to it." Dennis pauses while he looks at his hands. He speaks his next words in a low voice, almost to himself. "I should have researched shock therapy myself before signing the consent forms. That one's on me. I owe it to Heather to fight this battle for her and kids like her."

Wendy and Susie exchange knowing looks, impressed by Dennis's strong testimony and apparent sincerity. Maybe there is another side to this man. They watch as Paul retreats to his seat and gives way to Ingram.

There is something defiant in Ingram's movement as he approaches the lectern. However, once he's there, his first words are conciliatory, not the tough questions that Wendy expected. In a gentle voice, he acknowledges that both he and Dr. Wright are truly sorry for his loss. Dennis sits stonily, not reacting to Ingram's sympathetic preamble.

In a casual way, Ingram asks, "If I understand you correctly, you brought this lawsuit to make the world a better place—a safer place. Is that the gist of your last few answers?"

Dennis responds tersely. "Yeah, that's about right." He obviously distrusts Ingram.

"Well, it sounds like you think I misstated something here. Have I?" Ingram asks.

"We don't want other parents to go through what Cindy and I experienced," Dennis says, his voice inappropriately belligerent. "If I can do something to make this less likely to happen, then I'm going to do it."

Ingram steps away from the lectern, walks toward Dennis, and stops about four feet from him. He smiles at Dennis and says confidentially, "You wouldn't be motivated by money, would you?" Ingram casually turns and scans the jurors' faces. He is mocking Dennis and wants them to be a part of it.

"Money is all that our law permits. If everybody took justice into their own hands, we'd have a world of chaos," Dennis replies.

"Did you and Mr. Schofield rehearse that answer?" Ingram asks. Wendy draws a sharp intake of air. This man seems to revel in insulting Dennis, and, by implication, her husband, too. Dennis does not answer.

Undaunted, Ingram continues. "You certainly would not boast to friends that you were going to become a millionaire from this lawsuit, would you?" Ingram asks.

"No," Dennis replies gravely, but Wendy hears some wariness in Dennis's voice.

"Do you have a long-haired friend named Tony that you occasionally drink beers with?" Ingram asks.

Wendy sees apprehension in Dennis's eyes. "I have a lot of friends named Tony," he replies.

"Well, you sat next to this Tony at the Foundry Kitchen and Bar in Elyria on—just a second, let me get the date." Ingram pauses, glances at a document in his hand, and returns his attention to Dennis. "On February 26, 2018, around five in the afternoon. You told Tony you were going to get rich from this lawsuit. Does that refresh your memory?"

Wendy and Susie exchange worried glances. The specificity of Ingram's question suggests that he is aware of a particular incident. Wendy looks to Paul, but he is facing away from her. She can only see his back, which seems to be slightly hunched—like a man ready to take cover.

"You're asking me to remember a conversation that took place over a year ago. I'm sorry, but I have no recollection. Zero," Dennis replies, trying to sound nonchalant.

"Let me help you," Ingram says as he looks at the document again. "You said: 'Yeah, the case will be over and it'll be payday for me.' Do you remember saying those words to Tony?"

Paul springs to his feet and objects. At the same time, Dennis shouts, "I absolutely never said anything like that." Although there is vehemence in Dennis's voice, Wendy noticed that Dennis flinched before he denied Ingram's accusation. No doubt, some of the jurors saw that, too.

"May we approach the bench, Your Honor?" Paul asks.

As Paul rushes to the bench, the judge activates the white noise machine to drown out the conversation between him and the attorneys. Ingram, however, remains at the trial table, engaged in a whispered conversation with his gawky associate. Although Wendy cannot hear what they are saying, Ingram's face is flushed and he points angrily to a wall monitor. With his arms held tightly against his chest, the associate shakes his head. Ingram says something to the young man, who then stuffs some papers in his briefcase and rushes out of the courtroom. As the associate leaves, Ingram makes his way slowly to the bench where the judge and Paul await him.

"I think he just got fired," Susie says.

"What?" Wendy asks.

"I'm pretty good at reading lips," Susie says. "He just told that kid that he's fired."

With so much drama unfolding at the bench, they cannot dwell on that possibility. Although Wendy cannot hear any of the dialogue, she can see that Paul is furious. He first points his right index finger at Ingram's chest and then jabs it perilously close to his opponent's nose. The judge also looks displeased, his bushy gray eyebrows furrowed in consternation. After several minutes, the meeting concludes and the attorneys return to their previous positions like boxers returning to their corners. Paul takes his seat at the trial table while Ingram, once again, stands at the lectern.

The judge clears his throat. "Ladies and gentlemen, you are to disregard that last question and answer. You may not consider it as evidence in this case."

"Is that all the judge is going to say?" Susie whispers incredulously to Wendy. "How can the jury unhear that testimony? I think Paul just got screwed."

Wendy nods. She, too, has a sinking feeling in her gut. Dennis has been exposed for what he is and the jury isn't going to ignore this.

Replaying over and over again what just happened, Wendy has trouble concentrating on the remainder of Ingram's cross-examination. Despite the judge's ruling, Ingram remains on the attack, focusing on entries in Heather's autobiography in which Dennis calls his daughter stupid, lazy, or worthless. Dennis lamely claims that Heather wrote some of these entries in anger after he'd forbidden her to see a nineteen-year-old boy who "was way too old for her."

Ingram ends his cross-examination with admissions that Dennis refused family counseling sessions, visited his daughter sporadically while she was in the hospital, and failed to ask Dr. Wright any questions about ECT before he signed the consent form.

Wendy wonders if Paul will try to rehabilitate Dennis with some questions on redirect. Although that seems like a losing proposition,

Paul stands and apparently will make the attempt. She believes this will be a huge mistake. Paul should just move on.

"Mr. Ingram has questioned you about entries in Heather's autobiography, but he has been very selective in what he's chosen, hasn't he?" Paul asks.

"I think that's true," Dennis says.

For the next few minutes, Paul asks Dennis to comment on entries that depict Dennis in a more sympathetic light. Many are recollections from Heather's childhood: raking leaves with her father, kicking a soccer ball, and a father-daughter dance that they attended when Heather was in junior high school.

Wendy looks at Susie and shakes her head skeptically. Susie nods in agreement. They watch as Paul walks away from the lectern and stands directly between Dennis and Ingram, blocking Ingram's view of the witness.

"Dennis, I know you don't want me to ask this next question, but I am going to anyway," Paul says, and then pauses. "Have you ever been treated for a psychiatric condition?"

Dennis looks away from Paul and does not answer.

In a quiet voice, Paul urges his client to respond.

"Yes, I have," Dennis says, his face exhibiting either embarrassment or shame—Wendy cannot tell which.

"What condition is that?" Paul asks.

"PTSD," Dennis answers.

"Which is . . . ?"

"Post–traumatic stress disorder."

"Where did you get treatment?"

"I got outpatient treatment at the VA hospital in Cleveland for about a year. I had trouble controlling my anger after I returned from Afghanistan. I witnessed some horrible things there."

"Do you still get treatment?"

"No, I haven't been there in years."

Paul ends his questioning there and sits down. After Ingram

declines to inquire further, the judge announces the midafternoon recess.

Susie and Wendy rush to Paul's trial table, intent on finding out what happened during the bench conference with the judge.

"Ingram hired somebody to spy on Dennis. He secretly recorded Dennis saying those things to one of his friends at a bar."

"Oh my God," Susie says. "How did you keep that out?"

"Ingram never sent me a copy. It was a blatant violation of the rules. Ingram claimed that his associate apparently screwed up and failed to send it to me. He told the judge that he'd just fired him on the spot for that mistake."

"I don't think that's what happened," Susie says.

"Well, I don't have time to talk about it right now. I've got to find my next two witnesses, Ms. Ranier, the art teacher, and Shelly Hunter, Heather's best friend. They're out in the hall somewhere and I need to touch base."

A few minutes later, the trial resumes with Eleanor Ranier on the witness stand. Ms. Ranier is a tiny, fragile-looking woman in her sixties with wild gray hair twisting in every direction. To Wendy, this woman looks like the quintessential art teacher, unconventional in appearance and dress. She wears a green blazer over a brightly colored print dress. As if to emphasize her individuality, she completes her ensemble with combat boots that look like they came straight from the army-navy store.

Ms. Ranier tells the jury that Heather was one of the most gifted art students that she'd ever taught, describing some of her pieces as "really magnificent." She thought Heather had a bright future in art.

"How would you describe Heather?" Paul asks.

"Well, I got to know the real Heather," Ms. Ranier says, smiling at the memory. "We loved to talk about art, her pieces, and what she was trying to accomplish. We had a lovely relationship."

"Beyond art, what was she like?"

"Well, she was quiet around the other students. But with me, she was just delightful. She had this unusual, low-pitched laugh that just tickled me. She was always very kind, even when I asked her to critique a fellow classmate's work as we often do in class. She was just a very nice girl. I can't say it any better than that."

When it is Ingram's turn to cross-examine the witness, he asks only a few questions. He first confirms that Ms. Ranier was Heather's middle school art teacher.

"You did not have any contact with Heather after she entered high school?"

"That's correct, but I heard from some of her high school teachers that she was taunted and bullied there. I wish I'd reached out to her. I really regret that."

Ingram frowns. He obviously does not appreciate the gratuitous comment about Heather being bullied. It doesn't fit into his narrative that Heather's abusive father is responsible for her suicide. He thanks the witness and sits down.

Paul's final witness is Shelly Hunter, Heather's friend. She apparently came straight from her Catholic high school, because she is still dressed in a uniform—a black and blue plaid skirt and a white blouse. She looks bewildered as she timidly scans her new surroundings. The girl presses her sweaty palms against her skirt's wool fabric, nervously trying to dry them.

Wendy whispers to Susie, "Paul is taking a gamble with this girl. He hopes that the jury will picture Heather through her friend. But the danger is that she knows a lot about Heather's relationship with her father. He's worked with her, but still, her testimony could turn out to be a disaster when she's cross-examined."

"Not a great way to end your case then," Susie whispers back, giving Wendy's hand a squeeze.

Despite the microphone, Shelly's first responses are barely audible. After Paul reminds her to speak up, she clears her throat and speaks louder. She explains that she and Heather met in kindergarten and, when they discovered that they lived only a block apart, became best friends and spent hours at each other's houses. Shelly liked Heather because she was such a "good listener," never ridiculed other classmates, and refused to join the cliques that other girls found so important.

"What can you tell the jury about Heather's family life?" Paul asks.

"She adored her mom and younger siblings. She thought her mother was very pretty and she wanted to be just like her. She got a kick out of her brother and sister, particularly when they were little." Shelly hesitates and then smiles. "As they got older, they could pester us, but she still loved them and enjoyed taking care of them. She was a good older sister."

"You didn't talk about Heather and her father. What did you observe about that relationship?" Paul asks gently. Wendy's heart begins to pound as she awaits the answer.

"Well, he did set down a lot of rules in that house and he wanted them to be followed," Shelly ventures, but seems reluctant to expand on her answer.

"And how did Heather react to that?" Paul prods.

"She didn't like it. I mean, I don't like my parents' rules either. Heather told me that he would yell at them when they didn't do what they were supposed to do."

"So she didn't like her father?" Paul asks.

"Oh no. I wouldn't say that. Sometimes we'd be in her room with the door closed and he'd open it suddenly and stick his head in and make some crazy face. We'd burst out laughing. Sometimes, her dad was just hilarious."

Susie nudges Wendy and whispers, "How much did Paul pay her to say that?"

Shelly explains that the two became more distant when they attended different high schools. Three months before Heather died, Shelly stopped over at Heather's house unannounced. She was unnerved by what she saw. Heather's skin was a pasty white and her bloodshot eyes revealed that she'd been crying. Although Shelly tried to engage Heather in conversation about school and boys, neither topic interested Heather, who seemed very tired and sad.

"I eventually told her that I had to go and stood up. She opened up her arms and hugged me. I mean, she hugged me hard. She was crying and I just didn't know what was going on."

Although Shelly promised Heather's mom that she'd come again, she never did. "In the end, I wasn't much of a friend."

Paul assures her that she was and concludes his questioning. Thinking that she is done, Shelly stands up.

"Mr. Ingram probably has some questions for you," the judge says. "Please take your seat again."

Ingram shuffles some papers on his trial table, apparently searching for a particular document. "Please just give me a minute, Your Honor." After a few moments of confusion, Ingram stands, straightens his tie, and buttons his suit jacket. He gives the witness a friendly smile and begins by asking Shelly how long she knew Heather.

"About ten years. As I said, since kindergarten."

"And in those ten years you spent considerable time at Heather's house, is that correct?"

"Yes."

"Well, here's the problem as I see it," Ingram says, his voice now stern. "In all that time, you told the jury that you never witnessed any turmoil in Heather's house, just her father making funny faces. Do I have that right?"

Shelly looks troubled by the question, glancing at Paul and then at the floor. "Nobody asked me that question," she says meekly.

"Oh, okay. Then let me ask it," Ingram says, smiling at the jurors. "Did you *ever* witness arguments at the Zurcher house when you were there?"

"I did," Heather says.

"Well, tell us about those times, please."

"Okay, I was over there once or twice a week for many years," Shelly begins, speaking rapidly. "And there was one time when there was yelling. Mr. and Mrs. Zurcher were in their bedroom and they were shouting at each other. We were in the family room and we just kind of ignored it."

"What do you mean—you just kind of ignored it?" Ingram asks.

"Well, Heather tried to make light of it, you know. I could tell she was really embarrassed."

"Weren't there other episodes?" Ingram asks.

"Not that happened in front of me," Shelly says.

"So you're telling this jury that in ten years, you only witnessed one argument." Ingram shakes his head in disbelief. "Is that really your testimony?"

"It is the truth," Shelly says.

His strongarming unsuccessful, Ingram says, "No further questions, Your Honor."

Paul tells the judge that the plaintiff rests and moves for the admission of his exhibits. Ingram asks the judge to throw out the case on a directed verdict, claiming that the plaintiff has not presented sufficient evidence on Dr. Wright's negligence. After Paul briefly summarizes Dr. Masterson's testimony on that point, the judge denies Ingram's motion.

Wendy and Susie watch as the courtroom empties. When the three of them are the only ones still in the courtroom, the women approach Paul, who looks exhausted.

"We've got a million questions for you," Susie says.

"Oh God," Paul replies, holding up his hand in protest. "Before you get started with them, your impressions first, please."

"At one point, I thought you were finished," Wendy says. "A father bragging that he's going to get rich over his daughter's death. That was brutal."

"And . . . ?" Paul prompts.

"After the judge told the jury to disregard what Ingram had said, I felt that there must be something fishy about it," Wendy says.

"Yeah, me too," Susie says. "Like it wasn't reliable."

Paul looks both relieved and pleased. "I hope the jury sees it like that too."

"Hey, what about this PTSD stuff? Where did that come from?" Susie asks. "You never mentioned that to me and I didn't see it in any of the medical records."

"Dennis told me about it this morning. It came out of the blue," Paul says.

"Did Dennis make that up?" Wendy asks.

"I don't know. I've learned not to trust anything he says unless I check it out. But in this instance, I was desperate. I needed to rehabilitate him somehow. I just had to go with it," Paul says.

"Well, it does make Dennis a more sympathetic character—a veteran damaged in the service of his country," Wendy says.

Paul lets out a deep breath. "Guys, I'm really tired. Can we wrap up this postmortem and go home?"

"Not yet," Susie insists. "One last thing. That geeky lawyer who stormed out of the courtroom—he was refusing to do something. I know it. Ingram was really upset. It's like Ingram expected him to project something on the monitors and he wouldn't do it."

"Really?" Paul asks.

"That's what I saw, too," Wendy says.

"Maybe it was the transcript of that conversation," Paul says. "I didn't think that weasel had the guts to defy his boss." Paul rubs his forehead as he contemplates this. "Well, we're only guessing. We'll never know."

Paul gathers up his loose papers and puts them into folders before placing them in his briefcase. As they walk toward the rear of the courtroom, Paul stops at the doors and looks back.

"Day three is over and I still have a shot at this thing," he says. He sets down his briefcase, puts his arms around the two women, and gives their shoulders a squeeze. They respond by leaning into him. Wendy picks up Paul's briefcase and they walk together, side by side, until they reach the elevator.

As they descend, Wendy is very glad that she's experienced a small part of this trial. She's learned something important today: trial momentum swings back and forth, sometimes dramatically, other times erratically, but always unexpectedly. And, unfortunately, this emotional roller coaster lasts until the jurors walk into the courtroom with their verdict.

CHAPTER 27
SEPTEMBER 26, 2019
PAUL SCHOFIELD

Dr. Morgan Samuels, a psychiatrist from the prestigious Arthur Institute of Psychology, appears relaxed sitting in the witness chair. He will be Ingram's only expert witness, but, because of his impressive credentials, he will carry the weight of several doctors. In his late fifties, Dr. Samuels has an engaging smile and athletic build that contrasts with his thick eyeglasses and thinning gray hair. He is a former president of the American Psychiatric Association and the author of over three hundred articles dealing with adolescent psychology and teen suicide.

After establishing Dr. Samuels's extraordinary qualifications, Ingram asks the doctor to provide a short history of ECT. Unlike Dr. Masterson's biting critique, Dr. Samuels describes a procedure that, despite its growing pains, is now able to safely treat a variety of psychiatric and other medical conditions when drugs and psychotherapy fail. Paul is amused when Dr. Samuels goes off subject and enthusiastically describes how ECT has recently been used to treat SIB, an autistic condition involving self-harm behavior. He's convinced that the jury is bored by the doctor's tedious discussion, and, like them, he finds it difficult to concentrate when Dr. Samuels veers onto one of his sidetracks.

"I understand that Dr. Masterson was here yesterday and told the jury that ECT was nothing more than a sham treatment, a placebo of sorts," Dr. Samuels intones. "I'd like to show the jury a video of Jeremy, one of my patients who has SIB. Part of the video was taken before he received ECT and some was filmed after the third treatment."

Paul objects to showing the video, arguing that a young man with SIB has no relevance to a teen who suffered from depression. Judge Hardwig overrules his objection, telling Paul that he opened the door by claiming that ECT was wholly ineffective. "The defense should be allowed to show the other side."

Before playing the short video, Dr. Samuels tells the jury that Jeremy is autistic and intellectually challenged, and, at the time of the video, was nineteen years old. Prior to the video, he went through periods where he slammed his head and body against walls and objects and was physically violent toward his parents. Although the condition had been controlled by medication for a long stretch of time, the medicine stopped working. "Here is Jeremy the day before he underwent his first electroconvulsive treatment."

Suddenly the courtroom monitors show a young man wearing a helmet and running wildly about a room with padded walls. As if the visual is not frightening enough, the man's screams and wild laughter blare from the monitors' speakers. Staring at the camera, the man turns and runs to the opposite wall, slamming his head against it. Paul watches in horror as the young man dashes across the room again, jumps into the air, and, this time, smashes his chest against the wall.

Dr. Samuels pauses the video. "When I restart the video, you will see Jeremy after three ECT treatments."

Paul cannot believe what he sees next; the transformation is nothing short of a miracle. The same man is sitting quietly at a table, talking to his counselor and responding reasonably and calmly to his questions.

"After ECT, Jeremy was able to return to school. He learned how to go to the grocery store by himself, buy items from a list, check out with a debit card, and prepare a meal at home. We never thought any of those things were remotely possible for him," Dr. Samuels says proudly. "We changed his medication and, with periodic ECT maintenance treatments, he has done marvelously."

The jurors stare at Dr. Samuels intently, absorbed by what they have just seen with their own eyes, proof that ECT works. With this three-and-a-half-minute video, Dr. Samuels has refuted Dr. Masterson's claims and exposed him as either an eccentric or, worse, a fraud.

What Paul feels is a combination of panic, dread, and anger. His case has been seriously undermined because he has allowed himself to be dragged along by that fat, pompous ass—Dr. Masterson. Paul realizes that he must take some of the blame as well. To win his case, he never had to prove that ECT was a sham. He simply had to show that Dr. Wright didn't follow standards governing ECT's safe use and failed to warn the family about the Tofranil. Like Sancho Panza, he followed his own Don Quixote down this idiotic path, tilting at windmills.

After shutting off the video, Dr. Samuels tells the jury that Dr. Wright was perfectly justified in pursuing ECT after two trials of antidepressants had failed and the patient's depression continued to be unrelenting and severe. Still reeling from the video, Paul struggles to concentrate on the doctor's testimony. However, Paul listens as Dr. Samuels insists that other, less important standards governing ECT are nothing more than window dressing. Dr. Wright has followed the most critical one, and, therefore, was not negligent.

Unfortunately, Dr. Samuels is not finished with his testimony. Since he is an expert on teen suicide, Ingram asks him whether any psychiatrist could have prevented Heather's suicide. Paul understands that Ingram is attempting to give the jury another reason to find in his favor. Even if the jury finds that Dr. Wright was negligent, his actions—negligent or otherwise—did not lead to Heather's death.

"The sad truth is that psychiatrists can't always prevent suicides. That's just an unreasonable expectation," Dr. Samuels says. He educates the jury about teen suicide, explaining that children with mood disorders are extremely vulnerable, and even more so if they have made a prior attempt to take their own life.

"There is almost always a stressful event that precedes the suicide attempt. This can be the loss of a girlfriend or boyfriend, disciplinary problems at school, or family difficulties," Dr. Samuels says.

"What likely happened here?" Ingram asks.

"I'd conclude that something stressful occurred at the Zurcher home. Heather had been home for about a week, no longer in the hospital's safe environment. She hadn't left the house, so that eliminates all other options."

"Can you eliminate Dr. Wright as the cause?" Ingram asks.

"Absolutely. He'd done everything he could. The parents had stopped their daughter's last hope, ECT, and then they'd taken Heather out of the hospital against their doctor's advice. They were supposed to safeguard the medication and keep a close watch on their daughter." Dr. Samuels lifts his eyebrows to emphasize his next statement. "Those weren't Dr. Wright's responsibilities; those were the parents'. And, of course, we don't know what stressful event happened at their home, but we know that it almost certainly occurred there."

After Ingram concludes his direct exam, Judge Hardwig announces the midmorning recess. As soon as the jury leaves, Paul feverishly reviews his notes for his upcoming cross-examination, highlighting some points and crossing out others. He knows that the case hinges on how well he can neutralize Dr. Samuels's testimony. Lacking the funds to depose Dr. Samuels prior to trial, he has secured several of Dr. Samuels's depositions from other cases—a poor man's substitute. He doubts that this will be enough.

As he reorders his points, Dennis interrupts him, claiming that the video is a fraud and Paul needs to expose this.

"How the hell am I supposed to do that?" Paul snaps. "For God's sake, just leave me alone and let me organize my thoughts."

For once, Dennis does not argue and slinks away.

A few minutes later, Paul faces Dr. Samuels for the most important cross-examination of his career. The first order of business is to discredit the video. He begins by gaining an admission that Heather suffered from depression and not the destructive autistic behavior known as SIB.

"She was not thrashing about in a padded room—banging her head against walls and biting caregivers?" Paul asks.

Dr. Samuels smiles and calmly agrees.

"She was tranquil and talked reasonably to her nurses and doctors, right?"

"Well, of course. She was also undergoing psychotherapy, which, in layman's terms, means talk therapy."

Paul realizes that he hasn't gained much ground, nothing more than a foothold at the base of a steep cliff. He next confirms that Dr. Samuels received a second opinion from another psychiatrist before he commenced ECT with his patient Jeremy—something required by the standards. After some initial resistance, Dr. Samuels concedes that Dr. Wright did not do this for Heather. When Dr. Samuels claims that this is an inconsequential departure from safe practices, Paul gains another admission that these standards are minimum requirements, not optional.

Paul is just about to move on to another topic when he recalls something Dr. Samuels said during his direct examination—that Jeremy required maintenance ECT. Did Dr. Samuels hesitate before disclosing this? Paul thinks that he did, but he concedes that he might be imagining this. Nevertheless, he decides to follow his gut feeling and take the biggest gamble yet in the trial. Was Dr. Samuels trying to hide the number of Jeremy's maintenance ECT treatments from the jury?

Although Paul has never bluffed during a trial, he will today. He does not trust Dr. Samuels to respond honestly to his next question. Holding up some stapled papers that have nothing to do with medicine, Paul says, "At the break, I asked my assistant to get me a copy of your published article about Jeremy." He points to Susie, sitting in the front row, who dutifully smiles back. "Dr. Samuels, how often does Jeremy receive ECT treatments?"

The doctor does not immediately respond but merely gives Paul an uneasy smile. Attempting to hide his mounting anxiety, Paul maintains a stern expression. If Dr. Samuels asks to review the *article* in Paul's hand, his ruse will be exposed. Not only will Paul look foolish, but he'll likely lose all credibility with the jury.

Paul urges the doctor to answer, almost goading him. "Come on, Doctor, Jeremy first received ECT in 2012, seven years ago. He's been your patient ever since. How often does he still get that treatment?"

Dr. Samuels looks sheepish but finally responds. "He gets the treatment about once every eight or nine days." Trying to make light of the number, he says, "And with excellent results, I might add."

Paul cannot hide his astonishment. He walks over to a blackboard and wheels it to a spot where the judge, the witness, and the jury can see the board. With chalk in hand, Paul computes the math. When he is done, he says, "Let's see. Forty treatments a year for the last seven and a half years is three hundred and four treatments. Did I get that right?"

There is no bravado in the doctor's voice as he quietly agrees. Paul pushes his advantage and spends the next few minutes establishing that ECT will continue for the rest of Jeremy's life, that Dr. Samuels does not know the cumulative effect of near-weekly general anesthesia upon Jeremy's health, and that the cost of the treatment as of today is close to a million dollars. When Paul looks at the jurors, several are either nodding or smiling at him.

"Yesterday, Dr. Masterson told the jury that ECT does not have any long-lasting effects on a patient. Would that also be the case with Jeremy?"

"Jeremy's case is not the norm, Mr. Schofield," Dr. Samuels snaps. "And it is very unfair for you to imply otherwise."

Paul smiles, enjoying Dr. Samuels's discomfort. "Wait a minute, Doctor, you chose to showcase Jeremy's case as an ECT success story, not me."

"Objection. Where's the question?" Ingram says.

"I'll get to my next question," Paul says, feeling an energy that seemed impossible twenty minutes earlier.

On the fly, he just delivered one of the best cross-examinations of his career. He knocked Dr. Samuels off his pedestal and gave the jury a reason to be wary of this man's opinions, showing that Dr. Samuels was hiding facts from them. However, Paul will have to do much more if he wants a chance of winning the case. The danger, of course, is that a skilled witness like Dr. Samuels can regain his footing, reestablish his dominance, and convince the jury that he is right. But Paul feels confident. The time to deliver more blows is now—when Dr. Samuels is still reeling.

Over the next fifteen minutes, Paul gains admissions that Dr. Wright ignored five standards governing ECT and Tofranil. Although Dr. Samuels is initially reluctant to criticize the informed consent form that Dr. Wright required the Zurchers to sign, he eventually concedes that the form is defective because it does not warn about death or permanent memory loss. A few minutes later, the doctor grudgingly concedes that he would not have prescribed Tofranil to a teenager. Still later, he says that he would have done more to convince the parents to keep their daughter in the hospital. Even though Dr. Wright broke these *rules*, Dr. Samuels steadfastly maintains that Dr. Wright was not negligent.

Paul must take his cross-examination one step farther. He must show the jury why Dr. Samuels will not change his opinion, despite evidence of Dr. Wright's substandard care.

"Your fees for testifying today are being paid by the defense, are they not?" Paul asks.

"Yes, I'm being paid for my time, not my testimony. I review the facts and let the chips fall where they may," Dr. Samuels says in a practiced tone.

When Paul asks the doctor how often he testifies for the defense in malpractice cases, the doctor shrugs and claims that he doesn't know.

"Really? You don't know?" Paul asks.

"My secretary keeps track of that. Maybe once a year," Dr. Samuels says.

Pulling out a deposition given by Dr. Samuels from another case, Paul hands a copy of it to the doctor, opened to highlighted testimony. "Here, let me refresh your memory from a deposition that you gave five months ago. In that deposition, you were asked to bring records of your medical-legal consultations for the last ten years and you provided a list that identified ninety-two cases."

"Well, I stand corrected," Dr. Samuels says, attempting to sound surprised. Turning his gaze to the jury, he explains, "I really don't keep track of this stuff. It's just not important to me."

One juror raises her eyebrows in disbelief while several others fold their arms against their chest. Paul knows that he's making significant progress.

"And out of those ninety-two cases, you were always testifying for the defense, right?" Paul asks.

"Yes, but there are times when I review the facts, conclude that the doctor was negligent, and refuse to get involved," Dr. Samuels says sanctimoniously.

"Oh, you do," Paul says skeptically. "But in the ninety-two cases of which there are *actual* records, you told a jury that either the psychiatrist did nothing wrong or that his actions did not injure or kill the patient. Correct?"

"Yes."

Paul has made his point. Dr. Samuels is biased in favor of the defense. Like many defense experts, Dr. Samuels sees himself as the knight in shining armor—the hero who aids a fellow doctor in distress. Not only is this financially lucrative for him, but it feeds his enormous ego.

Turning to the second prong of Dr. Samuels's testimony, Paul will attack the doctor's opinion about causation. He will begin by confronting Dr. Samuels with statistics cited in one of the doctor's own medical articles.

Dr. Samuels confirms that about two million adolescents attempt suicide each year, but only two thousand of these attempts result in death. He also agrees that only one-third of the attempts require any urgent medical care.

"Given that 99.9 percent of suicide attempts are not fatal, can we conclude that the majority of teenagers do not really intend to take their own lives?" Paul asks.

"Yes."

"It's a cry for help? A cry for change?"

"It can be, yes."

Focusing the doctor on Heather's suicide attempt, Paul reviews the facts of that incident with him. The doctor understands that Heather crawled from her bedroom to a hallway before she collapsed. He also acknowledges that while this was happening, her family sat in the family room watching television.

"In your communications with Mr. Ingram, did he tell you how close Heather had crawled toward her family before she collapsed?" Paul asks.

Dr. Samuels says, "Let me check my correspondence." For the next minute, the doctor busies himself by scanning through letters and notes in his file. Finally, he says, "I can't see that he did, but I can't say for sure."

"Could that information be important in determining whether Heather wanted to be saved after she ingested the pills?"

"I really don't know," Dr. Samuels says, his face tense.

"She was just out of their field of vision, not more than twenty-five feet away. What does that tell you?" Paul asks.

"I don't want to speculate," Dr. Samuels says, shaking his head.

"You had no trouble speculating that a stressful event in the Zurcher home precipitated the suicide attempt, right?"

No longer the confident witness, Dr. Samuels looks diminished and tired. His eyes flutter before he speaks. "That's completely different," he says. "I'm basing that on statistics and studies."

Ignoring the answer, Paul asks, "Do you think she wanted help?"

"I don't know," Dr. Samuels says with a sigh.

"Do you think she wanted the drug reaction reversed?" Paul asks, his voice louder as he moves closer to the witness.

"I don't know. What more can I say?"

"She wasn't on her way to get a snack from the kitchen, was she?" Paul asks, mocking the doctor now.

"No."

Paul speaks in a whisper. "She wanted to live. She wanted to live, didn't she?"

"I wish I knew," Dr. Samuels says.

"Heather had no idea that this drug was more lethal than any others that Dr. Wright had prescribed?" Paul asks.

The doctor does not respond immediately.

"She couldn't possibly have known, could she?" Paul presses.

"Probably true," Dr. Samuels says, staring at his hands.

Paul repeats the doctor's answer and sits down. On the witness stand, Dr. Samuels looks beaten; he shakes his head and closes his eyes momentarily.

Undaunted, Ingram decides to conduct a redirect examination to rehabilitate his witness. However, he wisely keeps the exam short, merely asking the doctor if any of his opinions have changed because of Paul's cross-examination. The doctor dutifully answers that they have not.

After lunch, Ingram calls Dr. Wright to the stand. Again, the questions and answers seem rote and unimportant. The jury seems bored by the doctor's self-serving explanations about his treatment. And they appear even more uninterested when he explains why he altered the discharge summary. Sensing that the jurors have heard enough, Paul declines to cross-examine Dr. Wright.

Paul has no illusions that the jury will definitely find in his favor. This is still very much an open question, but, as the trial is reaching its end, he will soon get the answer. After the midafternoon break, he and Ingram will give their closing arguments and then the case will finally be in the hands of the jury.

CHAPTER 28
SEPTEMBER 26, 2019
ROBERT INGRAM AND PAUL SCHOFIELD

As Paul Schofield delivers his closing argument, Robert Ingram sits at his trial table, edgy and distracted. He's plagued by the promises he's made to Emily McDonald and Dr. Wright. Like a fool, he's predicted victory. And now he could lose a case that everyone expects him to win.

None of this is his fault, however. Who could have foreseen that his associate would betray him at a critical moment? He needed Wilchuck to post Dennis Zurcher's incriminating statement on the courtroom monitors and then the little shit lacked the guts to do it. Then this morning, Dr. Samuels fell apart during cross-examination. Time and again, Schofield trapped him, making him look like a total shill by the time he skulked out of the courtroom.

Ingram barely listens as Schofield summarizes the evidence on negligence and proximate cause. His opponent seems tired, his voice lacking emotion. Schofield's earlier battle with Dr. Samuels has probably sapped some energy from him—the only good thing to result from the doctor's unimpressive time on the witness stand.

An even-keeled Schofield returns to his "rules of the road" analogy, something he introduced in his opening statement. Using the court's video presenter, he projects six rules on the monitors, standards that Dr. Wright allegedly violated. For each rule, he quickly summarizes the evidence on each point. Next, Schofield moves on to Dr. Wright's alteration of the records, something he calls a signed confession of fault. Ingram is so tired of this story that he could scream. He scrunches his shoulders in a *So what* gesture and hopes that at least one juror notices his exasperation.

When Schofield begins his discussion of money damages, Ingram perks up and begins taking notes. Although Schofield is very businesslike as he discusses numbers, Ingram can sense that the jurors are shocked by the final figure—a request for two and a half million dollars. His opponent has gone too far. For the first time that day, Ingram feels energy pulsing through his body. He can exploit Schofield's money grab and regain the advantage.

And then suddenly, Schofield stops and reserves the remainder of his time for rebuttal, as allowed by the rules. Schofield has used only twenty-five of his allotted forty-five minutes, an unorthodox move from Ingram's standpoint. He expected his opponent to lose track of time, like most undisciplined plaintiff's attorneys, and be left with only a few minutes for rebuttal. But not Schofield. That clever bastard will have twenty minutes to make a final push to sway the jury. That thought makes Ingram uneasy, but there is nothing he can do about it. His job is to focus on his own presentation, destroy the plaintiff's case, and make Schofield's last appeal meaningless.

After thanking the jurors for their attention throughout the trial, Ingram tells them that this is not a difficult case to decide. He shakes his head and looks sympathetically at the jury.

"Heather Zurcher was a troubled girl—a severely depressed teenager whose depression was deepening despite every available treatment known to medicine: psychotherapy, group counseling, antidepressants, and even ECT. Dr. Wright did not create this tragic situation; he inherited it and tried to fix it. It's not his fault that he could not cure Heather Zurcher. No one could and it is terribly unfair to blame him for this. But in America, people like Dennis Zurcher file frivolous lawsuits every day, clogging our courtrooms and doing their best to subvert justice."

Ingram pauses as he slowly scans the jurors' faces. "I want to be totally direct with all of you," he says, his voice and eyes brimming with sincerity. "There is something terribly wrong about this case. We've all felt it from the very beginning." Like a seasoned actor, his voice suddenly becomes indignant. "This lawsuit was brought by Heather's father, a man who made her life a holy hell." He spits out each word bitterly to show his distaste and then spreads one arm in a grand gesture of scorn. "And now, he wants to be rewarded for his abusive behavior. Unbelievable, isn't it?"

He allows his words to sink in before he turns his back on the jury and faces Dennis Zurcher and Schofield. Like the preacher ready to shame a member of his congregation, he points his finger at Dennis Zurcher. "This is the man Heather called a monster and he wants to profit from her death." He pivots and faces the jury again. "This is sick. This is perverted. I can't believe Mr. Schofield had the audacity to ask you for money. It's so twisted."

Ingram feels the effect of his words upon the jury. They, too, look troubled. "Can you believe that Mr. Schofield asked you to award money for mental anguish and loss of companionship? It shocks the conscience, doesn't it? My God, Dennis Zurcher brought this misery upon himself by his own reprehensible behavior.

"But that doesn't seem to bother Mr. Schofield. He wants you to award two and a half million dollars to the man who made his daughter's life a living nightmare." Ingram shakes his head in disbelief. "Folks, you did not leave your brains in the parking lot when you entered this courthouse. Give money to this man? What could be more vile than that? Frankly, I can't think of anything."

He's reaching the jurors. Not only can he see it in their faces, but he feels it. He feeds off their energy and his words come spontaneously, spilling out one after another. For the next twenty minutes, he summarizes the evidence, spinning it wildly in his favor. Whenever he feels a juror's interest beginning to wane, he talks about Dennis Zurcher again, reminding the panel of Dennis's unworthiness to receive a penny from this lawsuit. When Ingram sits, he knows he has delivered one of the best closing arguments of his career. He will win this case.

Rising slowly, Paul Schofield looks thoughtful and calm. He is not surprised that Ingram focused on Dennis in his closing argument and pounded him relentlessly. It is why Paul reserved twenty minutes for rebuttal. But Paul underestimated Ingram's rhetorical skills and was caught off guard by his opponent's passion and persuasiveness. Although Paul has a planned response, he worries that it may not be enough.

"That was quite a closing argument you just heard," Paul begins. "Very moving, very emotional, and very persuasive. It was also very clever." He pauses and flicks his eyebrows to emphasize his point. "It was designed to divert you from the real issues in this case." He gently points his finger at the jury, as if to remind them. "Did Dr. Wright make mistakes? And if so, did those mistakes cost Heather Zurcher her life?"

Gesturing toward his opponent, Paul says, "Mr. Ingram didn't really talk about that, did he? No, he fired away at Dennis Zurcher, as I knew he would—I daresay, as you knew he would.

"He attacked Dennis Zurcher and told you he was a flawed individual. That's nothing new. We haven't hidden that from you. After a tour of duty, Dennis came home from Afghanistan a different person. Post–traumatic stress disorder can do that to people, gives them a hair-trigger temper that can last a lifetime. Dennis took the witness stand and admitted to his faults and his mistakes with Heather. He spoke of his regrets."

The jurors are listening, but Paul sees skepticism in many of their faces. He needs them to distrust Ingram if he hopes to win them back. "Here is where Mr. Ingram tried to deceive you," Paul says, his voice low and controlled. "Dennis Zurcher's behavior is not a defense to Dr. Wright's negligence. When Judge Hardwig reads the jury instructions to you, that won't be in there.

"What is Mr. Ingram really saying?" Paul asks. He focuses on one juror and asks, "What is he trying to sell you?" There is an intensity in Paul's eyes now. "He's telling you that you don't have to hold a doctor accountable for his recklessness. Yes, just ignore his behavior, even when his mistakes cost a young girl her life. It's allowed—says Mr. Ingram—because the patient's father has many flaws." For the first time, Paul's face reflects outrage. "Well, that's not the law and it never will be."

Although he's said it several times, Paul reminds the jurors that their job is to assess Dr. Wright's actions and whether they led to Heather's death. He, again, tells them that Heather, although playing a dangerous game, wanted to be saved—something that was impossible because of Dr. Wright's mistakes.

Paul reads disappointment in the faces of several jurors. They've heard this before and hearing it again is not swaying them. He needs to empower the jurors, make them believe that their decision will have far-reaching consequences.

"Let's get one thing straight: Dr. Wright never warned Cindy Zurcher about the Tofranil. Does he own up to this? Of course not. Instead, he commits fraud, deliberately altering the medical records." Paul does not have to manufacture anger at this; he feels it. "Then, when I ask him about this in his deposition, he out-and-out lies." Before Paul delivers his next words, he pivots and looks directly at Dr. Wright. "He lies *under oath* to deceive me and try to save himself.

"But Mr. Ingram is telling you to give Dr. Wright a free pass here by finding in his favor." He pauses and shakes his head incredulously. "You simply cannot do that." Paul stops again and, this time, scans their faces one by one. "You are the conscience of the community. A jury speaks through its verdict. And when it does, everyone must pay attention: doctors, lawyers, politicians—everyone." His voice becomes solemn. "What kind of message will you send if you allow doctors to change their records and lie about it under oath? This is wrong and will always be wrong. You can't condone this."

He knows he may have gone too far. Some jurors may find his statements grandiose, while others may be offended, believing that Paul is lumping all doctors with Dr. Wright. But, at this point, what choice does he have?

He scans the jury again, trying to assess whether he's regained their trust. Several jurors still will not meet his eyes. The stumbling block must be Dennis. For obvious reasons, they find it repugnant to award any money to him.

The irony is that he feels the same way. If there is a money verdict, Paul wants Dennis to receive as little of it as possible. And, if things work as planned, this is exactly what will happen. Perhaps he can hint at that possibility. He isn't sure how to do that, but he hopes that the right words will come as he talks.

"I want to return to Mr. Ingram's closing argument once again. He told you not to award any money to this family because Dennis Zurcher is so undeserving." Looking at one of the two jurors who wouldn't meet his eyes earlier, he asks rhetorically, "Isn't that, in essence, what he told you?" The juror feels Paul's stare and glances up at him.

"Okay, he can make that argument. I expected him to make that argument, but he's ignoring that there are three other members in that family who have suffered," Paul says, now turning his attention to the other juror who ignored him moments before. She looks at him and nods.

Paul continues. "Cindy Zurcher lives in pain every day. And is Cindy some kind of monster? You heard testimony from Heather's best friend, and what did she tell you? Heather loved her mother and wanted to be just like her. That tells you all you need to know about that relationship.

"What about Heather's siblings, Travis and Melissa? You learned that Heather loved them very much and they loved her back. These are relationships that should have lasted for decades and generated countless memories. Instead, their time together was cut drastically short and the memory that will be burned in their minds forever is the sight of Heather in the hallway, clinging to life. An awful thing for anyone to experience, let alone young children.

"They were also in the emergency room when the doctor told the family that Heather had died. That's a horrible memory. These are scars that they'll bear for the rest of their lives. But, according to Mr. Ingram, they, too, are undeserving of a single penny."

Paul glances at Ingram for a moment. "Mr. Ingram wants you to believe that all of the money awarded in this case goes straight into Dennis Zurcher's pocket. Well, there's something Mr. Ingram did not tell you—something he did not want to tell you. When you deliberate, you make one award for the entire family and someone else divides the money between the family members."

Although Paul and Ingram have addressed the jurors for over an hour, Paul has their attention. They are intensely interested in what will happen if they make an award to this family. "This is a wrongful death case and the Lorain County probate judge decides how the funds are to be divided, all of it." Paul pauses and smiles. "Does that surprise you? After you reach your verdict, Judge James Walker, one floor below us, will decide if Dennis Zurcher receives any money."

Ingram stands and objects. "Your Honor, this is highly improper. You tell the jury what the law is, not Mr. Schofield. His closing argument has gone well beyond a discussion of the evidence and you need to rein him in."

Judge Hardwig trains his turquoise eyes on Ingram and scowls.

Recognizing that he has offended the judge, Ingram tries to backtrack. "I mean I would *respectfully* ask this court to curtail his discussion of the law."

Considering the objection, the judge looks toward the ceiling and then down at his bench. Finally, he says, "So far, I haven't heard Mr.

Schofield misstate the law. I'll allow him to go a little farther, but be careful, Mr. Schofield."

"Thank you, Your Honor. I'm just about done," Paul says. "As I told you, the probate judge will decide how much money any particular family member will receive from your verdict. The probate judge will hear evidence about Heather's relationship with each family member. The judge can also receive written documents—for example, Heather's autobiography. Then, after considering all of that, he'll divide the funds as he deems fair. That is his job, not yours."

Some of the jurors seem relieved—at least, that is Paul's impression. He glances at Dennis, who does not appear upset by his last comments. Knowing Dennis, he probably believes that he can control the narrative reaching the probate judge. And, if not, he'll ultimately control the funds awarded to his wife and children, as he does with everything else in their lives.

Before he sits down, Paul tells the jurors that he is confident that they will return a verdict in favor of the Zurcher family. "Not only will you render justice for this family, but you will send a message to everyone about ECT and about doctors who dishonestly change their records for their own benefit. Thank you for your attention."

After a brief recess, the judge reads the jury instructions to the panel. At around four, the jury retreats to its jury room. The judge tells the attorneys that he will send the jurors home around five, giving them just enough time to elect a foreperson and briefly discuss the case.

When it is five o'clock, the judge adjourns for the day. As expected, the jury has not reached a verdict. They will reconvene the following day at nine. In all likelihood, the verdict will come tomorrow. For Paul, it will be a sleepless night, replaying the trial in his head and thinking of all the things he should have done differently. But for now, as he packs up his briefcase, he is relieved that his part is over. Now it is up to the jury.

CHAPTER 29
SEPTEMBER 27, 2019
WENDY SCHOFIELD, ROBERT INGRAM, AND PAUL SCHOFIELD

As their morning begins, the four members of the Schofield family sit at the kitchen table, slightly bedraggled and lost in thought. Dressed in a skirt and blazer (her preferred secretarial garb), Wendy wordlessly spoons oatmeal into her mouth. As if playing a board game, the girls push cut pieces of toast around on their plates. Wendy glances at Paul to see if he's touched the now cold scrambled eggs that she set in front of him twenty minutes earlier. He hasn't.

In a few minutes, she will see the girls off for school and leave for Paul's office, where she will hold down the fort while Paul awaits the verdict in the courtroom. She wishes that she could wait with him, but someone needs to answer the phone and interact with clients.

Wendy barely slept the night before, her thoughts dominated by the jury that will determine not just the Zurchers' fate but their own. Likewise, Paul didn't sleep much last night. When she trudged into the kitchen at four a.m. for a glass of milk, he was in the family room watching one of the many *Rocky* movies. She hoped it was the one where Rocky knocked out his opponent. Optimism is in short supply in their house and any dose, even fictional, is welcome.

Their balloon payment is due in about six weeks. They have a plan if Paul loses this case. They'll sell the house and hope to stave off bankruptcy. She fears that bankruptcy would spell disaster for Paul's legal career. To their clients and potential clients, bankruptcy screams mismanagement and incompetence. She imagines that Paul's clients will abandon him in greater numbers than after his uncle's death.

Glancing at her husband again, she sees that he's pushed the plate of uneaten food away from him. "Do you want me to dump it all in the garbage disposal?" she asks.

Paul nods. As Wendy reaches for his plate, her elbow catches Alyssa's glass, causing it to tumble and spill orange juice all over the table. "Damn it, damn it, damn it," Wendy says as she rushes to grab a dish towel. As she begins wiping up the mess, she looks at the girls. "I'm sorry I said those bad words. I guess I'm even more nervous about your dad's case than he is." And then as an afterthought, she adds, "But that's no excuse."

The girls smile but say nothing. Looking at them, Wendy can see only their crooked teeth. She forces a smile at Paul. "You'll call me immediately after you get a verdict, won't you?"

He nods.

"Good or bad. I want to know right away. Okay?"

"I promise," he says. "I'll even let you know if the jury comes back with a question before the verdict."

"Oh, yes. Please do that," Wendy says. She knows that these questions often give lawyers their first glimpse of how the jury intends to resolve the case.

"Did you bring the Fowler file home for me?" Paul asks as he stands up from the table. "I'll work on it while I wait for the jury."

"It's in the study," Wendy says. "That man calls every day. I try to sweet-talk him, but he's definitely getting impatient with you." Mr. Fowler is just one of many clients whom Paul has ignored while focusing on the Zurcher case. Until Paul completes their legal work, they will not be paying him, further compounding his cash flow problems.

When Paul returns with the file, he sets it down on the kitchen table. "Oh geez, I forgot that was wet," he says, wiping the file with his hand before setting it on his chair. With his hands free, he hugs his wife and kisses his daughters on the tops of their heads.

Wendy gives him a thumbs-up as he walks out the door. "You'll call me, remember," she says, hoping that she doesn't sound like a nag, but she needs to know as soon as he does. She watches as her husband walks to his car, turns to her, and gives her a final wave.

●●●

Checking his emails, Robert Ingram sits on a bench in the Justice Center's hallway, outside Judge Hardwig's courtroom. He can feel the sun's warmth as it streams through the long rectangular windows that reach from the floor to the ceiling. Although juries are unpredictable, he feels reasonably certain that this jury will rule in his favor.

Two hours pass without incident as the jury deliberates again this morning. Schofield sits in a small conference room outside the courtroom, apparently trying to focus on other legal work, while Ingram's client, the charming Dr. Wright, sits in the courtroom, presumably reading a book. He can't keep track of the Zurchers, who are sometimes in the courtroom, other times in the hallway, or occasionally in the elevator on their way for some fresh air or a smoke. Anyway, they are Schofield's responsibility to locate in case of a verdict, not his.

Ingram is answering an email from one of his girlfriends when he feels someone press a hand on his left shoulder. Startled, he looks up to see Judge Hardwig's bailiff, Frank McCloskey, towering over him.

Taking in McCloskey's solemn expression, Ingram's feeling of confidence vanishes and a wave of anxiety flushes through him. "What do you have for me, Frank?" Ingram asks, his voice tense.

"You're in trouble," McCloskey says loud enough for anyone in the hall to hear.

Ingram cringes as he surveys the people in their vicinity, trying to determine if any are connected to the Zurcher case. None of them are. Doesn't this idiot realize that he needs to be discreet? "We can't talk here, Frank. We need to go somewhere more private," Ingram says.

Ingram points to the end of the hall in front of another courtroom where no one is milling about. An overweight man with a sizeable paunch, McCloskey waddles alongside Ingram as they make their way to the more private area. Ingram can't help but notice that the bailiff's sports jacket clashes with both his shirt and his tie. Why does he have to associate with losers like McCloskey, a man who failed in his office supply business and lost handily in his one attempt to become an Elyria councilman?

But McCloskey is his mole, and a very useful one at that. When they golfed together a few weeks ago, McCloskey promised to keep Ingram apprised of the jury's deliberations. As a bailiff, McCloskey routinely interacts with juries during their deliberations and learns of their progress. In previous trials, McCloskey has fed Ingram invaluable information about developments in the jury room.

When they are isolated at the far end of the hallway, Ingram asks, "Okay. What's going on with the jury?"

His face grim, McCloskey raises his eyebrows and says, "Well, I always check on the jury around eleven to see if I need to order them lunch. When I went in, the foreperson—you know, that woman with frizzy hair—tells me that they've reached a verdict and are working on damages. She tells me to order lunch, but that they might not need it."

If the jury is working on damages, Ingram realizes that the jury has found in favor of the plaintiff. "Oh shit," Ingram says, more to himself than McCloskey. "What kind of numbers were they talking about? Did you hear?"

"The foreperson had a piece of paper in front of her and she'd written down some numbers on it. I couldn't get a good look at it, but I think that all of the numbers were over a million dollars."

"Tell me more about those numbers," Ingram demands.

"I don't know. She had four or five numbers on the paper with dollar signs in front of them. Like I said, they all appeared to be in the millions of dollars. I don't know if she went around the table and asked each juror to give her a number. I'm just guessing here, Bob. That's all I can tell you."

"And you didn't ask her any additional questions?" Ingram asks, visibly upset that McCloskey is unable to provide more details. Ingram shakes his head at McCloskey, communicating his displeasure with the bailiff's incompetence.

"Sorry, Bob, that's all I got. I thought that would be enough," McCloskey says. He sounds like a child who expected a parent's praise but has been roundly criticized instead.

"It'll have to do," Ingram says as he turns abruptly and walks away from the bailiff. While on the move, Ingram grabs his iPhone from his breast pocket and dials his insurance adjuster's phone number.

* * *

Paul hears someone knock and then open the witness room door. Paul does not look up from his file, expecting Dennis to be there with one of his inane questions about the jury deliberations. Instead, Ingram stands there, halfway in the hall and halfway in the room.

"Can I talk to you for a minute?" Ingram asks, his voice surprisingly cautious and respectful.

"Sure," Paul says. "Do we have a verdict?"

"Oh no, nothing like that," Ingram replies. "But I do have some news that may interest you."

"Oh," Paul says.

"The insurance company wants to make an offer."

"Why now?" Paul asks as he pushes his chair away from the table.

"To be perfectly honest with you, I think they're getting a little nervous," Ingram says, and then shakes his head. "They expected a defense verdict, like, within an hour, and they're getting antsy." He smiles and then laughs. "Insurance companies—I don't try to figure them out anymore."

By Ingram's easy demeanor, Paul senses that the offer will be next to nothing—a meaningless gesture meant to irritate rather than resolve anything. Paul decides to play along; he doesn't have any other choice. "So what's the big offer?"

"Four hundred and fifty thousand dollars," Ingram says, and raises his eyebrows as if to emphasize that this is a significant sum.

Paul's pulse quickens as the number sinks in. He expected much less, maybe one hundred thousand dollars, but Ingram's figure is not trivial. He quickly calculates his attorney fee from the proposal and realizes that it might just be enough to rescue him from his impending financial disaster. However, he will feign disinterest. Paul shrugs and says, "Oh."

"Is that all you can say?" Ingram says. "In my opinion, it's a gift and totally against my recommendation."

"Well, you're going to have to do better than that to interest us," Paul says.

Ingram masks his surprise with a frown. "Well, aren't you the tough guy. If I were in your shoes, I wouldn't be so cavalier."

Paul decides to maintain his bluster. "I could sell them on six hundred thousand a lot easier than four hundred and fifty thousand. You know my client."

When Ingram smiles, Paul knows that he's blundered. Ingram apparently realizes that if Paul can work with six hundred thousand dollars, he can do the same with four hundred and fifty thousand. Ingram's smile quickly fades and his face takes on a resolute air. "Let me be perfectly clear. The insurance company will pay four hundred and fifty thousand dollars and not a penny more. I can commiserate with you about your client, but that's not the issue. Either he takes what's offered or we see what the jury does."

Paul says, "Of course, I'll communicate your offer to my client. I'm duty-bound to do that, but don't hold your breath."

"One more thing: The insurance company doesn't want this to drag out all morning. They want an answer right away. They told me to give a deadline of fifteen minutes for your reply."

"You've got to be kidding," Paul says.

"I know that sounds like a pressure tactic and I don't like it any more than you do. Believe me, I'm not going to be sitting here with a stopwatch, but you get the idea. It's a one-time offer, no negotiating. Those are my instructions."

Paul's head feels like it is being squeezed in a vise. Time is of the essence; the jury could reach a decision at any minute. He despises what the insurance company is doing to him, but he understands the dynamics and will have to deal with it.

"This is unrealistic. My clients will have a thousand questions," Paul replies as he quickly gathers his papers from the small table and puts them in his briefcase.

Ingram shakes his head. "From my experience, the only question your clients will ask is how much money they'll net after expenses and attorney fees. Everything else is just window dressing." As if to emphasize his point, he gives Paul a condescending smile.

Ingram's cynicism irritates Paul. "It's not that easy and you know it."

"Well, go answer their questions then. I'll advise the judge about our offer and wait for you in his chambers." As if to further goad Paul, Ingram makes a show of glancing at his wristwatch.

Paul rushes from the witness room and brings his clients from the back of the courtroom to the same room where he and Ingram just talked. The three sit down, Paul on one side of the table and the Zurchers on the other.

Paul explains that the defendant, through his insurance carrier, has made a one-time, take-it-or-leave-it offer. When Dennis asks why, Paul provides the same explanation that Ingram gave him.

"They are offering four hundred fifty thousand dollars to resolve the case at this time," Paul says, looking directly at Dennis. "My fee is one-third and we have expenses of approximately twenty-five thousand dollars. The expenses are deducted from your share of the settlement, meaning that you would net approximately two hundred seventy-five thousand dollars." Paul does not disclose that he has a co-counsel arrangement with Scott Worthington that will reduce his share of the attorney fee from $150,000 to $90,000.

"This offer is an insult," Dennis says, slamming his right hand against the tabletop. "Is that all Heather's life is worth? If so, they can all go to hell."

Trying to calm his client, Paul explains that the insurance company's offer is not a valuation of their daughter's life. Instead, it reflects many factors: the uncertainty of a plaintiff's verdict, the jury's difficulty in assessing damages for loss of companionship and mental anguish, and prior Lorain County wrongful death verdicts, which are traditionally quite modest.

For the next ten minutes, Dennis goes on a rant, berating Dr. Wright and insisting that his daughter's death haunts him each and every day. While Dennis acts out, Paul thinks about the potential fee and what it would mean to his family. Plain and simple, it would be their savior, staving off financial ruin. After applying that money toward their house debt, he would have no difficulty refinancing it. But he is only kidding himself. His narcissistic client is out of touch with reality and will never agree to the settlement. Paul realizes that hoping for resolution is nothing short of self-torture.

Paul eventually holds up his arms, signaling Dennis to stop his diatribe. "Can I conclude that you want to reject the offer and roll the dice with the jury?" Paul says.

"What do you recommend?" Cindy asks, surprising both him and Dennis, who jerks his head and stares at her with his mouth open.

Paul senses that Cindy is interceding on her attorney's behalf. She doesn't care about Dennis, but she wants Paul to get paid something.

Although Cindy asked the question, Paul stares at Dennis as he answers. "There's no guarantee that the jury is going to find in our favor. At the end of the day, we could walk away from the courthouse with nothing. That's fine with me, but the defendant's offer is not unreasonable under the circumstances. We might do better with the jury, but who knows? It really depends on your tolerance for risk."

"Are you sure the insurance company has no more money to offer us?" Dennis asks, his voice sullen. Apparently, his theatrics are over and he wants to assess the offer realistically.

"I'm ninety-nine percent sure that this is it. We really don't have time to have any more back-and-forth in the negotiations. The jury could come back at any minute. Either you want it or you don't." Paul looks at Dennis for an answer.

"I really don't want to accept it, but I don't want to end up with nothing," Dennis says, the bravado gone from his voice.

"I think that's a reasonable way to go," Paul says before Dennis can change his mind.

"I hate to do this. I really do, but I want this to be over," Dennis says.

"Okay, I'll let Ingram and the judge know," Paul says before he walks from the room.

For a moment, he feels immense relief—as if he has navigated a ship through a storm into the safety of a protected harbor. But that feeling vanishes as quickly as it came, replaced by disappointment and guilt. Has he sold himself short? Has he lacked the courage to see the case through to the end? No, he is merely the messenger. He remained neutral on the offer, didn't he? Well, maybe not. He emphasized the likelihood of a defense verdict and suggested that they'd be "rolling the dice" with a jury verdict. Perhaps he pushed them in the direction that he wanted them to go.

By the time he reaches the judge's office, he feels apprehensive and anxious to finalize the deal. When he enters the judge's office complex, it appears that almost all of the judge's staff are gone for lunch except for his civil secretary, Amy Morgan, who sits at her desk in the open area. Paul intends to walk past her and enter Judge Hardwig's private chambers, where he assumes Ingram and the judge await him.

As he approaches Amy, Paul smiles at her. Several months ago, Amy's daughter, Melanie, shadowed him for half a day, watching a bench trial in municipal court that Paul won. Melanie continues to play on the soccer team that he coaches, and, through her, Paul has gotten to know her mother. Truth be told, Amy can be something of a pest. She often intercedes on her daughter's behalf, asking if she can change positions or get more playing time. Amy can monopolize a conversation and he needs to stay clear of her at any cost.

Despite his desire to avoid her, Paul is perplexed when Amy does not return his smile. Did he yell at her daughter at practice or injure her pride in some other way? Glancing at the judge's open door, she whispers, "I need to talk to you in private." She quickly pushes back her chair, stands, and beckons Paul to follow her into the vacant court reporter's office. Whatever she wants to discuss, this is not the time.

Paul doesn't want to be rude and make an enemy, but he can't allow himself to be drawn into an emotional conversation that probably involves the hurt feelings of a girl on his soccer team. "Look, I'm supposed to join the judge and Ingram in the judge's chambers," Paul says, unable to keep the impatience from his voice. The settlement could fall apart at any moment if the jury returns a verdict or if that prick Ingram decides to withdraw the offer. "If this is about your daughter, I don't have time right now."

"God no, it's not about Melanie. It's about your case." From the expression in her eyes, she looks like she wants to grab him by the shoulders and shake him.

"What about my case?"

"You're being played. At least, that's what I think."

Chastened, Paul replies, "You've got my full attention."

He follows her into the court reporter's office, where Amy partially shuts the door, leaving it about four inches ajar. Clearing away several transcripts from the court reporter's desk, Paul sits on its edge, his eyes boring into hers.

Amy entwines her hands in front of her chest and takes a deep breath. "I think Frank McCloskey, our bailiff, has been feeding Ingram information about the jury deliberations."

Schofield is initially speechless. When he speaks, he asks the only question that matters. "Are you sure?"

Amy clenches her teeth and then blows out a puff of air. "No, I'm not positive, but it sure looks that way."

Schofield hoped to hear something more definite. Hiding his disappointment, he says, "Tell me what you know then."

Amy takes a deep breath and begins. "Well, around eleven a.m. Frank tells me he is going to check on the jury. He wants to find out if the jurors are close to a verdict or if he needs to order them lunch. About ten minutes later, the judge comes out of his chambers and asks me where Frank is. I tell him that he went to check on the jury and hasn't returned. The judge is in a big hurry to schedule something and he wants me to locate Frank pronto. I knock on the jury room door, peek in my head, and they tell me that Frank just left. I figure that he's in the courtroom, but when I go in, he's not there.

"I walk straight through the courtroom and into the hallway. At the end of the hall, I see Frank talking to Ingram outside of Judge Gary's courtroom. I walk toward them and Ingram looks distressed, almost panicked. As he passes me, he's digging his cell phone out of his suit jacket. When I reach Frank, I ask, 'What's that all about?' He looks away at first and then he says, 'Oh, nothing.' I raise my eyebrows at him. Then he says, 'Well, if you need to know, we were just arranging a golf game at the Westwood Country Club, where Ingram belongs.'

"This kind of surprises me because I know the judge frowns on this kind of thing and he's warned Frank about accepting any gifts from attorneys practicing in our courtroom. I say, 'Since when does the judge allow an attorney to pay for your golf game at a fancy country club?' Frank gets defensive and says, 'It's not a big deal, Amy. Bob and I are friends.' And I think, *Oh, that's rich; you guys are friends*, but I keep that to myself. Instead, I tell him, 'Well, it's not right.' And he scrunches up his eyes and uses this prissy voice on me. 'Oh, so you're going to tattle on me?' It's like I'm some schoolgirl. Inside, I'm burning up, but I don't show it. I tell him that the judge wants to see him immediately about scheduling something.

"And then Frank walks away from me. As I'm watching him head back to our courtroom, I'm thinking, *Why is Frank talking to Ingram before he reports back to us?* I mean, what's going on here?"

Both of Paul's hands instinctively ball into tight fists. He slowly tilts his head back, stares at the ceiling, and fights the impulse to scream. Ingram's late offer never made sense to him, but now it does. The jury has probably decided in his favor and are trying to agree on damages.

Amy continues, "Then, of course, ten minutes or so later, Ingram comes waltzing into our office and asks me if the judge is in his chambers. When I tell him that he is, Ingram says that he just made a settlement offer to you and wants to tell the judge personally about it. He's all puffed up, pleased with himself—you know the way he gets. And then he asks, 'Can I go back?' The judge's door is open. I say that the judge doesn't have anyone in with him right now and he can announce himself and walk in. Ingram says to me, 'When Schofield arrives, tell him to join us.' I nod that I understand but I think to myself, *You snake, he'll join you only after I've talked to him.*"

"Thank you, Amy. Thank you," Paul says. Five minutes ago, he wanted to avoid her, and now he wants to hug her. Instead, he grabs her right hand and squeezes it between his two hands.

Amy appears startled and somewhat embarrassed, and Schofield releases her hand. She opens the door before she speaks. "I could never have lived with myself if I didn't tell you," she says. "You are so nice to my daughter, Paul, and I've worked with Wendy on some PTA events. No need to thank me. You'd do the same for me if things were reversed."

"Well, still. Thank you." He looks at his watch. It is 11:50. "I've got to talk to my clients again."

"I figured you would."

Schofield nods before hurrying out of the office. He hasn't taken two steps before he realizes that he isn't sure how to approach Dennis. His client is a volatile, unpredictable man. If he tells Dennis what the bailiff has done, he might go berserk—physically assault Ingram or the bailiff or both. And then there is the possibility—remote as it is—that Ingram and the bailiff were only setting up a golf game. Amy has not overheard their conversation; he has no direct proof that the bailiff has breached his duty of confidentiality.

When Paul returns to the courtroom, his clients are sitting in different rows of the spectator benches. As soon as Dennis sees him approaching, he jumps to his feet and asks, "Is it done?"

"No, not yet. We still need to talk," Paul replies. Although they have the courtroom to themselves, Paul knows that someone could enter at any time. "Let's go back to the witness room."

Dennis shakes his head but nonetheless follows Paul, trailed by Cindy. Just beyond the courtroom's inner doors, Paul opens the door to the witness waiting room. As soon as Paul shuts the door, Dennis stands about six inches from him, intentionally invading his space. "I'm through talking, Paul. Your job is fucking simple. You just go back there and tell them yes and we all go home."

Paul backs away from Dennis before replying. "You're making a mistake. I'm convinced of it."

"Jesus, that's not what you said ten minutes ago. In case you forgot, you asked us if we wanted to gamble with a jury verdict and we said that we didn't and you agreed with us. Then I instructed you to nail this thing down. Instead, you come back and say we need to talk more. What is this?"

"Just hear me out, okay? That's all I'm asking," Paul says. "Ingram was trying to pressure us into a quick decision."

"That's what a good salesman does," Dennis replies. "I negotiate with people every day at the dealership. Sometimes you've got to apply pressure."

Paul shakes his head. "It's more than applying pressure. Why would the insurance company suddenly want to settle this case?" Paul asks rhetorically. "Because they're damn scared. They expected a defense verdict in an hour and now three hours have gone by and the jury is still hashing things out. They're frightened that we're going to get a big verdict."

"I don't care if they're scared. Nobody knows what the jury is going to do. Not you, not Ingram, not the insurance company. While everybody is scared, I want to take their money."

Paul silently acknowledges that his client's instincts and analysis are correct. Worse yet, Paul practically said the same thing to Dennis a few minutes ago when they initially discussed the offer. It is no wonder Dennis scorns Paul's new "insight."

Paul decides to take a different tack. "Dennis, the only way you're going to expose ECT's dangers is if there is a large verdict here. If you settle, you will allow everyone to bury this. Do you really want that?" For two years, Paul has listened to Dennis spout this same mantra as the justification for the lawsuit.

"This case has never been about money for me," Dennis says, astounding Paul with his brazen insincerity. "I've made my point. They're paying us almost half a million dollars. I'd say we've won."

"If you take the money, you won't change anything," Paul responds. "Let me remind you that the settlement will be confidential. Nobody will learn anything from this case. However, right now, you've got an incredible opportunity to make a difference. You've got a jury deliberating, ready to announce to the world that shock treatments are horrible, that they can kill people."

"You don't really believe your own bullshit, do you?" Dennis asks.

"This case isn't going to change anything for anybody, so we're going to take the money."

Paul purses his lips, trying to think of another reason to let the case go to the jury. When he can't, he decides that his only option is to reveal what he suspects about Ingram and the bailiff. However, before he can say anything, he hears an announcement on the public address system that tells him to report to Judge Hardwig's chambers immediately.

He can't just deliver this revelation—it is a bombshell—and then leave. He needs time to divulge his suspicions to Dennis gently and then calm him down. He will go directly to the judge and ask for additional time with his clients. "I'll be back in five minutes and we can finish our discussion then," Paul says as he opens the door.

"There is no more discussion," Dennis replies. "You've told me all along that this is my call. I'm directing you—no, I'm commanding you to accept the offer." Paul suspects that in the last ten minutes, Dennis has already decided how he plans to spend the entire settlement.

"I'm telling you that's a mistake—a big mistake."

"I'm telling you to settle the case."

"Okay," Paul says as he stares at his intransigent client.

A few minutes later, when Paul enters the judge's offices, Amy looks at him expectantly. In response, he blows out a deep breath in exasperation. Unable to explain his situation, he merely shakes his head and walks past her toward the judge's chamber.

As he approaches the open door, he can hear Ingram talking but cannot make out his words. Once inside the office, he sees the judge sitting behind his desk, while Ingram occupies one of two upholstered chairs facing the judge. Paul takes a seat in the vacant chair. The judge and Ingram end their conversation abruptly and stare at him.

"I understand you've been talking to your clients about the offer. Do we have a settlement?" the judge asks.

"We're not quite there yet," Paul replies. "I still need about ten more minutes with my clients before we can give you an answer." Paul tries to exude calm, but his eyes flutter as he glances from the judge to Ingram.

"What do you say, Bob?" Judge Hardwig asks. "Ten more minutes?"

Ingram raises his eyebrows and scowls. "My instructions were to give plaintiffs fifteen minutes to decide."

"It's your call, Bob, but what's the harm in letting Paul carefully respond to his clients' questions?" the judge asks, telegraphing what he wants Ingram to do. Ingram nods and gives the judge an ingratiating smile. Paul relaxes.

Before Ingram can respond further, Frank McCloskey rushes into the room. "The jury just buzzed us and I went in. They've finished their deliberations. They have a verdict."

A feeling of dread starts in Paul's stomach, spreads to his chest, and clutches his neck. Adrenaline shoots into his bloodstream, making it impossible for his brain to think rationally. *Everything is going wrong*, he thinks, *Everything.*

As Ingram begins to speak, Paul struggles to focus on Ingram's words. "This was a very generous offer. I fought hard to get the insurance company to pony up. Despite our sparring, I like Paul. I think he's a good young attorney. You know, after forty years, this is just another case for me, but I sense that this is a critically important one for Paul. I'd hate to see him come away with nothing. Are you telling us, Paul, that Mr. Zurcher is not interested in our offer? Has he rejected it?"

Perspiration beads on Paul's forehead. His client has accepted the offer and he knows his duty. "I just need more time," Paul croaks, his voice faltering.

The judge sighs and taps his fingers on his desktop. "Paul, I'm sorry, but the jury has reached a verdict. I'm sure that they all want to go home. Unfortunately, it's decision time. If your client is being stubborn and won't take the offer, then he must suffer the consequences if the jury disappoints him."

Paul's shoulders slump. He's run out of options. As much as his brain rebels at accepting the offer, he has no choice but to do that. His client has told him to say yes in no uncertain terms. He has to accept the offer before it is withdrawn.

Paul begins, "I've talked to Mr. Zurcher about the offer and he has instructed me—" And then he stops. The next words leap from his mouth involuntarily, almost as if another person has hijacked his brain and is speaking for him. Later, Paul will conclude that the emotional part of his brain overruled the rational part.

Looking directly at Ingram, Paul says, "I'm convinced that you received inside information about the jury deliberations this morning."

For an instant, Ingram's face shows surprise and guilt, but that quickly dissolves into indignation. "This is preposterous. How dare you accuse me of anything so heinous."

Paul turns to the judge's open door, where Frank McCloskey stands, awaiting instructions for the jury. "Your bailiff told Ingram that the jury had reached a plaintiff's verdict around eleven this morning."

Unlike Ingram, McCloskey looks flustered as he shakes his head emphatically. "I talked to Ingram around that time, but we was talking sports. I don't know—the Cleveland Browns—something like that."

"That's interesting. When Amy Morgan confronted you about this conversation, you told her that you were arranging a golf game with Ingram," Paul answers coolly.

Ingram jumps in. "In fact, that is exactly what we were talking about. Frank and I always play golf together a couple of times each season."

Paul stands and glares at Ingram. "Do you deny that immediately after you talked to the bailiff this morning, you made a phone call to your insurance adjuster?"

His face red, Ingram jumps up and wags his finger at Paul. "Are you cross-examining me now? I will not have you impugn my integrity."

Paul asks, "You didn't answer my question. Did you call the insurance company after you talked to Frank?"

Ingram looks at the judge and speaks directly to him. "Judge, for the record, I have had the authority to make this offer since we concluded our closing arguments yesterday. My instructions were simple: if the jury deliberated for more than three hours, I was to extend this offer. I have had no contact with any of my insurance representatives today."

Ignoring Ingram, the judge stares at his bailiff and says evenly, "Frank, did you tell Mr. Ingram anything about the jury's deliberations? Yes or no?"

Frank attempts to follow Ingram's lead; however, his feigned indignation is not convincing. Unable to maintain eye contact with the judge, Frank stammers, "I—I'm an officer of the court. I would never betray my oath."

"Yes or no?" Judge Hardwig presses.

Frank's face has turned white and he backs away from the judge. "There's no way, Your Honor. I told him nothing about the jury deliberations. You've got to believe me." Frank sounds desperate and he begins wringing his hands. To Paul, these are not the words of an innocent man, but of a cheater who's been caught.

Paul glances at the judge but can't read his face. The judge's expression shows either sympathy or barely contained rage. For whatever reason, the judge seems paralyzed by indecision.

While the judge dithers, Paul presses on. "Your Honor, I'd like Mr. Ingram to hand over his cell phone to you. If he didn't call or text his insurance representative after he and Frank talked, I'll drop this."

Before the judge can answer, Ingram screams, "I'm doing no such thing. Who does he think he is? He has absolutely no right to invade my privacy and see my personal texts or calls. This is still America, isn't it?"

For the first time that day, Paul smiles. "Thanks, Bob. We reject your offer."

The judge sits with his eyes closed, not speaking. Finally, he says, "We're going into the courtroom to receive the jury's verdict." With his head bowed, the judge rises slowly from his chair and points toward his door. "I'm deeply troubled by these allegations," he says. "Very troubled."

When Paul enters the courtroom, Dennis and Cindy are seated in the back again. As soon as Dennis sees him, he jumps up and runs toward Paul.

"Why is everybody returning to the courtroom?" Dennis asks. His eyes dart from Paul to Ingram to the judge, who is taking his seat behind the bench. "You got the case settled, right?"

"The jury has rendered its verdict, and in a few moments, we're going to find out what it is," Paul says as he moves toward the trial table.

Before Paul can pull out his chair, Dennis grabs him by the shoulders and spins him so that they are face-to-face. "What about the offer?" he asks, his voice both desperate and angry.

Paul whispers, "I rejected it but it's going to be all right."

"What the fuck?" Dennis shoots back. "You can't do that. You can't do that."

"You're just going to have to trust me, Dennis," Paul replies. "Now, sit down."

As Dennis takes his seat, he snarls, "If you're wrong, you're getting sued."

"I know," says Paul. "And this time you won't have a difficult time finding a lawyer."

"What's that supposed to mean?"

"It means you'd have a damn good case."

CHAPTER 30
SEPTEMBER 27, 2019
PAUL SCHOFIELD

With a seething client seated next to him, Paul nervously searches the jurors' faces as they file into the courtroom. Scrutinizing them is an exercise in futility; it's impossible to learn anything from their expressions or demeanors. As if to prove the point, none of the jurors makes eye contact with him; they look either straight ahead or down at their feet.

He's convinced that they will return a plaintiff's verdict, but the amount of the verdict is still an open question. Over the decades, Lorain County juries have routinely been conservative when assessing damages, rarely passing the million-dollar threshold. What if this jury's award is less than Ingram's offer? It's not inconceivable. When a jury is troubled by some aspect of the plaintiff's case, it may reach a compromise verdict—finding for the plaintiff but awarding only partial damages.

After Judge Hardwig tells everyone to be seated, he asks the jury if it has reached a verdict. One of the jurors, a frizzy-haired woman who is apparently the foreperson, stands and presents a thick, sealed envelope to the bailiff, Frank McCloskey. Walking woodenly toward the bench, McCloskey stops and, with a noticeable tremor in his right hand, gives the envelope to the judge. Thrusting his left arm toward his bailiff, the judge grabs it without looking at him.

Noisily flipping through the forms, the judge gently rocks his torso back and forth while his eyes remain focused on the documents. As the judge reviews the papers, Paul looks about the courtroom. Although Ingram sits erect and maintains an impassive expression, his shoulders suddenly quiver. His breathing labored, Dennis repeatedly clenches his right hand into a fist and then relaxes it. Only Dr. Wright seems composed, stifling a yawn while he awaits a verdict that, even if adverse, will be paid by his malpractice insurance carrier.

Fueled by a combination of adrenaline and anxiety, Paul feels his pulse pounding in his eardrums. Attempting to relax, he takes a deep breath. When he hears a woman cough in the back of the courtroom, he turns to see who it is, hoping that perhaps Susie has returned to await the jury's decision. However, the only person there is Cindy, who sits in the far corner of the back row. Paul catches her eye, raises his eyebrows, and smiles.

Clearing his throat, the judge says, "I've reviewed both the verdict forms and the answers to the jury interrogatories. They are consistent, and, therefore, we have a verdict that I will now read."

The judge looks up from the documents and glances at Ingram. Paul cannot be sure, but it appears that the judge is suppressing a smile. Pushing his eyeglasses back to the bridge of his nose, he begins, "'We, the jury, being duly sworn, find in favor of the plaintiff, Dennis Zurcher, Executor of the Estate of Heather Zurcher, deceased, as against the defendant, Sheldon Wright, MD, in the amount of One Million Eight Hundred Thousand Dollars.'"

After that, Paul cannot focus on the judge's words. Two years of struggle have culminated in this verdict and he can barely contain his pent-up emotions. His body and brain surge with elation, and if he were not in a courtroom, he would be yelling *yes* in celebration and pumping his right arm in the air. But with no outlet for his energy, his heart races and his knees tremble. His brain replays the events of the last hour: Ingram's unexpected offer, Amy Morgan's revelation, and his decision to override his client's direction to settle. Somehow, it worked out. Preoccupied by these thoughts, Paul barely listens as the judge thanks the jurors for their service.

"Before I discharge the jurors from their obligations, is there anything more from counsel?" the judge asks, looking first at Ingram and then at Paul.

These words jolt Paul from his reverie. He stands and says, "No, Your Honor." Not bothering to rise from his chair, Ingram shakes his head. His vacant expression suggests that his mind is elsewhere, perhaps contemplating the possibility of disbarment or criminal prosecution. As the jurors stand to leave, Judge Hardwig catches Paul's eye and gives him a sly, congratulatory wink.

Paul expects Dennis to be grateful that he overruled him, but that doesn't happen. When Paul holds out his hand, his client grudgingly shakes it. Dennis refuses to meet Paul's gaze, and his voice takes on a derisive tone. "Unlike you, I always knew we had a strong case," Dennis says, shaking his head in disgust. "And if I hadn't held your feet to the fire, this never would have happened. Never."

Paul rolls his eyes but says nothing. The verdict is not more than five minutes old and already Dennis is rewriting history.

Before Dennis can say more, Cindy rushes from the back of the courtroom, ignores her husband, and gives Paul a heartfelt hug. "You did a wonderful job. Thank you so much," she says.

As they embrace, Paul whispers, "I know none of this will bring Heather back, but it's all that the law can do."

Upon hearing those words, Cindy squeezes him harder. After they release each other, Cindy says quietly, "I know it won't bring her back. The important thing is that you fought for Heather. That's what matters to me."

As this unfolds in front of Dennis, his face contorts with anger. Cindy's show of affection will undoubtedly lead to a rebuke or worse when they return home. Taking her by the elbow, Dennis forcefully pivots her in the direction of the exit doors.

"I'll be in touch about my money," Dennis says as he leads Cindy away. When the couple have walked about ten feet, Dennis pauses and looks over his shoulder. "And it better not take too long," he warns, wagging his right index finger at Paul. Unfazed, Paul does not reply, knowing that Dennis's day of reckoning is coming soon.

After the Zurchers resume their walk to the exit, Paul turns and begins gathering his materials from the trial table. Curious, he glances in Ingram's direction and sees that his opponent made a speedy retreat. In his apparent haste to leave, Ingram left a mess on his table: a half-empty water bottle, a scattering of paper clips, and several crumpled pages from a yellow pad.

Digging his cell phone from his jacket pocket, Paul is poised to phone Wendy when four jurors approach him. Although he desperately wants to give his wife the good news, this call will have to wait. These jurors seem eager to explain their verdict, and just as eagerly, he wants to know what persuaded them.

For the next ten minutes, they talk, one person interrupting the other in a jumble of competing words. They explain that, although they did not like Dennis, they disliked Dr. Wright and his attorney even more. After weighing the evidence, they were convinced that this teenager should never have been subjected to ECT and that Dr. Wright failed to warn the family about the antidepressant—all of which they believe directly caused Heather's death. They uniformly express sympathy for Cindy and lavish praise on Paul and his performance.

After thanking them for their jury service and kind words, Paul returns to his trial table and sits down. As soon as the last of the jurors files out of the courtroom, he calls Wendy.

"Hey, it's me," he begins, his voice betraying no emotion.

"Well, what happened?" she asks, her voice desperate with anticipation.

"We won," he says. As soon as the words come out, he grins broadly, a grin that is impossible to suppress.

"You won. Oh, my God!" Wendy screams. "I knew you would. I just knew it." Her breathing becomes rapid and Paul suspects that she is jumping up and down. "How much was the verdict?"

He hesitates before answering. If he tells her over the phone, he'll be further deprived of witnessing her excitement firsthand. Over the years, his wife's wild reactions have been an experience unto themselves—funny expressions, jerky dance moves, or even piercing coyote howls. Can he wait to give her the details in person? He's only a five-minute walk from his office.

"So how much?" Wendy asks again, impatience creeping into her voice.

He can't keep her in suspense any longer. "One point eight," he says, letting each word drop like a bomb.

"As in one point eight million dollars?" Wendy asks incredulously.

"Yes."

"Paul, you did it. You really did it," she gushes. She unleashes a series of Indian battle whoops that nearly shatter his eardrums. Maybe he *can* appreciate her reactions over the phone. In fact, it might be safer.

"And I almost settled for four hundred and fifty thousand dollars a few minutes before the jury reached its verdict," he adds.

"What are you talking about?" she asks. "I thought Dr. Wright's insurance company wasn't going to make an offer—ever."

"It's a long story," Paul says. "I'll tell you when I get back to the office."

"Get moving," she orders. "And then I want every detail."

EPILOGUE

Judge Hardwig fires Frank McCloskey minutes after the jury trial ends. That afternoon, the judge also contacts the county prosecutor and asks him to begin an investigation into the incident. Because no one overheard the two men's conversation, the judge reasons that a conviction is unlikely unless one of the pair is granted immunity and testifies against the other. The judge is unsure which one is more culpable: his bailiff or Ingram. He will leave that to the prosecutor.

Two days later, Cindy begins executing the plan that she, Susie, and Wendy devised. When Dennis is at work, she moves her belongings and those of her children out of Dennis's house and into the home of Susie's in-laws. Cindy's divorce attorney files the initial papers several days thereafter, seeking a restraining order and requesting temporary support payments.

Because Cindy and Dennis cannot agree on the proper division of the jury award, the probate court sets a hearing to decide the issue. Both Cindy and Dennis hire separate attorneys for the hearing, while the court appoints two attorneys to protect the interests of the two surviving Zurcher children. After the probate judge, James Walker, considers all the evidence describing Heather's relationship with her parents and siblings (including Heather's autobiography), he limits Dennis's share of the proceeds to fifty thousand dollars. Dennis is livid but is told that he has no grounds for an appeal. With more than a million dollars directed to Cindy and the two children, they look forward to a healthier life, no longer financially dependent upon Dennis or subject to his abusive behavior.

After paying Scott Worthington his co-counsel fee, Paul Schofield nets an attorney fee of $360,000. With this influx of capital, he is able to refinance his home loan, retire his and Wendy's student loans, and negotiate a final payment for Kirsten's outstanding medical bills. Three weeks after the verdict, both Alyssa and Kirsten have their first appointment with an orthodontist.

ALSO BY DAVID MIRALDI

The Edge of Innocence: The Trial of Casper Bennett
The Edge of Malice: The Marie Grossman Story
The Edge of Doubt: The Trial of Nancy Smith and Joseph Allen

ABOUT THE AUTHOR

David Miraldi is an author and attorney hailing from Lorain, Ohio. With a career in civil law that spans over four decades, David has dedicated himself to championing the cause of the common man against insurance conglomerates and corporate giants.

A graduate of The College of Wooster (1975), David earned his law degree with honors from The Ohio State Moritz College of Law where he met his wife, Leslee, also a lawyer. Driven by an innate sense of duty, he returned to his hometown to practice alongside his father and brother, serving the community that shaped him.

An author with a flair for narrative nonfiction, David made waves with his debut book, *The Edge of Innocence: The Trial of Casper Bennett*, which was crowned the 2018 Book of the Year by the prestigious International Rubery Book Awards.

He further cemented his reputation as a storyteller with his sophomore release, *The Edge of Malice: The Marie Grossman Story*, earning accolades from Kirkus Reviews as a "superbly crafted nonfiction drama" and receiving a shortlisting by Rubery for its 2021 awards.

His third book, *The Edge of Doubt: The Trial of Nancy Smith and Joseph Allen*, examined the tragic dynamics of a wrongful conviction. After the book's publication, David spoke frequently about the issues raised in the book, including a presentation to all of Ohio's appellate judges.

Beyond the courtroom and the written page, David's creative spirit finds outlets through photography and music. His evocative photographs often grace local exhibits, and he generously donates the proceeds from their sales to charity. A pianist with eclectic tastes, David composes original pieces and has a predilection for classical, ragtime, and contemporary music. He is also a fitness enthusiast and engages in tennis, swimming, cycling, pickleball, and gardening.

David shares his life with his beloved wife, Leslee, who also edits his books. They are the proud parents of three children and doting grandparents to three grandchildren. They continue to make Avon, Ohio, their home.

www.ingramcontent.com/pod-product-compliance
Lightning Source LLC
Chambersburg PA
CBHW060452030426
42337CB00015B/1558